NOT PEACE
BUT A SWORD

NOT PEACE
BUT A SWORD

Wing Commander Patrick Gibbs, DSO DFC and Bar

Think not that I am come to send peace on earth:
I came not to send peace, but a sword.
MATTHEW x. 34

GRUB STREET · LONDON

Published by
Grub Street
The Basement
10 Chivalry Road
London SW11 1HT

Originally written in 1942 and published by Cassells in 1943
This revised version published 1993 by Grub Street, London
Text copyright © Patrick Gibbs

A catalogue record is available on request from the British Library

ISBN 0-948817-68-2

Typeset by BMD Graphics, Hemel Hempstead

Printed and bound in Great Britain by
Biddles Ltd, Guildford and King's Lynn

With special thanks to Mrs J M Buckberry at RAF Cranwell,
Roger Hayward, Norman Hearn-Phillips and Norman Franks

CONTENTS

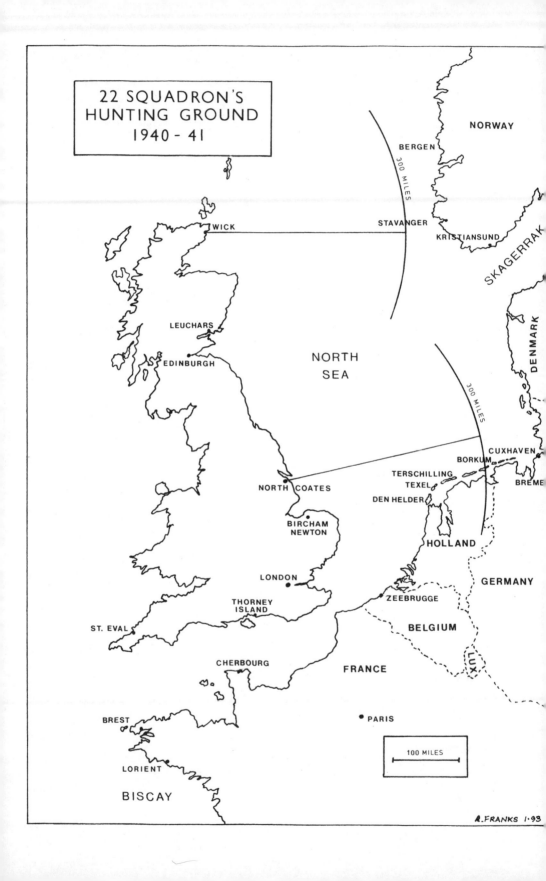

22 SQUADRON'S
HUNTING GROUND
1940 - 41

NORWAY

BERGEN

300 MILES

STAVANGER

KRISTIANSUND

SKAGERRAK

WICK

DENMARK

LEUCHARS

EDINBURGH

NORTH
SEA

300 MILES

CUXHAVEN

BORKUM

TERSCHILLING

BREME

TEXEL

NORTH COATES

DEN HELDER

BIRCHAM
NEWTON

HOLLAND

LONDON

GERMANY

THORNEY
ISLAND

ZEEBRUGGE

BELGIUM

ST. EVAL

LUX

CHERBOURG

FRANCE

PARIS

BREST

100 MILES

LORIENT

BISCAY

R.FRANKS 1·93

CHAPTER I

THE BIRTH OF A STAR

REMEMBER peace-time? Then you recall trivialities, an abundance of petrol, the brightness of lights in the streets in the hours of darkness, freedom to buy from shops anything you could afford, ease of travel, absence of petty grievances and restrictions; above all, the care-free days and nights without disturbance. You recall a life without inflicted pain, fear and sudden death.

Do you remember the occasional silver aeroplane with gay red, white and blue circles on wings and fuselage which droned overhead, perhaps disturbing your game of golf, some afternoon walk in the countryside or peace-time gardening? It was an RAF aircraft, and who knows but that its pilot, some young officer of twenty, is not now the decorated bearer of a famous name, acclaimed to-day for fine leading of a Fighter Wing or some tenacious bombing mission on which he led his squadron?

Yet that silver aircraft and its pilot did not then command attention; it was peace-time, with war seemingly remote; aircraft were rare in the air, and the Royal Air Force, a few thousands of airmen, a few hundreds of aeroplanes with their quota of pilots, was no more remarkable and rather less credited in the country than just another factory in an industrial town. Flying was no longer new; it had lost man's enthusiasm for a novelty, was established and little thought of, an accomplished and forgotten fact.

Then came fear of war, increasing with the roll of martial drums; the Abyssinian Crisis, the Austrian Anschluss and Munich-time were cymbal clashes in the rising crescendo heard throughout the world. Finally, and almost as a relief to rumoured nerves, came war itself, and with it all heads are inclined towards the sky, eyes focussed with interest and admiration on each aircraft speeding through the air, no longer silver but in the grim paint of war. The Royal Air Force is young and bold, brave and victorious, recognized throughout the land; hands are stretched out to greet men in blue and boys with wings, lips smile for them and eyes search for them. In a night the ignored of yesterday have awoken to find their service, their aircraft and their work of first interest and the object of discussion, not only in Britain and the Empire, but in all free countries, and no less, I imagine, in enemy territories where our Air Force is known and feared.

There has been a change indeed in this country's attitude to flying in the last decade, which I saw come about intimately and from within, for I joined the Air Force at the age of eighteen and have grown up with her from a childhood of peace to an age of war. How I came to join the flying service is a story in itself, and one which must be briefly told, for it is in fact an inseparable part of the wider story of flying and the war.

I left school in 1933, without a single idea as to what I was going to do then or how I should earn my living. This aimless attitude, with which I had passed through school, was very much my own fault, for despite the frequent suggestions from school authorities that the matter of a future career should be given serious attention, I still left with nothing decided on, and little done.

In truth, my parents were more than a little to blame for my lack of ambition for a career, but the absence of decision on their part was by no means without reason. There was a family business, founded by my uncle, John Angel Gibbs, in which four brothers had been the original partners and the greater part of the capital subscribed by their relations; sisters, cousins, brothers and their families all held shares. It was a true family affair, in which only a few outsiders were interested; the business was shipping and the firm, which bore the family name, were shipowners. My parents must have seen no reason why I should not welcome the opportunity which the firm offered of an apprenticeship, to be followed by a partnership, and so they had not encouraged my ambitions in any other direction. They were not to know that I would grow up with a marked antagonism to such a career, an attitude fostered by vivid childhood impressions, and that, when at last I should feel a strong attraction from another quarter, its appeal would be irresistible. While I was growing up only negative influences were at work on the course of my future, but they led me directly towards a very potent star, whose light, once seen, I immediately followed. That star was, of course, flying.

I was three years old at the time of the Armistice which concluded the last war, when I saw flags hanging from our nursery windows and heard the sounds of hooters and sirens rising from the city near by. I did not know then that the ships which the firm owned had been sunk by the enemy, three vessels of about 8000 tons, nor that the firm's founder, my uncle, had been killed on the Western Front after being awarded the DSO for bravery. I did not question why my father was not fighting; it was many years before I realized that he had been placed in the lowest medical category and was unfit for service.

Yet the firm had not been unlucky; if ships had been sunk it was not before they had made both lucrative and valuable voyages, and before this present war of reserved occupations, the firm was lucky to have been able to keep the surviving partners' experienced hands at the helm to guide its fortunes. I am not sure that those were not the great years of shipping firms in South Wales, notwithstanding the fact that they were war years. There was money in Cardiff, the result of prosperity and activity, and although shipping was then, as today, an essential national service, I often wondered during the post-war era if the firm could not be labelled with the contemptible title then on everybody's lips of "War Profiteer". On reflection today, this very suggestion seems an injustice. The firm never wasted time valuable to the country in bargaining over freights, the ships were run with no eye to profit; they carried essential goods of every kind and continued to do so as long as they floated. If the business was profitable, profit was incidental and service was its first concern.

My father, who had lost one brother and partner, was actively supported in the business by another brother, orders for ships were executed in due course, and soon three ships were sailing again under the firm's name: one a 10,000-ton vessel and two slightly smaller. There was, apparently, never any thought of not replacing the lost ships or of winding up the business to a profitable conclusion at the end of the war; the partners were still young and of considerable shipping experience, and there must have seemed no reason why the business should not be carried on as successfully as in pre-war days. There was no visionary who foresaw a changed future for shipping, no one in the whole of Cardiff who anticipated the dire results of the post-war over-building of shipping tonnage. The city had become rich from its docks, on the exporting and importing of coal and grain during the war years. In the early nineteen-twenties there was still money being made in Cardiff around its docks; there was yet no shade of the cloud which was to break on her, and money, if easily made, was being carelessly spent. No one foresaw a change.

I cannot say that as a child I ever thought that I should eventually

join the firm, and carry on the tradition of the business. In all probability, I regarded the future of earning my own living as delightfully
remote, and considered it inevitable that I should some day work in
the offices I knew so well. I was not at this time averse to a business
life, as I became later, nor had I any strong feelings about a career,
both because office life seemed distant and I had no great ambitions
in any other direction.

In 1925 I first went away to school, and in that year business
continued its steady decline in Cardiff. Freights were less profitable,
cargoes scarcer; the slump was starting. There was, as yet, no general
alarm, certainly not among the established firms, although there were
nevertheless some immediate failures, involving for the most part
speculators with small reserves, the unlucky or the unwary who had
ordered ships on anticipated profits and now found a ship delivered
for which they could not pay. There were soon too many ships available and too little merchandise for them to carry—bluntly, not enough
business to go round; the market had become overcrowded, and
sellers outnumbered buyers.

But this black picture is anticipating the end of the decade; 1925
sounded only the first warning, which passed unheard and so
unheeded. Few families tightened their belts against the needs of a
future day, few firms made economies or augmented their reserves at
the cost of reduced dividends. There was still money to be made in
Cardiff, but it was to become less easy, and profits steadily decreased
until the real depression years following 1929, when firms sailed their
ships at a loss rather than keep them idle, when small companies failed
or sold out at a ruinous price to some larger and more resourceful
firm, whose strength might enable it to weather the storm of depression behind which prosperity might be waiting. Meanwhile many fine
ships were actually laid up and could be seen tragically lying rusty and
idle in the rivers and estuaries around our coast. Such a sight I saw
for myself each summer when we went to Cornwall for our holidays,
and the unforgettable picture of great ships rusting at anchor in the
Fal and Helford river had a greater influence on my opinion of the
shipping business than any impression I obtained in Cardiff. The
humbled grandeur of ships lying hidden and unwanted in lonely back-
waters made a sad sight, and brought home to me the tragic depths
which shipping was then plumbing.

I was at school during the whole of this period and so was spared
the continuous spectacle of the effects of declining business on a once
prosperous city. But during school holidays I would often go to the
docks when father was driven to the office, or called for in the

evenings. I saw queues at the labour exchanges, crowds of unemployed at street corners, signs of poverty in what I had known as the busiest of dockside squares. A hush seemed to have descended on the firm's offices; the ships sailed, but voyages were profitless, the business was dead. It was recognized that the game was at least temporarily played out; no one could foretell when they might be given another innings, or if it would occur in their lifetime. Shipping had always been a variable business, very dependent on outside influences, with bad years alternating with profitable ones, and it was known that its day would come again. Meanwhile the only solution was to keep the business together, to hang on and wait.

From private school I was sent to Public School at Oundle. This was 1929, when I was fourteen, old enough now to feel the effects of the decline in the firm's prosperity, yet young and irresponsible enough not to let it worry me unduly. I believed, if I considered the matter at all, that business might improve before I finished school. Years then seemed to take long in passing and nothing seemed imminent. Looking back now, it is clear that I was aimlessly drifting through school with no end in view. The days when money had been plentiful were not so far away in the past as to be beyond remembrance. Memories of a peaceful, gay and unworried home persistently refused to become dim; in fact, life at home in the few brief weeks of school holidays appeared after all not to have changed so very much since childhood.

It did seem strange that all our fortunes appeared almost literally to be sunk in one ship, the family business, and that my father had not invested at least a part of the post-war profits in some concern far removed from shipping influence. I learned later that during those years when he had been educating his children, keeping up the house which we loved, and maintaining all the time the air of not being too severely hit by the slump, the successful appearance so necessary to a business man, all this time he was drawing on his outside capital. The shares in the firm had at all costs to be held; it was a family concern, with strong sentimental associations, and I can imagine that this was a point of honour. In any case, a return to prosperity and the whole future of the family depended on the retention of our interest in the business. Father had backed shipping heavily enough, and perhaps rightly, when he gave no thought of selling out in the boom years. Now, he backed it virtually with all he had. Outside shares often with good prospects, more often and more heartbreakingly actually paying good dividends, shares which had been acquired against such a situation, were gradually and over a long period of years sold to keep the family and home together in the same way as the firm was kept afloat.

Father was backing a return to prosperity in Cardiff against the final parting with the whole of his outside capital; it was a wager against time, in which the firm was backed to recommence dividends before other capital was exhausted.

Nor were we favoured by that elusive good luck which could have contributed so greatly to making this system work smoothly. Just after I left school, Father was found to be suffering from consumption, and was given but a few years more to live. The inability to fight in the last war was now fully and belatedly explained. He must have been an ill man throughout the nineteen-twenties, and a very ill man indeed in the next decade, when fortune was furthest from him and worry ever present.

All this time I was at school, oblivious of tragedy near me, working not over industriously and paying more attention to games than to study. I was enjoying life, little worried about the seemingly far off and unsettled future, certainly not regarding any home anxieties as my own, or remotely realizing the precarious structure of the family edifice. In my second year I passed the School Certificate Examination, gaining five credits and so matriculating, but above all I played games, undoubtedly to the detriment of my school work. Nobody pointed out how present study would help a future career, and I was too young and irresponsible to reach that conclusion myself; games must have seemed much more attractive.

Love of games was a legacy from Father, who played rugby for Wales many times in the years before the last war, and toured Australia and New Zealand as a member of a British touring team. He was, I suppose, famous in his day, the great period of Welsh rugby, but those were days before specialization, and his ability was not confined to this one game only, for he was an all-rounder, playing cricket for his county, and a sprinter of some distinction. Every game came naturally to him; at golf his handicap was in single figures, on the billiard table he might make a hundred break, and to this great facility for ball games it must be added that he was a brilliant and formidable card player. So it was not surprising that the legacy of a love and interest in games fell strongly to me, but sadly the great ability was withheld. I tried, I was madly keen, and I practised assiduously, yet I was never anything more than mediocre. All the same, I played games at school to the exclusion of study, and although they stood me in good stead later, at Cranwell and in the service, I was to regret the wasted working hours which could have assured me the choice of a future career.

I left Oundle in 1933, much at my own instigation, for at my age I could have stayed on for another year, and my parents wished me to do so. By now I was less blind to the difficulties at home, and was unwilling for my parents to continue subscribing expensive school fees, which I felt to be without return. Still, no decision had been made as to what career I was to follow; I had no ideas on getting a job, for school had endowed me with no particular qualifications. In reality I knew that it was tacitly understood in my family that I should enter the business; so much was already staked on the recovery of trade that the small addition of my future to the wager would make little difference.

Emphatically I thought otherwise; the prosperous years were far in the past and vanished further into oblivion before the vivid picture of depression formed in my mind by the recent past and present. The true state, not only of the shipping business but of our family affairs, could no longer be withheld from me. The impression I received was one of insecurity inevitably coupled with continual anxiety for the future. If to embrace shipping was to cost this price, it was certainly not one I intended to pay; nor did the seemingly easy fortunes of the earlier period appear to me any more desirable. I did not want continued risk, backed by the phantom of failure, nor yet a fortune; still less did Cardiff itself appeal to me. If I were to enter the business I would be anchored to Cardiff indefinitely, all my life, and the city's associations were identical with those of shipping. The slump years had played on my nerves, the boom had failed to impress me by its impermanency, and I doubted that either my future or happiness were to be found in Cardiff, from which I felt estranged.

So I flatly refused to consider entering the firm, a refusal that was accepted with a good grace—in fact it was expected, for I had for some time been protesting unwillingness to enter a firm which appeared to be dying a slow and agonizing death, and which I had never clearly remembered as living. My future was in this way quickly and negatively settled: I was not to go into the business. Meanwhile, and by way of marking time, I was sent to France to learn French, without any decision being reached as to what I should do afterwards. I was still drifting, still aimless, but at last, and not too soon, tiring of it.

I travelled to France by air liner. The French family with whom I was to stay as a paying guest lived at the now notorious political centre, Vichy, at that time a pleasant resort with no sinister associations. If the journey had been made by boat and train, necessitating a change of stations at Paris, it would have taken two days, but by flying to Paris and travelling on by train it could be accomplished in a single day. This method of travelling must actually have been cheaper, for I had no difficulty in persuading my parents to let me go that way. I did not know then, nor could I have guessed, that I was taking the first step on the road which was to lead me directly to a choice of career, for to fly seemed to me then merely an expeditious means of travel and nothing more. Yet I was not unexcited, for this was to be my first flight.

I travelled by Imperial Airways, and visiting their office in the Haymarket booked an outside seat which I selected from a plan of the air liner's interior. The aircraft was due to leave Croydon at nine o'clock in the morning, but I had to be at the company's terminus at Victoria an hour earlier, where I was weighed on a large machine complete with my luggage, then taken with other passengers by coach to the airport.

At Croydon there was no time to collect impressions of the exciting activities of a busy airport; we passed quickly through the airport building on to the concrete apron of the aerodrome, mounted steps into a Hannibal class air liner and were soon in our seats. The engines started, the aircraft taxied slowly over the grass surface, gathered speed, and in a moment was in the air, heading for the coast. Immediately I liked flying—in a short time I was mad about it. The three features of flying, which have since become so familiar, appealed strongly to me from the first. The wonderful aerial view of the sky and land, the sensation of rising curiously above the world, not only physically but in spirit, and the feeling of being one with the sun and sky, cloud and rain, an identification with the elements. The view, the weather, and the sensation of power are always together in flying.

It was a cloudless day of sunshine and blue sky, to make the colours of countryside, towns and water stand out brightly as if from some magic map containing life within its paper. The south coast looked a remote and beautiful beach as we towered some hundreds of feet over Lympne, setting out to cross the little Channel, whose opposite bank, the French coast, could easily be seen. Passing high over Le Touquet, we flew inland with Beauvais cathedral beneath us; then followed unrecognized countryside, intersected by straight poplar-lined roads, and all too soon the serpentine Seine wound itself into this map from the horizon ahead. Before I had time to marshal the new sensations of the air and to wonder at Paris itself, with its radiating streets and meandering river, the flight was over; we had landed at Le Bourget. But if my feet were reluctantly on the ground once more, my spirit had started on a timeless flight which is not yet ended.

I have not forgotten that flight of nearly ten years ago, for it was a stepping-stone to my career and is fixed in my memory. I had seen aircraft before, been close enough to touch them, and watched them landing, taxi-ing and taking off at Cardiff's little aerodrome, yet surprisingly the appeal of flying as a spectacle and sensation had never before touched me; I had been aloof from it until now, but this flight, together with the sight of sleek new aircraft at Croydon and Le Bourget, ready to take wing and fly to all parts of Europe, fired the dormant ambition in my mind and filled my imagination. I already felt that I was drifting no longer, but at last making way, and although no action had yet been taken, I saw my future for the first time distinctly; it was in the air. My first letter home from France told my surprised family that I wanted to join the Royal Air Force.

At the end of my stay in France I again travelled back by air, this time in a De Havilland Dragon air liner of Hillman's Airways, which had just started a service direct from Vichy to London. But flying was now no longer a novelty to me, for I had often spent an afternoon sitting on the aerodrome boundary gazing fascinated at the flying taking place, and had seen this particular aircraft come and go a dozen times. The feeling that I had a future in the air was ever present, and strengthened my decision to break away from the shipping ties and all they involved; the RAF was first in my thoughts.

On this occasion the weather was wintry, with rainstorms and bumps in the air; consequently I felt far from well during the return flight, a large part of which was spent in thick cloud. Yet it would have taken more than an unpleasant experience to influence my decision now; on my return home I was more full of enthusiasm than ever, and carried my parents with me. They agreed, without much persuasion, to let me try to enter the RAF College and so make the service my career. I hardly questioned that they would find the two years' fees for my stay at the college, and thoughtlessly did not realize that theirs was a gesture of considerable sacrifice thus to hold open to me the door to a career which must otherwise have remained closed; it was 1933, and the depression at its worst.

However, money alone could not take me to Cranwell; I had first to pass a competitive examination and be approved by a Selection Board. This was the first examination which had ever been of real importance to me, and I set to work for it with so much industry that I surprised even myself. I worked mostly by myself, with some help from a tutor, whom I visited for a few hours each week. But I was virtually my own master, and determined not to let his pupil down; I would go into the examination room with the confidence that nothing had been left undone.

Meanwhile my parents thought it wise for me to go before a preliminary medical board at the RAF Headquarters in London. It would be heart-breaking and a waste of time, they argued, to see my work rendered useless by succeeding with the papers yet failing medically. Medical examinations demanded a very high standard in those days, which were before the expansion of the Air Force and long before ideals were crushed in the press of war.

In due course, after my return from this medical examination, intimation came that my heart was below standard and it was most unlikely that I would be accepted by the medical board proper. This was a blow made doubly heavy by the fact that it was completely unexpected. I had never been seriously ill, always played games without sign of strain and had continuously enjoyed good health. I considered this to be a blow well beneath the belt, at the same time being convinced that I was sound medically; this conviction I passed on to my parents, who allowed me to continue preparation for the examination, which I took, together with a second medical board, in November.

Afterwards I was confident that I had passed, even thinking that I had done quite well in most of the papers. It was on the result of the medical examination that all seemed to depend, and this we awaited with apprehension; I was far from confident of this result, and none of us would have been surprised if I had failed, so when we heard that I had passed, joy was tinged with astonishment at the good news.

The result of the written examinations was now awaited with confidence; November became December, for the news to be expected daily. But when the letter came, it was to say I had failed, finishing twenty-seventh on the list, from which only the first twenty-one had been taken. This was a complete reversal, and bitter news after thinking to have done well, but disappointment turned to frustration when I found that one of my papers had been completely excluded from the total marks on a point of regulations. There had been a choice of subjects available, with not more than two foreign languages permitted. I took French, German and Latin, not considering this a modern language, and had thus fallen into an error which, uninstructed, I would make again today. This mistake had cost me a possible 300 marks which I could have gained in another subject, for in accordance with the regulations my best paper of the three languages could not count in the total marks. The six places by which I had failed were covered by less than twenty marks, and I had thrown away a possible 300!

This was a costly mistake, for there would not be another opportunity of sitting the examination again for six months, while the necessary revision and preparation for the second attempt would not now take longer than a few weeks. A future success, which seemed assured, offered no solution as to what I should do during the intervening period. Inevitably, and quite willingly, I went to work in the business. Each day I walked, caught bus or tram, morning and evening to and from Cardiff docks, and sat from nine till five in the outside office, adding figures, checking accounts and running messages, an office boy, earning ten shillings a week.

Sadly there was all too little to do, and my surmise that the business was at least temporarily dead proved correct. There was perhaps an hour's work for each of us daily, the typist, the clerk and myself, with not much to occupy the partners, who lived in a hopeful but admittedly distant future, when prosperity might be regained once more.

Ships made voyages of which I could now see for myself the losses at the bottom of balance sheets, only an occasional profit keeping heads above water and hearts beating. If I could see the most distant glow of romance and fortune in old records within the offices, I had only to look outside in dockland at the unemployed poverty of the present for illusions quickly to vanish. I was happy enough to work in the firm during those few months only because I doubted that I should ever do so again. I was glad to have worked there if only for a short time, for the impression office life made on me strengthened the conviction that my choice to break away from it was a right decision, and one I would not regret.

I sat again for the Cranwell Entrance Examination in June, and this time I passed without difficulty. Amazingly, my first failure returned now in the guise of a blessing, for I passed in second on the list, a position which made me eligible for a prize cadetship, a form of scholarship to the college. This was a success outside my whole range of expectation, and so the more surprising and warming. It placed me not only on the road to my future career, but firmly on that road, and there seemed no reason why I should ever have cause to look back. The future seemed great, and it seemed to be so especially for me.

CHAPTER II

FIRST FLYING

THE Royal Air Force College into which I had passed was at Cranwell in Lincolnshire. There had been an aerodrome, in fact two adjacent aerodromes, in this remote spot ever since the last war, when it had been a Naval Air Station, surprisingly far removed from the sea. I believe that even in those early days flying instruction took pride of place over many other activities at Cranwell, and it has been so ever since.

The college was little younger at Cranwell than flying itself. After the war the naval camp passed into the hands of the newly formed RAF, and it was natural that when the college was founded in the early nineteen-twenties it should be situated at Cranwell so that cadets could use the enormous southern aerodrome and other facilities of an established camp.

Aerial fighting in the last war was originally shared by the Royal Flying Corps and the Royal Naval Air Service, and it was not until the war was nearing an end that an Independent Air Force was proposed, to become the seed from which the RAF was to spring. Lord Trenchard had been largely responsible for the formation of this independent flying service; he had overcome much opposition to secure its formation, and once formed, the same energies were determined to see it continue and prosper.

So it is not surprising to find that the virtual founder of the RAF was also the prime mover for the founding of a college for Air Force cadets, on the lines of those at Woolwich and Sandhurst, from which the service would draw it officers. In this way it would be ensured that the flying traditions handed down from the war would not be lost in the new peace-time service.

But the RAF was not only a very young, but also a small service, and the post-war decade was one of Treasury-imposed retrenchment, not of expansion. So the RAF College never became comparable with the Military Academy at Woolwich or the college at Sandhurst, which together sent hundreds of officers each year to the army, for Cranwell was dealing only in tens.

Nor for a whole decade was the college housed in a building worthy of its name. The old camp at Cranwell was a hastily constructed city in the wood and corrugated iron of war-time huts, now made by a tight-reined Exchequer to suffice until richer days, and naturally enough in these surroundings the college became a superior but nevertheless wooden building of one long low storey.

This lack of a pretentious background to the early years was of no account. The tradition in which the young service was to grow up could not be drawn from a building or any such inanimate object bound to the earth; it was to come strongly and directly from the sky itself, originally from the flying and aerial fighting of the last war; it was born naturally in a young service which possessed the freedom of the air, and whose members were ever under the strong influence of the sensations of flying, the curious feeling of spiritual power, the identification with the elements combined with the changing beauty of the aerial view. It is not surprising that pilots appear to possess a curiously detached independence of body and of mind, for flying breeds detachment from earthly ties. The college personified this abstract, indefinable spirit, and it is unimaginable that there was lacking among the cadets of former years the enthusiasm and keenness of expectation of flying which I felt on the first day I joined the college, and which has been with me in some degree ever since.

But materially I was luckier than those early cadets, for on my arrival at Cranwell in August 1934 I found the college housed in a magnificent and brand new building. We were the first entry to start our full time in the new college, for although it had been occupied by cadets for some months, they had all moved across from the old dilapidated wooden structure, now unbelievably the home of the college for at least twelve years. Thus we were, without then realizing its implication, a completely new generation of cadets at Cranwell, who did not pass by the old building, remember its discomforts and thank Providence for the luxury of the new college, as our senior terms might; we took a fine building for granted as our own right, and as a natural provision for the service of the future.

I never made any secret of the fact that it was flying and flying alone which attracted me to the service. I had no eye on a military career, nor had I given a thought to the difference between civilian and service life, about which I was completely ignorant. Ambition to fly was the spur; just as I had surmounted all difficulties to reach the college, so was I now determined, whatever might be demanded by the service, to allow no sacrifice to deter me if it were made in the name of flying.

But it soon transpired that there was little flying for cadets in their two years at college; life was not lived in the shade of the hangars to the roar of running engines, or in a whirlwind of propellers. Hardly had the new term of Flight Cadets been assembled than we were addressed by the Commandant of the college. Almost his first words contained the seemingly blasphemous statement that flying was but one of the many subjects we had to master during our stay, and neither more nor less important than any other. Worse still was to come, for he went on to explain that time allotted to flying in the college time-table was no more than proportionate to its importance, and only amounted to a few hours each week.

Not a single cadet of the new term assembled there took the slightest notice of these words; no one believed them. Aircraft were flying around outside, and visible from the windows of the room in which we sat attentive; if our eyes dared not stray openly to the windows, our ears could nevertheless hear distinctly the hum of aero-engines. Was this not the Air Force College and flying our star? Certainly and finally we dismissed from our minds this implication that anything imaginable could rank in importance with flying, and forgot this warning determinedly and wishfully for the two years at the college, perhaps for ever.

To become accustomed to the ways of the college did not take long, nor was the life different from what I had expected. The routine did not differ greatly from that of a school, but the atmosphere, superficially at least, bore no point of resemblance; here there was more freedom and greater aspirations, and the college seemed a half-way house between school and university. As was to be expected at a military establishment, discipline was strict, but not uncomfortably so, for the service was young and had not weighed itself down with a burden of regulations and restricting conventions. Daily morning parades appeared only as preludes to the day's flying periods; tiresome, seemingly useless subjects in class would be forgotten in expectation of the evening's games. There was little to dislike and much that was very pleasant about life at Cranwell, a life which I was later to find typical of all Air Force messes.

Class subjects were largely mathematical; this did not suit me personally, since I had always at school avoided mathematics, for which I had substituted languages, now no longer required. Now, I found mathematics of all kinds in the forefront, with many periods allotted in the timetable to their study, for these subjects went hand in hand with the practical side of engineering which was taught in workshops. The emphasis on engineering was not without reason, for the RAF is a mechanical service dependent entirely on complicated machines, and it is not only desirable for a pilot to be an amateur engineer, but essential, in order that he may understand his aircraft.

The other half of our time in class was devoted to service subjects: engineering practice, aircraft armaments, signals, including wireless and the morse code, air navigation, air force law, meteorology, hygiene, administration and many others of equal importance. With so many subjects to master it was not surprising that flying itself could not occupy more than a limited share of our time.

Cadets were also strongly encouraged to play games, for flying demands a high degree of physical fitness from a pilot; a clear head and quick reaction are essentials, and the playing of games was considered a sure way to keep in flying condition. So it can be readily understood that a cadet's time was fully occupied; while not working he was expected literally to be playing, and his free time was only a relative term. Nevertheless, we enjoyed this full life in which every hour was employed, and the little real leisure we received was the more appreciated.

Yet all other attractions at Cranwell were belittled by the fascination of learning to fly; games and study were variations on known tunes, while flying was a completely new and unexplored theme. Fitting ourselves at the clothing stores with flying suits lined with warm "teddy bear" material, trying on helmets, testing their intercoms and being issued with goggles, were preliminary thrills of the pleasure to come.

We had our parachutes adjusted to fit correctly in the parachute section, from whose roof hung the white silk canopies of other parachutes drying after their periodical inspection. All their mysteries were in time unfolded to us, and we were all able later to pack or hang one if the need should arise. It was sufficient now just to know the simple way of opening the canopy in an emergency, by pulling the rip-cord with the handle which comes conveniently to the right hand. Normally a parachute is forgotten, or seen by a pilot merely as the not very comfortable object on which he is sitting, and for years it may thus do silent duty, only to be suddenly wanted and present at a critical time. Forgotten and ignored, a parachute can still be a pilot's best friend.

Equipped with all these necessities of flying we reported to our "Flight", which occupied a huge corrugated-iron hangar on an elevation facing south over the flat grass-covered aerodrome. Inside were aircraft, some with wings bare of fabric, others lacking wheels or undercarriage and supported on trestles, one or two mere skeletons of aircraft without fabric covering, wings or engine; all were in the hangar for repair or routine overhaul. The predominance in our time-table of engineering subjects needed now no explanation or excuse, the purpose was revealed in one first brief survey of the hangar.

At the back of the hangar were some offices and a pilots' room containing metal lockers for our flying clothing and parachutes. Next to this room was the Flight Commander's office, from which could be heard the voices and occasional uproarious laughter of the instructors. On the inter-communicating door a notice read: "F/Lt. H. M. Pearson, OC 'C' Flight", and below was printed the legend: "We can teach cows to fly, but they must try!"

This humour was at once friendly and comforting, for I think most of us had a secret dread lest we should turn out to be indifferent pupils, be air-sick, or worse still, lack aptitude to such a degree that the authorities would decide it was insufficient for the demands of the service. Such a decision would result in a cadet leaving the college with his dreams unfulfilled, a failure through no fault of his own. The standards of the RAF were high; it could in those days afford to pick its pilots by demanding a high medical standard, and would not waste time on excessively long instruction of some backward pupil whose ability was questionable. I think my term was lucky, for if one of us left through inability to fly it must have occurred within the first few weeks, before we all knew each other, and I have forgotten all about it.

My instructor was the Flight Commander himself, a former Cranwell cadet, as were the majority of the staff, who had become instructors after some years spent in squadrons. I was more than a little in awe of his experience and probable intolerance of stupidity, but when he came into the pilots' room and talked to me for a few minutes he seemed quite human, saying I was to ask him at any time if there was anything I did not understand, and let him know if I was having any special difficulty. Then he took me out to show me over an aircraft, one of many lined up on the "tarmac" outside the hangar. Any solid ground outside hangars is invariably called tarmac in the service, though it is more often made of concrete.

The aircraft was an Avro Tutor, a biplane and two-seater, well known as being "fool proof" and, of course, fitted with dual control. I could see at a glance that both front and rear cockpits were identical, crammed with instruments and appearing very business-like, especially in comparison with the upholstered interior of an air liner, which was my only standard. The Tutor was painted silver, with the usual red, white and blue roundels on fuselage and wings, as well as wide vertical stripes of the same colours on the rudder. On the sides of all college aircraft were painted enormous black letters or numbers, by which a particular aircraft could be recognized; many erring pupils had crimes nailed at their door by some instructor who had "taken their number".

It is hard to realise now that this was still exclusively the era of the biplane; not only were biplanes present to the exclusion of all other types at Cranwell, but throughout the whole service, and this was less than ten years ago! Several years were to pass before the first tentative introduction of simple monoplane types, with such revolutionary features as retractable undercarriages, landing flaps and variable pitch airscrews, features which in their turn were to become commonplace. But I did not need to look forward then, the present was good enough, and the Tutor seemed the best aircraft in the world, for I was to fly it.

Clad in flying suit, with helmet and goggles on and parachute slung over my shoulder, I made my way through the hangar, past the grinning skeleton aircraft out on to the tarmac, where the Tutor stood in the open, under a sky which had never before looked so wide, yet at the same time so intimate. The engine was running to warm up, with an airman sitting in the cockpit, for a running aircraft may not be left unoccupied. As I approached he got out, and, knowing that I was a novice, helped me settle myself in the front cockpit, where pupils always flew, and fastened the safety straps of the harness over my shoulders.

There I sat, harness tightly fastened, intercoms plugged into their socket, goggles ready to be lowered, waiting for my instructor. He appeared from the depths of the hangar, quickly got into the rear cockpit and, before I had realized what was happening, had "run up" the engine, tested the magneto switches and signalled to the waiting airmen to remove the wooden chocks from in front of the wheels. I was trying to sort all this out, when a voice asked in my ear: "Can you hear me quite clearly, Gibbs?", to which I replied into the speaking-tube with alacrity that yes, sir, I could. My first flying lesson had started.

Flying instruction consists initially of demonstration by the instructor and imitation by the pupil, later by experiment and trial on the part of the pupil, who makes deductions from his results. A pupil can learn a great deal from his instructor, but he must teach himself so very much more. An instructor can ensure that he starts out on the right path, and return him to it at intervals when he strays, but real progress depends on the pupil himself and his application. Learning to fly calls for concentration and hard work, but how much easier does this work become when it is aided both by natural ability and enthusiasm. None of us coupled flying even remotely with our conception of work, but everyone tried his hardest.

So great were my expectations that this first flight might easily have been an anti-climax, but this did not happen; far from bringing any feelings of disappointment, its result was to increase my zeal for flying to such a pitch that for weeks afterwards other subjects had no existence in my thoughts and other topics of conversation palled. Yet at this first lesson I was only shown how to taxi!

The key to good taxi-ing is "slowly and surely", to go no faster than a walking pace, all the time looking ahead for obstructions on the ground and searching the sky for aircraft coming to land. Brakes were fitted, but their use was discouraged except in an emergency, for aircraft brakes, even now, have a habit of letting a pilot down, often when they are most wanted, and not to place reliance in them is to avoid the ignominy of taxi-ing into some stationary aircraft and helplessly watching the propeller chewing hundreds of pounds' worth of avoidable damage.

I eventually succeeded in taxi-ing to my instructor's satisfaction, but not before we had made some gyrations reminiscent of a waltz and I had been reproved for making too much use of the brakes. He then told me to taxi to the down-wind boundary of the aerodrome, and telling me to keep my hands and feet lightly on the controls, turned the aircraft into wind and took off without further ado.

He flew around for about ten minutes so that I could feel the movements of the controls beneath his hands in all manoeuvres and become accustomed to the experience of flying. The college building, with its white façade of vertical pillars, could be seen almost in plan view below; the enormous south and smaller north aerodromes were dotted with aircraft crawling like insects over their surface, and the sky itself seemed filled with flying activity. The countryside extended open and flat as far as the eye could see, looking like a beautiful three-dimensional map in lifelike colours. But before I could marshal my feelings of wonder, the new and delightful sensation I was experiencing, we were on the aerodrome again after the lightest of landings and the voice of my instructor was saying, "Taxi in now; you've got her". We reached the tarmac outside the hangar without incident, the aircraft was turned into wind, the engine switched off and chocks placed behind the wheels to prevent it running away. My first lesson was over.

Walking up the slope towards the hangar beside my instructor, I listened eagerly as he talked of what we should be doing in the next few lessons, unfolding for me a magic immediate future of turns, landings, spins, loops, rolls, all the things which I knew I should do, but which had seemed unreal until this moment, when he spoke so naturally about them. Discussion on every aspect of flying was rife amongst first-term cadets to the exclusion of all other subjects, and if opinions were uninformed and facts often fantastically removed from truth, the entertainment and speculation of such conversation persisted tirelessly. By contrast these quiet, natural and informed words from my instructor appeared of immeasurably great importance; this was the real thing from one who knew.

I stowed my parachute in its locker, unpeeled my flying suit, then, sitting at the desk in the pilots' room, wrote in my brand-new flying log book the first entry: "Aircraft: Avro Tutor; Pilot—F/Lt. Pearson; Passenger—Self; Flight—10 minutes' Air Experience", and also the date: "September 21st, 1934".

After nearly five hours' dual instruction I could take off, make reasonably accurate turns, recover from a spin, climb and glide, make a passable approach to the aerodrome—in fact, everything necessary for a solo flight, except land. My landings were erratic; sometimes I would flatten out too high and stall the aircraft at ten feet above the ground, resulting in a heavy landing and an agonized silence from my instructor, who would soon recover imperturbability and patiently tell me to try once more. At other times I would do exactly the opposite, and leave flattening out from the glide until too late; the wheels would touch before the speed had fallen to the stall and we would bound back into the air, a gigantic bounce to thirty or forty feet. Wearily my instructor would take control, open the throttle and climb up again for me to make another attempt.

This could clearly not go on; I felt quite confident, yet each time, when I thought I had succeeded, the landing would turn out to be a bad one. As a last resort my instructor took control and flew me over the aerodrome surface just above stalling speed and at a height of only three or four feet, a fine example of accurate flying. After he had flown several times up and down the long aerodrome in this manner, he handed over to me, and although the wheels touched the ground occasionally, I managed to keep the aircraft fairly steady. In the end I had a shrewd idea of what the aerodrome grass looked like from the correct landing height, and afterwards had no more landing troubles.

During my next flight I made two or three landings in succession which seemed to satisfy my instructor; he taxied in to the tarmac rather earlier than usual, and instead of switching off the engines told me through the telephones that I could go up and make a few circuits and landings—solo! Here was a milestone, my first solo flight, but curiously it seemed then in no way remarkable, but a natural event; my feelings were not of apprehension of something going amiss, but of relief that I had at last reached the required standard. I was full of confidence, for during the last few lessons I had handled the aircraft throughout without help from my instructor. Moreover, during the whole of my flying he had occupied the rear cockpit, out of my sight and so out of my thoughts, and his presence would not now be missed, for the vacant back seat could not be seen.

There was no glamour about this first solo flight, or any other at Cranwell; it was a matter-of-fact affair, and an everyday occurrence. I taxied out from the tarmac, slowly and carefully, turned into wind, made the necessary adjustments in the cockpit and took off without hesitation. From the ground the aircraft could be seen climbing steadily to a thousand feet, then turning on to the aerodrome circuit it came round and made a safe landing into wind. While I taxied back ready for another take-off, my instructor, who had stood on the tarmac watching my first effort, turned his back on the aerodrome and vanished into the hangar; he had seen enough to judge that I was flying safely. From now on I had much to teach myself.

Flying is fascinating; in those days it was nearer an art than a science, which it now approaches more closely. The mechanical complexity of a modern aircraft, with its long range and comprehensive equipment, causes actual technical knowledge and flying routine to be placed highest among a pilot's qualifications. "Flair", the natural aptitude of a pilot endowed with instinctive ability, was the coveted attribute in those biplane days, when aircraft were mechanically simple and flying itself the goal. To be painstaking, conscientious, to be thorough, seemed alone not enough; without flair a pilot would lack, and be seen to lack, a final polish.

A change in the character of flying has taken place in the last decade, a change dictated both by progress in aircraft design and the specialized demands made on flying by the war. Today the training of pilots is more comprehensive, the aircraft unrecognizable from our Cranwell biplanes, more difficult to master technically and to fly. A new system of instruction has been evolved for the mass production of pilots to fly and fight the modern aircraft; inevitably the former individual touch has been lost as gradually the pilot himself becomes less important than the machine. The game has become a business which must not fail.

Yet, to me, a backward glance still brings a tinge of regret at the passing of the former individual touch on flying, when the aircraft and pilot were one entity. In those days of leisurely instruction at Cranwell we could afford to have other gods, which our easy and simple aircraft did not deny us. Flying was then nearer to a game than a business, with which it is now comparable, and flair akin to natural games ability. I was to make the change, spanning the years between biplane and monoplane flying, but today or yesterday, flying to me is still fascinating.

To us first-term cadets flying instruction seemed to proceed at an exasperatingly leisurely pace. While a whole period of an hour and a half was given in our timetable to flying each day, this did not mean that each pupil spent all this time in the air; a multitude of circumstances might prevent him flying at all during this period. Bad weather, with its gales and squalls, rain, low cloud and, worst of all, fogs and mists, would cause a black cone to be hoisted outside the Chief Instructor's office to signify there was to be no flying, a signal greeted by audible moans from the cadets, but, I imagine, by silent cheers from some weary instructors. Thus in a foggy week—and Cranwell suffered much from such weather—we would do no flying at all. Also there were not always enough aircraft to go round; even in those days of uncomplicated aircraft it was a struggle to keep sufficient numbers serviceable, and a pupil might have to sit for a whole period disconsolate on the tarmac, enviously watching others flying. At all events, we were lucky if we actually spent forty minutes of this period in the air.

So, although flying was our star, its light was rationed to us in what we considered miserly quantities; the whole of every day of the week devoted to flying would hardly have satisfied our appetite. Yet interest never flagged, as the first unbounded enthusiasm became tempered with reticence born of first-hand knowledge; love for flying itself did not die, but it was spread among the many facets and intricacies of the game, which were constantly being discovered to fill our expectations anew.

When at the end of my first term the college closed for four weeks' Christmas leave, the senior term passed out into the service, to become no longer Flight Cadets but Pilot Officers, and take their place in the various squadrons to which they had been posted. Their transition seemed remote to me, for there were four terms at the college, of which I had completed only one, and the three before me still seemed an eternity. Although happy, I was looking ahead and impatient to achieve complete independence, not least in the air.

Ironically I found at home and in Cardiff a spark of prosperity burning; shipping, ever dependent on industrial influences, was becoming a little more active, though there was a long leeway to make up before dividends would flow once more. The threat of a far-off war, which was soon to cause the Air Force to expand, was already urging industry forward to greater efforts, and shipping was beginning to follow the trend.

So nothing depressed my leave, indeed I made the pleasant discovery that a flying life excited interest everywhere; although flying was no longer a novelty, the average person was not intimate with it. The RAF was then a small service and not widespread, and the reach of Civil Aviation was limited; the man in the street was then as ignorant about flying and the Air Force as he is knowledgeable today. To have chosen a career then far from commonplace was satisfying to my sense of adventure; if I were thirty years too late to be a flying pioneer, I was just in time not only to be included in the microscopic pre-expansion Air Force of biplanes, but also to belong to the first generation in the new college. I had only flown for about forty hours during the whole of that first term, but I had passed the necessary examinations and played some games for the college; the life seemed good and I was satisfied with my choice.

More periods of leave came and went, to divide the terms as the months passed by. Subsequent terms never held that novice's enchantment in a new kingdom which that first term possessed for me, yet their promise was wholly fulfilled. Flying still dominated our thoughts, but differently, more subtly, for we were growing in experience, not only of flying, but in the service way of life. Days seemed less full, and we were more masters of our own leisure, while every new term of cadets appeared more madly enthusiastic and even more breathlessly occupied than we had been. The life was no longer new and strange, the college routine came to us automatically, classwork was not so arduous; above all, there were no sinking doubts lest we should fail in flying or examinations. Our confidence increased as terms passed on to make way for new; we could fly and we would succeed.

The first year's flying was done entirely in the faithful Tutor, to which we became deeply attached, for if easy to fly and completely without vices, it was nevertheless full of character. It was an ideal trainer, and not its least feature was strong construction, frequently the object of praise by some cadet who had made a heavy landing without damage to his aircraft. In the air it was slow, as might be expected from the low power of the engine and its blunt lines, and we only cruised at 110 miles an hour, but it handled beautifully and was an ideal aircraft for aerobatics.

By no means all our Tutor hours were solo, for throughout the whole year's flying we were receiving dual instruction at intervals. In this way our progress was checked regularly for bad habits to be detected and corrected before they could take root, and on almost every dual flight there was something new demonstrated, to be practised and repractised when we flew solo. No more comprehensive system of instruction can be imagined, with the instructors themselves setting the seal on the system by the interest they took in each individual pupil and by their own polished flying, always before a pupil as his model.

The whole sequence of instruction followed naturally after my first solo flight; then I could make circuits and landings in fair weather, but very much more than that was needed before I could be called proficient. Forced landings in confined spaces had to be mastered, for which special fields in the neighbourhood were used; spins, inverted spins, loops, rolls and half-rolls, stall turns, every aerobatic was learnt, for they confirmed a pupil in mastery of his aircraft in any attitude, requiring the precision and judgement so essential to accurate flying, together with a cool head and quick thinking. Map-reading, practical air navigation, flying on compass courses, bad-weather flying, low flying at the height of tree-tops, blind flying by instruments with the pupil beneath a hood, all these were taught by demonstration, practised solo by the pupil, and checked at intervals by the instructor. The instruction was thorough, and, changed in detail as it is today, the basis of the system still survives as the rock on which the enormous edifice of war-time flying instruction is built; that also is thorough, and its thoroughness is repaying us today with a flow of pilots well trained to fly and to fight.

The year of flying Tutors, the *ab initio* trainer, came to an end, and we were ready for more advanced flying than that type could give us. The next step was to fly a service type of aircraft, identical with those in use with Air Force squadrons, but divested of war equipment. Machine guns, bomb racks and the like were removed, for only flying pure and simple was taught at Cranwell; the application of flying to warfare, the firing of aircraft guns and dropping of bombs, could easily be hung later onto the framework of accurate flying which the college aimed to give every cadet.

At this time three types of service aircraft were in use at Cranwell: the Atlas, an army co-operation machine; the Bristol Bulldog, the standard air force fighter; and the Hart, a day bomber, which was the latest thing and considered very fast and formidable. I was placed at the end of my first year in the Hart Flight, and by this a little disappointed, for I had an inclination towards fighters. While I felt lucky to be flying the more modern aircraft, I knew I would be more likely to be posted to fighters at the end of my time if I were in the Bulldog Flight.

Today or yesterday, most new pilots and, if the truth be told, many old have this leaning towards fighters, and it is understandable. Then, flying itself was at its most exacting and enjoyable in the small and manoeuvrable types of fighter aircraft, while today Fighter Command is perhaps the only branch of the service in which fair and pure flying ability are still recognized and have something of the importance of former days.

The difference between a fighter squadron and any other was not in those days as marked as it is now, when it has been accentuated no less by the great divergence in design of fighter aircraft from others than by the influence of the specialized nature of fighter operations. In time past the majority of aircraft were manoeuvrable single-engined types, all capable of aerobatics, while now almost the only aircraft of this type are in Fighter Command. But perhaps the most attractive feature of fighters is their wartime role, which is essentially that of attack. It demands an individual effort and initiative, in which a pilot is master of his own destiny and much dependent on flying flair. Fighters will always be different and are always coveted.

If I felt disappointment at missing fighters, it was soon to be forgotten in the delight of flying the Hart, which produced a sensation of mastery of speed and power lacking in the Tutor. Its 500 horse-power Rolls-Royce engine and sleek lines gave a performance in the air which was at first breath-taking; the open exhausts made a staccato roar, and the controls were sensitive to the slightest touch. After the docile Tutor, the Hart seemed incredibly fierce and tricky.

So flying instruction began all over again, with the same fascination as before; dual circuits and landings, ending with a first solo flight in a service type, started once more the whole sequence of instruction which I had completed in Tutors. I made several cross-country flights, disgracing myself on one of these by getting lost and landing at an unrecognized aerodrome. Forced landings were practised as before, and on one attempt I carried the top foliage of a hedge away with my undercarriage by cutting the approach too fine. Luckily no one had taken my number, so authority was none the wiser. Aerobatics were practised now more than ever, for the Hart's fast rate of climb made the ascent to a safe aerobatic height a matter of seconds, for which the old Tutor had seemed to take an eternity.

I flew for about seventy hours in Harts during that last year at Cranwell, of which about a third of the time was spent in dual instruction. By the time my last term came, whatever first disappointment I had felt in my lot had faded away, for I was becoming attached to the Hart and quite willing to join a day bomber squadron when I passed out into the service, a time which was approaching fast. The two years at the college seemed to have passed at the speed of aircraft; only yesterday I had made the first entry in my log book, in which many pages were now filled with flying, though my memory of the day when my instructor had adopted a last resort to teach me to land was still quite clear.

My last term had only a few weeks more to run, and in these I competed for the flying prize, a silver trophy more sought after than any of the other prizes for college subjects, even ranking higher than the sword of honour, awarded for all-round excellence; as always, flying took first place. In the competition two cadets from each flight carried out a set programme of flying which was witnessed and marked by the judge, an independent instructor sent from the Central Flying School.

I was lucky to be one of the six selected to compete, for the standard in my flight was not very high. Actually I made no serious mistakes, rolling across the sky in a nice straight line, first to the right then to the left, and judging my forced landing fairly accurately. Yet I am sure I came nowhere near to winning; only the winner's name was announced, others were not placed, but from what I saw of his performance it was faultless and polished, in quite a different class from mine. The winner has been in fighters ever since leaving Cranwell, and was later in No. 111 Squadron, the first to be equipped with Hurricanes. Today he commands his own fighter squadron, was recently awarded a DFC and has several enemy aircraft to his credit. Promise has not failed.

Final examinations were taken amidst the appropriate apprehension and last-minute panic of revision from which they are inseparable. I was not sure now that the increased leisure which I had found as my term advanced through college had not been obtained by a sacrifice of study. An occasional week-end leave, Sunday afternoon's golf or evening cinema made inroads into good intentions for work. In short, the library and study had been somewhat neglected.

Nevertheless all turned out well, for I finished in sixth place in my term's final order, a result not quite so satisfactory as the second place in which I had passed into Cranwell, but then I had deliberately devoted time to games, playing in three college teams, as well as concentrating on flying. I had attempted to strike a mean between work and play, and was not dissatisfied with the result.

Since cadets were given a measure of choice in their first postings, I gave as my selection fighters, for I was still optimistic, still under the spell which is never for any pilot quite impotent and even today is not yet dead to me: a longing for single-seaters. But this time I felt no disappointment when I found myself posted to a day bomber squadron, which had been my second choice and little behind the first in my estimation.

Reading the list of postings pinned to the notice-board, I realized that my term of thirty cadets, which for two years had shared not only one roof and the same daily round, but also the same enthusiasms and aspirations, was now to be parted and spread over the country. Only a handful were posted to fighters, the remainder distributed among flying boats, army co-operation squadrons, torpedo carriers and heavy night bombers; all dispersed to stations in remote places, some soon to go abroad.

While parting was sad, the hopes of what the future might hold were comforting as ever. We were all filled with anticipation of our new life in squadrons, an independent life, free from school-like supervision, with a sky of almost boundless flying. I passed through the last parade hardly realizing that we stood for the last time together on the parade ground on which we had stood daily for two years, when, watching the blue ensign ascend slowly to the mast against an equally blue sky, every cadet had wondered silently if the weather would hold fine for his flying period!

No long partings: we packed, shook hands and went our ways, often to meet in the next few years, for flying made light of distances and friends could be visited. There was a month's leave before joining our squadrons, when we would be no longer Flight Cadets but Pilot Officers, and in the RAF at last. I felt that I was setting out on another exciting journey, with the path still leading the way I had chosen; to day bombers and No. 98 Squadron.

CHAPTER III

GOOD-BYE, "98"

98 SQUADRON was stationed at Hucknall, just outside Nottingham, an aerodrome which I had already visited on a practice cross-country flight from Cranwell. Its aircraft were Hawker Hinds, identical with the Hart except for a more powerful Kestrel engine, giving it a speed of just under 200 miles an hour. If a Hart had once seemed immeasurably superior to the Tutor, my first flight in a Hind revealed a performance to place the Hart in a class to be remembered tolerantly as "old and faithful", but nevertheless outmoded. The extra power of its engine gave the pilot an exhilarating push in the back as he opened the throttle to accelerate rapidly over the ground, and it enabled him to climb steeply and rapidly away from the earth. After four weeks of leave I was out of flying practice, but the Hind handled just like a Hart, and after a few circuits and landings I was at home in the air once more.

Curiously, I was very ignorant of quite what to expect of an RAF station; if the college had taught cadets a hundred things about their service, it had imparted only the theory, and so painted an ideal picture from which any departure in practice was unimaginable. Cranwell had been a hothouse in which we grew in knowledge, completely isolated from the service around us. If cadets left the college finally full of learning, they still knew nothing of what they were to find outside in reality. The picture in a cadet's mind of his service in a squadron was an idyllic one and destined to be unfulfilled. When eventually the true situation was appraised and service life accepted at its own valuation and not that of the college, initial disappointment might fade away, but the first discovery of this misconception, fondled for two long years, seemed something of a foul blow, and one from which some cadets never quite recovered.

The blow, generally, was caused by imperfection. The college itself had been efficiently run and well organized. Objectives were to be achieved there to make life seem sweet and worth living. We had our goal before us for the two years, which was reached when we passed successfully from the college out into the service. In comparison, life at a station seemed aimless and lacking in direction, and soon I began to feel let down by the college, which had continually rung bells which appeared now to be unjustified by the procession which they heralded. These feelings, I see now, were the aftermath of over-enthusiasm. I had built in my imagination a shining tower of the service from the idealistic plans the college had drawn for me, and not unnaturally the tower was tottering now in the open, unsuited to the winds and rain of a real climate. I had expected so much, and now found so little; frankly, I was bitterly disappointed with this new life.

98 was a new squadron, and when I arrived in August 1936 it was just three months old. The wind of war was rising in Europe, to make an uneasy government, not completely unmindful of the future, embark on an expansion of the Air Force. In my last year at Cranwell the course of the Abyssinian crisis had given rise to wild speculation on a probable aerial war; there had been rumours of sudden movements of whole squadrons from home to Malta and the Middle East; squadrons actually waited on desert aerodromes for word of war. There had been a buzz of activity in the RAF, which only died down with the country's ignominious withdrawal. Nevertheless a lesson must surely have been learnt; the implication that the Italian Air Force was superior to our own could not be allowed to pass unchallenged. As Winston Churchill vigorously opposed the Government's appeasement policy and attempted to shake off the mantle of lethargy from the country with the grim picture of Germany's aerial might, growing daily, the expansion of the RAF began. Yearly the service was to grow, as one expansion scheme was deemed inadequate to meet the demands of the changing political situation, to be succeeded by another scheme, and yet another even more sweeping than before.

Before my term left Cranwell, evidence of the expansion was before us in several forms: promotion was accelerated, new squadrons were forming, modern aircraft had been ordered and new aerodromes were being built. The Treasury purse was at last opening its strings to the neglected services. Air estimates were in that year the highest of all peace-time, only to be exceeded regularly in successive years. New Flying Training Schools were being opened and many more pilots were called for annually; the RAF was spreading over the country and so becoming known.

Many, attracted by flying, now saw a chance to learn, and joined the RAF, with the easily obtained short-service commissions. The tiny Air Force of former days was swallowed up in the expansion before I could reach it. The service doubled itself, redoubled and multiplied again and again as the snowball of expansion rolled down the decade to war. I was there, I saw it happen. At first expansion was slow, later it became an avalanche. I stood within to witness, rather sadly, the old, select and lovable service of biplane days, in which I had chosen my career, vanish from sight without my ever knowing quite what I had missed. I was now in a new squadron of a new service, one unknown to the college or to me. Herein was the true reason for disappointment.

Although 98 was new, it would have been the same disappointing story even in a squadron which had been continuously in being since the last war, and so full of tradition and memories. For the expansion was demanding new squadrons, and the method adopted for forming one was to take a complete flight away from an established squadron and use it as the basis on which to form the new unit. A squadron normally consisted of three flights, of which two might now be taken to form new squadrons; old squadrons were mutilated mercilessly in this manner, and lost unavoidably much of their former character and individuality.

Previously a squadron had been an entity, with its own peculiarities and customs, reputation and habits. A newcomer among its officers was a rarity, its airmen knew their officers and loved the aircraft, which they nursed as their own. These were the ideal conditions I had expected, which had now to give way to a new order, a situation comparable with the abandonment of handicraft for mass-production. Throughout the Air Force in these years it would have seemed the same; nothing was permanent, everywhere there was change. I had to dream my future again and forget the microscopic Air Force in which squadrons were teams and flying the game they played.

No. 40 Squadron at Abingdon had given birth to 98 by breaking off one of her flights. For a few months parent and child had shared the same hangar, until 98, receiving airmen, officers and equipment at a great and bewildering rate, had formed two flights of its own and was ready, literally, to fly away. One morning the few aircraft which were 98 Squadron taxied out over the aerodrome at Abingdon, laden with suitcases, squash rackets, golf clubs and all the paraphernalia of a peace-time move, and left their parent, to fly away and fend for themselves at their new home. When I arrived at Hucknall, the squadron had been there for a month and was finding its own feet.

If 98 had been hastily formed and was without tradition, spirit and keenness were not lacking, but were all-pervading, not only among pilots but throughout the squadron. Rivalry was thus born and kept alive between us and another Hind squadron, No. 104, which was the only other squadron on the station. Friendly competition with 104 was continuous; we considered our aircraft shined more brightly, our landings better, our pilots more skilful and our formation flying closer than our rivals. This attitude was typical of the peace-time service, in which competition of some kind kept bright the flame of interest, which might so easily burn low for want of direction. The distant question of "Where are we going?" was never asked.

98 had only two flights when I arrived, "A" Flight and "B" Flight. Flights are always known by letters, for while all squadrons have different numbers, all use the first few letters of the alphabet to distinguish their flights. I was placed in "A" Flight by the Squadron Adjutant, to whom I reported on my first morning. I had already met him, and most of the other officers, in the Mess the previous evening, when I learnt in conversation nearly all there was to be known about the squadron. Surprisingly, all these officers were only Pilot Officers, except the Squadron Commander himself, who was appropriately a Squadron Leader. This strange state of affairs was directly attributable to the expansion, for the tiny former Air Force, which was to be the keystone of the new building, had contained only enough officers to occupy the key positions in the expanding service, and the squadrons' vacancies for Flight Lieutenants and Flying Officers went unfilled for lack of officers in those ranks. Now short-service officers were beginning to pour into the service to supply the deficiency, and all the squadrons' Pilot Officers held short-service commissions, while the most senior had finished his training only six months before.

That the short-service officer was in the ascendancy was something about which Cranwell had not warned its cadets; this discovery was yet another surprise. The short-service scheme was one imposed on the RAF by the nature of its work in war-time. After the last war it was realised that casualties in any future aerial war would be very heavy, and that a large reserve of pilots would be required to maintain continuously an adequate force of aircraft in the air. However, a pilot cannot be made in a day; some months of training are required before he can take his place in the air and on the ground with sufficient knowledge and skill to be of use to the service. It was this very urgent necessity for a large and well-trained reserve which gave rise to the short-service system.

In the small pre-expansion Air Force this system had been working well, and was almost as old as the RAF itself. Then the service was a skeleton of permanent officers, built up to a full form by the presence of short-service officers, who would enter, stay a while, then leave for civilian life and the Reserve, always to be replaced by another and yet another batch of officers, also to be trained, stay and eventually go their own ways. The skeleton itself had been kept alive by the steady but small Cranwell output, together with those to whom permanent commissions were granted as graduates of Universities, and those very few lucky short-service officers who were retained beyond their normal five-year term.

When the expansion was planned, it must have seemed that the easiest way to increase the number of pilots was to multiply the number of Flying Training Schools turning out short-service officers. Such a method would also show a quick result, since the course of their training took only eight months, not being elaborate but confined to essentials, a time which compared favourably with a cadet's two years at the college, learning mostly theory. So Flying Training Schools sprang up on all sides, flooding the Air Force with short-service officers to fill the vacancies caused by expansion. Yet the college did not increase its output, and the skeleton was neglected in the race with time; the Cranwell officer was to become a rarity in the growing service, inevitably always greatly outnumbered by short-service officers. In many ways it was sad to witness the passing from the college of its influence on the service, almost before it was old enough to be felt, yet the short-service officer was no mere substitute in an hour of need; he was an invaluable pillar of strength in these difficult times, when the service was suffering from growing pains, and much is owed to him.

"A" Flight of 98 Squadron had no provoking rhyme on the office door such as I remembered in the Cranwell hangar; in fact, it was not even hung with the name and rank of the Flight Commander, Pilot Officer Harrison. He was a natural pilot, handling his aircraft brilliantly, but remembered above all as a humorist and raconteur, and the five officers of his flight who shared the office spent most of their time in fits of laughter. The Hinds, being new to the service, were suffering from trivial technical troubles, sufficient to keep them continually in the hangar under repair. There was not therefore much flying to be had, but a great deal of leisure, for which the inhabitants of the Flight Office were good company. Day aimlessly succeeded day in which very little was achieved.

The most notable event in the first few weeks was my learning to fly in formation. Harry taught me by patiently flying his aircraft on straight and level courses while I did my utmost to keep mine at least within sight. But practice produced results, and before long I could keep in position half a span away from my leader in dives and turns, take-offs and landings. Formation flying inspires me with a sensation of confidence, present to this day; the proximity of other aircraft is comforting, and to be one of a flight droning through the sky together as one aircraft increases the feeling of exhilaration and power, which for me is inseparable from flying. Certainly nothing looks more impressive than a well-drilled formation crossing the sky, and I have still some photographs of 98's Hinds flying together which show, even by my present standards, that we were not quite incompetent.

Squadron flying was desultory; at first it seemed entertaining and varied, but soon began to appear somewhat aimless. I was enjoying the actual flying no less than I had always done, and the same enthusiasm was still there, but flying alone did not now seem enough. I had achieved my ambition to enter the service and fly, and that ambition now seemed an empty one. My Cranwell days had been made bright by the light from the star ahead, and I had trusted blindly in the future, but now suddenly I was lacking in confidence, wondering if the expanding service had cheated me of the life I had chosen. For the first time I had chosen my career correctly, doubts which were to recur increasingly often in the coming years.

Meanwhile I lived a life which I was to find typical of the service in these years. In working hours there was occasionally some flying to be done, but this never approached a surfeit, or nearly as much as I would have liked. But flying a Hind was still fascinating, and there were yet new things to be done in the air, fresh countryside to fly over and unknown weather to fly through. Apart from actual flying, there was little to occupy us during working hours; in bad weather, indeed nearly always, we would congregate in the Flight Office, there to drink interminable cups of tea, idly talk or read. Every well-run flight has an organized tea "swindle", in which all its pilots contribute pennies to some airman, who produces in return tea of dubious quality, ostensibly half-way through the morning and afternoon, but in reality at any time of the day. A tea swindle is a feature of flight life throughout the service, no doubt made essential by the lack of occupation during working hours and the consequent necessity of continually whiling away the time.

Games I still played, for the service allows more time and gives greater facilities for these than can be found in any occupation outside it. This was a feature I found most attractive, at one time thinking it might compensate for all other deficiencies which the service held for me. If life during working hours was somewhat empty, I could make up for it during leisure, of which there had been so little at Cranwell that to find my time so free was almost an embarrassment.

I was at first surprised to find it a practice for officers to go away from the station almost every week-end, certainly for three out of four, but soon I fell in with the custom and went home for an occasional weekend leave. There was certainly nothing urgent to keep us back which could not be attended to in the ample week-day working hours. I was beginning to see how life should be lived, and to question if I wanted to live it.

Yet in spite of these misgivings I was starting to settle down. If I had doubts about the Air Force, there were none about my squadron; 98 was the best in the world. All its Pilot Officers were still far from promotion, all joined together by the common tie of flying, which made us friends. It is impossible for officers of a squadron to live together, play games together, fly together and still remain unknown to each other or estranged. There is a great tie between people who have served together in a squadron. If two of us meet to-day, conversation will go straight back to "The Squadron"; although we will both have served in many others since, our loyalty will not have strayed.

These were good companionable days, and, like so many other good things, it has needed the future to point out their merits. By the end of October I had been in the squadron three months, recovered from my first surprise at our Squadron Commander calling us all by our Christian names, part-exchanged my car, which was something of a habit among junior officers, and done sixty hours' flying in Hinds, of course all solo. I was hoping vaguely to remain with the squadron for at least two years, which was a normal time to remain in one post, and eventually to become a Flight Commander. At this worst of all moments, just as I was settling down and shelving my discontents, a signal came, posting me away from the squadron. I was to say good-bye to 98 Squadron almost before I knew her.

The service can be an exacting master, not least in the demands it makes in the matter of postings. To move often and at short notice has been my lot during this war, when it has naturally been acceptable, but to be liable to move often and rapidly in peace-time is, in my view, one of the great disadvantages of life in a service. You may be settled in your work, comfortable at your station, making friends in the neighbourhood, when suddenly you will be required to sever all ties and remove yourself elsewhere, to start again the struggle for a reasonable existence in some strange place. It was not only the actuality of a sudden posting which became so disturbing to me in the peace-time service, but the liability of such a happening which was so oppressive. If you like to settle down, the service is not for you. For years I was constantly wondering what was wrong with the life. In the end I discovered that it was something wrong with me: I am a settler.

My posting signal read: "P/O P. Gibbs is specially selected for posting to the FAA. He is to be attached from 12/11/36 to Leuchars for a course, on completion of which to report to Calshot for a course. He is to be posted to Gosport for No. 5 Torpedo Course commencing 3/1/37."

This signal contained far too much of the unexpected for my liking. The thought had not remotely crossed my mind that I should be posted away after such a short time in the squadron, much less that I should have to go to the Fleet Air Arm, about which I knew as little as of some far-off country. I knew that the RAF supplied some of the pilots for aircraft carriers, but until this moment I had not thought to inquire where they were drawn from. Now I found that three were to be taken from this station, two from 98 and one from 104 Squadron.

I recalled with misgiving that one or two of the Cranwell instructors had served at one time in aircraft carriers, and their opinion of the posting was a low one; they had heartily disliked the life at sea, so different from that on an RAF station, and could never get used to a way of living which had been thrust on them and was far removed from that of their choice. With this recollection I could not help feeling doubly depressed at the upsetting course of events. That I should have to leave my squadron, where I was happy and settled, was in itself bad enough, but to have suddenly to prepare to embrace without option an entirely new life seemed to be asking too much of adaptability.

There is no questioning a posting signal; it said "go" and we went. Not one of the three "specially selected" officers was pleased at the prospect before him, but we had no alternative but to obey orders. The "specially selected" phrase added a particularly bitter touch, for these were words with the implication of present-giving, insinuating that we three had been singled out from hundreds of other officers with identical qualifications, all struggling to obtain such a posting and jealous of our luck. We imagined some fiend at the Air Ministry picking names indiscriminately out of a hat, then with a saturnine smile inserting the phrase "specially selected" in the posting signal, adding salt to our already bitter fate. The true story of how we came to be chosen was not pieced together until later.

Meanwhile, it was packing again, with hasty farewells and the disconsolation of parting from friends. We were turning our backs not only on our squadrons, but on the RAF itself. The road ahead was a watery one, more of the sea than our chosen sky. It was good-bye to "98".

CHAPTER IV

THE SCENE CHANGES

LEUCHARS, the first of the stations to which the posting signal had ordered us, was in Scotland, and the three of us, travelling up together by train, duly arrived at the Mess the evening before the date on which we had to report for duty. After being shown our rooms, we filtered through to the ante-room, where we were greeted by two surprises. Firstly, the room was full of the dark-blue uniforms of naval officers, outnumbering the RAF present by about ten to one. We had not expected to find ourselves in the midst of a naval life so soon, for Leuchars was an RAF station.

The second surprise, equally unexpected, was a very pleasant one; sitting there in the ante-room were two officers from my term at Cranwell, Eddie Culverwell and Jackie Fishwick, who had suffered the same fate and had come to Leuchars to join us on the course. The presence of old friends cheered me tremendously and improved the black outlook. They knew no more about the posting than we did, but were equally disgruntled at leaving their squadrons. Before long we were having a hearty communal moan against what we considered to be our bad luck.

But if the future looked black, the present had something to commend it; there was some interesting and new flying to be done. We were at Leuchars to gain experience in being launched from a catapult, a unique possession not found on any other aerodrome, but used in naval vessels. Its presence here was due to Leuchars being used exclusively for naval training, for this was the Flying Training School where naval officers entering their air arm learnt to fly.

A whole week was to elapse before we were shot off the Leuchars catapult, for a delay was caused by adverse winds. Although the catapult was mounted on a turntable, there were some directions in which it might not safely be pointed, and one of these was towards the two-storeyed Officers' Mess. Perversely the wind blew from over the Mess day after day, and since a catapult launch had to be made, like any normal take-off into wind, we waited impatiently for a change.

Meanwhile we put in some flying practice on the type which was to be used for the launch, a Hawker Osprey, yet another of the famous line, little different from the Hart or Hind, except for special strengthening to stand the strain of catapulting, and folding wings for easy stowage in the restricted space of a ship. We had no difficulty with the Osprey, though I failed to remember that, like all FAA and coastal command aircraft, the air-speed indicator had a scale reading in knots instead of the customary miles per hour, so I kept approaching the aerodrome too fast to land. Eventually I tumbled to my mistake and felt very foolish, for the others had been watching with amusement my many efforts to touch down well above stalling speed.

Flying at an aerodrome nearly always has an audience standing on the tarmac, whose standard is not easily satisfied, for candid criticism of other pilots' flying is considered quite legitimate. Also a flight's offices are usually in front of the hangar facing on to the aerodrome, and nothing is pleasanter than, with cup of tea in hand, idly to gaze out of the window at the miscellaneous flying going on outside, and to comment on incompetent landings. So someone will always see your poor performances, and only when you do your best landings does nobody appear to be looking.

When not actually flying we waited impatiently on the weather, but it was not until the end of the week that the wind finally changed and we prepared to be shot into the air. A crane hauls the aircraft up, its engine running all the while, and deposits it on to the catapult cradle, drawn back to the end of its short run. A ladder is placed in position up which a pupil climbs gingerly to the cockpit, a little breathless in his precarious position high above the ground. The ladder is withdrawn and a charge of cordite the size of a medium shell placed in the breech. With everything now ready, the pilot opens the throttle fully, as for a normal take-off from an aerodrome, and with engine roaring the aircraft strains to be free, but is held fast to the cradle. The pilot raises his hand to show he is ready, a few seconds are allowed for him to brace himself for the shock of acceleration, then, with a noise like a gun firing, the charge is detonated, the aircraft is shot down the catapult track and hurled off the end into the air.

Cordite dislikes the cold; for it to be effective it must be above a certain temperature, and at Leuchars it was kept in a specially heated store by the side of the catapult. But the electric heating of this store went wrong, and the month was a very frosty November in Scotland. The first few launches went smoothly, but the door of the store was being opened after each launch to bring out more cordite, which became colder and colder as time went on, the effect being to reduce its explosive power. As launch succeeded launch it became apparent that the Osprey was leaving the catapult with less speed every time; indeed, rather than being shot away with flying speed, it was dropping limply off the end at just above the stalling point, its wheels just missing the ground as it gained speed to climb away.

At last the inevitable happened; one of us left the catapult at much less than flying speed, the Osprey's wheels hit the ground with a sickening crunch, and although it bounced off into the air and climbed away, it had obviously been damaged. It was landed gingerly and taxied in from the aerodrome, not towards the catapult but to the hangar.

After this episode, two decisions were made: we were to wait for a warmer day or the repair of the heater, and use not an Osprey but a Fairey III F, which needed less speed of launch. So we had now to do some practice flying in a III F, an obsolete warhorse, fitted with the famous Napier Lion engine. She was quite nice to fly, and we welcomed a new type to enter in our log books. Eventually we carried out the required number of catapult launches without further incident, and were sent off to Calshot for floatplane training.

Flying floatplanes was to prove great fun, but if the catapult had been capricious to delay us at Leuchars, it was the weather which we were to curse at Calshot. It was now late November, and depressing in its winds and rains as we gazed from the pilots' room window at the waves lashing against Calshot spit, a narrow causeway projecting into Southampton Water. Only five hours' solo flying in a floatplane were demanded here, after which we could go on leave until the start of our next course at Gosport. The sooner we finished at Calshot, the longer would be our leave. But the weather persistently threw obstructions in our way. If the sky was clear, the sea would be too rough; if the sea were smooth, it would be foggy, or else there would be rain and low clouds. Liners passed the window steaming up the "water" to Southampton, dice rattled on the pilots' room floor, and even snores resounded from more than one corner. In the end we finished a few days before Christmas.

The sea is an unbounded aerodrome on which to alight, but a slipway is a small target at which to taxi in a floatplane. Briefly this summarizes floatplane flying; the flying itself presented no difficulties, it was the seamanship which kept us guessing. The aircraft were Swordfish on floats, a Fairey aircraft, best described as an overgrown Tutor. It was even as easy to fly as that old trainer, and had a hundred hidden but endearing qualities, not the least of these being its strong construction and reliable engine, a 700-hp Bristol Pegasus. It was not fast or advanced in design, but very solid and reliable.

The whole procedure of floatplane flying is reminiscent of motor-boating. The aircraft is pushed out of the hangar down the slipway on a trolley, which is then withdrawn by airmen wading in the water, and at a movement of the throttle it glides away, skimming over the surface. In a choppy sea the waves just touch the tips of the revolving airscrew to send little spurts of spray up over the open cockpit, making an alarming and indescribable noise of blade cutting water.

The take-off is an exhilarating dash through the waves with spray thrown up all around; as it accelerates, the aircraft begins to feel lighter under the hand, becoming, as the speed increases, less a speed-boat and more an aeroplane, until suction of the water on the floats is overcome by the lift of the wings for the aircraft to unstick and rise dripping from the surface. Alighting on the sea (it was still always called landing!) was easy, since the accurate approach called for by the narrow confines of an aerodrome were superfluous here, where sheltered waters stretched wide on every side.

But taxi-ing in to the slipway was a different matter altogether. At the end of a period the aircraft had to be brought ashore, and this was a most intricate business, for while the machine was designed essen-tially for good control in the air, it had now to be made to behave like any trim surface craft and belie its ancestry. Admittedly there were rudders fitted at the ends of the floats and controlled by the rudder bar, but neither these nor the air rudder were effective at slow speeds to keep the aircraft heading in the desired direction. Reliable or erratic, I could have done with conventional aircraft brakes.

Allowance has to be made for both tide and wind when approaching the slipway, and not the least distressing feature of this manoeuvre is that the engine must be switched off before the slipway is reached, since the airmen who wade out to secure the floats would be endangered if the propeller were still turning. Thus the last few yards of the approach have to be covered under the aircraft's momentum, with little hope of recovering if the slipway is missed, for with engine stopped the pilot is without control and helpless, to drift where tide or wind take him. Altogether the manoeuvre requires skill, nautical knowledge of wind and tide, and practice, and it was not unknown for aircraft to drift helplessly up against a nearby jetty, causing not a little damage.

Not surprisingly, there were plenty of incidents in our stay at Calshot, none however very disastrous, but the usual critical spectators found more to amuse and comment on than could be discovered on any aerodrome. The sight of one pilot having inadvertently stopped his engine, drifting impotently towards the *Queen Mary* steaming down Southampton Water, was one which aroused a frenzy of delight, only slightly lessened as he was seen narrowly to miss the stern and then to be subjected to a tossing in the great liner's wake, while a launch sped out to tow him in to safety. Also floatplanes bounced. Sea seems as hard as concrete at landing speeds, and a faulty landing results in a bounce off water no less than off land, but with the distinction that it is accompanied by an enveloping shower of spray. In every way this was entertaining flying, and we went on Christmas leave with our verdict on the posting a little more reserved.

"... to Gosport for No 5 Torpedo Course commencing 3/1/37" had read our posting signals, and so we all arrived there on the appointed day after our few days' leave. The Mess was wonderfully situated, looking out across the Solent to Ryde, in whose roads some great liner would often be lying, so large and near that it might be on the doorstep, or at least no further away than the bottom of the garden. The good-looking German liners, *Bremen* and *Europa*, were occasionally there, their presence then without particular significance. I was later to recall their peaceful appearance, when in wartime they became two targets for my squadron, but now they merely looked majestic as only fine ships can.

I was now in Coastal Command, the headquarters which administered the Fleet Air Arm when ashore and so was responsible for our present training, and I have remained under this Command when serving in the U.K. As the very name implies, its aerodromes are almost without exception near the sea over which its squadrons keep watch. Some aerodromes are the sea itself, those of the flying-boat squadrons, but even from the majority of its land aerodromes it is possible to throw a stone into the sea from some point on their boundary. If you are fond of both the sea and the air Coastal Command would be your choice in the Air Force.

The six of us who had been together at Leuchars and Calshot were together again at Gosport, and of these six, three were short-service officers and three former Cranwell cadets. We were all of a rank, Pilot Officers, and only a few days separated us in seniority. By chance I was looking through our flying log books one day when I noticed that we had all been assessed as "above the average" pilots.

Not only are details of every flight he undertakes entered in a pilot's log book, but also an assessment of his flying ability is made at intervals by his Commanding Officer or instructor. In this way a log book is truly a flying pedigree, for from its entries can be seen exactly what a pilot has done; how long he has been flying, on what types he has experience, in what units he has served and how he flies, well or badly. It is a cryptic diary, in which a single entry may conjure up vivid details of a flight from the past, and now, in wartime, a log book has become more than ever a treasury of unforgotten stories told barely in half a dozen pregnant words.

Certainly, in the face of this discovery, it did not appear we had been posted quite at random to the Fleet Air Arm; there were too many points of similarity between us. We were all from Hind squadrons, all from Bomber Command, and were identical in rank, experience and ability. The riddle was solved for me by a knowing instructor, who explained that pilots were taken for the Air Arm after three months in single-engined squadrons; only above the average pilots were selected, and half the number had to be former cadets. So, briefly, the whole plot was laid bare, but I cannot say that this knowledge made us any happier, as each silently wished he had failed to meet one of these qualifications.

Our course at Gosport was to last three months, during which we had to learn torpedo dropping, the tactics of a torpedo attack, night flying and deck-landings. The variety of the flying and the attraction of something new, to which I was always susceptible, kept intervening to drive doubts about the future from my mind. The present persisted in being deeply absorbing. Torpedo Training Unit, in which we were now pupils, was a flying training school in miniature, with a more advanced and specialized line of instruction. It taught not only pilots destined for the Fleet Air Arm, but also those who were to go to torpedo squadrons in the RAF. This was an exiguous branch of the service, comprising only a few squadrons, then equipped with the Vickers Vildebeeste biplane, already obsolete but which was still to be in use at the outbreak of war.

Our party of six, who were by now firm friends in our misfortune, were now joined by a similar number of naval officers who had just finished their training at Leuchars, consisting of Lieutenants and Subs. They were no less keen on flying than we were, and surprisingly good in the air when it is remembered they had come straight from their flying training school, whereas we had been in squadrons, and considered, on rather doubtful grounds, that we were already quite experienced.

We had heard vaguely that the RAF and the Navy did not "get on" together, with a result that for the first few days no communication took place between the two camps, although we were all sharing a not very large pilots' room. In the end someone audaciously broke the ice, the atmosphere thawed completely, and we got together and never afterwards looked back. The RAF even pulled the Navy's leg unmercifully, teasing them about their conservatism. The "nautics" would talk about "going ashore" when they were already on shore and meant going into the town, and of closing the "scuttle" when they referred to a window. These peculiarities we jumped on, but they were later to have their sweet revenge when we embarked in a carrier, very ignorant of naval terms. But we did become friends.

Swordfish were our aircraft again, this time the floats giving way to a normal wheel undercarriage so well designed that any but good landings were almost impossible. The torpedo was carried on a special rack slung under the aircraft, and to drop it correctly into the water was a skilled art not quickly learnt. As a preliminary to actual torpedo dropping, we flew around the Solent low over the water, to get accustomed to handling our aircraft just above the waves and to learn judgement of height above the surface. It was not unknown to catch a wheel or wing tip in the water on these exercises, but we had no incidents—in fact, this business of skimming over the waves did not seem too difficult, since our floatplane experience helped us. After a few hours of this low flying we were expected to be competent in judging our height above the water, but to do this really accurately requires much more experience, as the surface of the sea varied from day to day, sometimes from hour to hour; swells, calms and white horses, together with many variations of light on the water, make a correct guess at one's height problematical, but nevertheless it is vital to a good torpedo drop.

We started actual torpedo dropping by using dummy cases bereft of their expensive and delicate mechanism, for the real thing was far too valuable to be hazarded by raw pupils. These dummies were dropped alongside a pinnace anchored in the Solent, and as they fell away from the aircraft to enter the water were photographed by a camera on the pinnace. The drop could afterwards be analysed from the result, for the height of the release and angle of entry of the torpedo into the water could be obtained from measurements on the photograph. If our early photographs provoked mirth and showed little else but the belly-flopping splash of a dummy dropped flat from some monumental height, later results showed that we were steadily improving.

Soon we became proficient enough to be allowed to drop Runners; the real thing except for the absence of the explosive head, for which a dummy was substituted, and it was satisfying to circle above watching the straight bubbly track of a torpedo running truly through the water after a correct drop. It was to become still more fascinating later, when we practised flight torpedo attacks against some naval vessel steaming off the Isle of Wight. Six Swordfish would dive simultaneously out of the sky to the surface of the water, drop their torpedoes together, and then make away hugging the waves, while six straight tracks pointed towards the speeding target.

If there was much to be learnt about the actual dropping of a torpedo, there was even more to be learnt about aiming one, and not a little about the tactics of an attack, and technically about the mechanism of the torpedo itself. The target is nearly always moving, sometimes very fast, and its speed must be estimated correctly when aiming which is done by simply pointing the aircraft. Range, too, ideally 800 yards, is not easy to judge, yet an error here will nullify a good drop. When it is remembered that fierce anti-aircraft fire is presumed, and that a pilot does well to hurry in and out of his target's gunning range, it can be seen that decisions affecting aim must be made in the span of a few seconds, and the actual dropping of a torpedo must be second nature.

All this was new flying, but night flying came into quite a different class of novelty; I had never flown at night before. It was not then part of Cranwell's programme, and had to be learnt subsequently as opportunity allowed. "98" had been starting night flying when I left, but at this time there was a general backwardness in flying at night throughout the whole Air Force, and it was to be some time before it became accepted as a normal event and taught early in a pilot's training. But the expansion could not look every way at once, and while deficiencies in equipment and training were legion, the building was going up all the same, large and solid; the new Air Force.

We learnt to fly at night from the Civil Airport at Southampton, since Gosport had become a sea of mud from February rains and was quite unusable for a few weeks. The aerodrome lighting there was excellent; the boundary was clearly marked by a chain of red lights, obstructions were lit up, and a floodlight illuminated the surface for landing as if it were daylight. Above all, these were nights before the total darkness of the wartime black-out, and lights shone brightly all around. Southampton, Portsmouth and Hythe were all pools of light from their streets, shop-windows and houses, and liners creeping up Southampton Water were floating fairy palaces with their reflections dancing in the water. It was not surprising that night flying in these conditions was attractive and presented no problems.

Yet before my first night take-off I was full of misgivings such as were never experienced before my first solo flight, but no sooner was I actually flying in the night air, challenging the unknown and finding my apprehensions unfounded, than complete confidence returned. I had no difficulty at all, and found night flying attractive by its very strangeness after all my daylight flying, which was perhaps already losing something of its first appeal.

At the end of the course I entered in my log book a total of three hours' solo night flying, in red ink to distinguish it from more usual daytime flying. I had no thought then that this was to be my last night flying for nearly four years, and that this meagre total would be unchanged in my log book when in wartime I was posted to a squadron operating largely at night. Now the ability to fly at night at all seemed sufficient in a service in which this was not yet usual.

Only deck-landing remained now to be mastered. This was a matter of being able to make the aircraft touch down "on a sixpence", and for practice a narrow area was marked out on the aerodrome to represent a carrier's deck, on to which we would land. After intensive practice in this we were considered competent for the real thing, and early one morning were taken aboard the aircraft carrier *Furious* lying at Spithead. Soon after our arrival she put to sea, and before long was circled by a flight of Swordfish flown out from Gosport by our instructors. As they landed on the deck in turn, we formed the usual critical audience, almost hoping that some instructor would make a mistake.

Here was novelty once more, to make flying seem a book without end, always another page grew into a chapter and the story continued, breathless and vivid. Not only was the flying new, but the environment quite strange. If aerodromes were beginning to seem commonplace and alike, the *Furious* was an unknown floating aerodrome, which, as she ploughed through the water, amazed us both with her novelty and impressiveness.

Deck-landing requires careful flying. It is not hazardous, but a pilot must be accurate. In harbour a carrier appears larger than several blocks of flats put together, a great island towering out of the water above nearby buildings and smaller craft. At sea, out of sight of land, a carrier viewed from the air is little more than a dot in the ocean to a pilot circling to land. If such a landing is not actually hazardous, it is at least a little tricky, for there is no room for error. However, there are two great aids provided for the pilot. While aircraft are landing, the carrier steams quite fast directly into wind, thus giving the effect of increasing the wind speed over the flying-deck, and so reducing the actual speed at which an aircraft touches down. Also there are "arrester" wires strained across the deck, on which a hook, specially fitted to all Fleet Air Arm aircraft, catches after landing. These two aids simplify the pilot's task immeasurably, and make pulling up within the length of the deck a fairly easy matter. For an aircraft to run off the end is almost an unknown occurrence; it is allowing the aircraft to drift sideways which must be avoided. The deck is long but narrow, and also high, with a drop of eighty feet to the water below. The pilot must not only make his aircraft touch down slowly and "on a six-pence", but keep it running straight up the deck, not on any account towards the sides.

This flying required no little skill, and was therefore the more attractive. Incidents were frequent, and an expectant group of pilots would always assemble on the flying-deck to watch aircraft landing. Accidents, if more frequent than at shore aerodromes, were rarely with more serious result than a broken undercarriage or tail wheel, though very occasionally an aircraft might fall over the side, sustaining not so trivial damage. For such emergencies a destroyer always followed the carrier, just a few lengths behind, ready to pick up any crew finding itself in the "drink", be the cause a bad landing or a rare engine failure while flying from the ship.

I cannot say I found deck-landing easy, but all of us succeeded in reaching the required standard, not before Fishy had spread a Sword-fish over the "after" lift by a heavy landing and there had been several other minor incidents and excitements. I was certainly far from polished in my performance and probably not a little dangerous in those six landings, which were the number required to complete the course. In the end I at least felt confident, but not over-confident, of my ability to land on the carrier, and it was to be some time before I was putting up a consistent performance.

By the end of a full day we had all completed our six deck-landings, and also done very much more; the ship had been explored from stem to stern. We had travelled on the great lifts which transport aircraft between the flying-decks and hangars, watched aircraft being smartly manhandled by a party of seamen on the deck, been entertained in the Wardroom, seen the complicated but spotless engine-room and innumerable times had lost ourselves in the labyrinth of passages, hatches and companionways which thread through the decks.

As the *Furious* anchored off Ryde that evening it no longer seemed that she was at the steps of our Mess at Gosport, but that the Mess and the shore itself were distant and remote objects vanishing in the dim light of a past existence. As a pinnace took us off to the shore the setting sun was disappearing behind the island, a greying mass silhouetted in the last light of a long day. The sheltered Solent Waters were calm as we drew away from the ship's side. It was a typical south coast spring evening, which was the essence of peace, evening to a day across which the towering hull of the great carrier had thrown the shadow of my new, unchosen life.

CHAPTER V

YEAR OF DISCONTENT

OUR course at Gosport was now finished, and we were posted to two Fleet Air Arm training squadrons, half our number to each. This did not mean we should be parted, for both squadrons were identical and belonged to the same carrier, the *Furious*. They were complete squadrons in every way, but had only a small permanent staff of pilots, used as instructors, the remainder being made up of pupils who stayed for one cruise only, on which they carried out advanced training. In fact, the *Furious* was a training carrier at this time, making three cruises each year solely to train pilots for the other carriers. Besides the two torpedo squadrons between which we were divided, there was also a similar fighter squadron flying Ospreys, and like our squadrons consisting of half RAF and half naval pilots, the majority of whom were under training.

We had ten days' leave before joining our squadrons, which were conveniently based at Gosport when disembarked, and we found them there on our return from leave. Meanwhile the carrier herself, having just finished her spring cruise, was in Portsmouth preparing for the summer cruise to Scotland. My squadron, whose number was 822, had a Naval Lieutenant Commander as CO, and my Flight Commander was a Naval Lieutenant, but notwithstanding this mixture of the two services, life seemed very similar to that in an ordinary RAF squadron. Indeed, when the day came for us to embark and we flew out to the ship in a squadron formation of twelve aircraft, there came back to me strong memories of "98".

Living in a ship I found difficult. After the first few days, passed pleasantly in wonder at the new surroundings, life began to seem blank. We had no less leisure than ashore, in fact much more, yet there were no games to play, no privacy, no room to move about, nowhere to go, and no permanency. I began to feel imprisoned, but knew there was no means of escape. This was a naval pilot's chosen life, and he had already had the opportunity of teaching himself how best to live it during his sea-time before learning to fly; he was a flying-fish, and a carrier sailed in his chosen water. On the other hand, the RAF pilots were completely unaccustomed to living in ships, and were unhappy away from their true setting on an RAF aerodrome, where the seemingly irresponsible and carefree attitude bred of flying was recognized and understood. Also, the naval pilots had duties in the ship in which we could not share; they kept watch at sea and in harbour, and took their part in the running of the ship. We, in the RAF, were restricted to a concern with the flying side only, and to add to our plight, there was very little actual flying to be done.

For if there were factors conspiring to limit flying from an aero-drome, they were few compared with those restricting flying in a carrier. If the ship were anchored, no flying could take place, since the wind speed over the deck would be insufficient. If the ship were moving and could not afford to delay, flying was impossible, as she would be required to turn into wind while aircraft were taking off and landing and so be diverted from her course. There was none of the casual flying beloved by RAF pilots. The half-hour's test flight in the morning, the short cross-country flight to visit a friend at another station, the practice circuits and landings, were all absent, sorely and genuinely missed. Such flying as there was from a carrier had to be arranged in advance, for it required a surprisingly wide organization to fly off even one aircraft. Hydraulic power had to be given to the lifts, a handling party turned out to push the aircraft, the flying-deck had to be cleared, the ship to alter course, and numerous other operations carried out. It was quite a performance compared with the simple request of a pilot to his Flight Commander on an aerodrome: "May I take up 'C' for a few circuits and bumps, Harry?"

When she had received her three squadrons safely on board, the *Furious* went north to exercise off May Island at the mouth of the Forth, and then further north still to the Moray Firth. Here other units of the Home Fleet were exercising during the summer months, and always at least a few destroyers would be lying in harbour at Inver-gordon, where we anchored most evenings and every weekend. Flying consisted of the now familiar routine of practice torpedo attacks and deck-landings, although we carried out some air firing at a target towed by another aircraft, and also practice bombing on practice ranges, neither of which I had done before. I welcomed anything new to lend a finishing touch to my flying, but flying experience means flying hours to make a creditable total in a pilot's log book, and unfortunately we flew rarely, and then not for long.

While we mourned for our previous easy flying facilities, we also appreciated that no real comparison was possible between aerodrome and carrier flying, but realization brought no cure for our air-starved lot. We were sick at heart, and this sickness was not the fault of the navy, for the ship did much to make us comfortable and happy in our strange surroundings. Many of the executive officers must even have resented our presence in what was patently their preserve, for they regarded the *Furious* as a ship, not an aerodrome, yet all were most kind. We knew we were helpless victims of strange circumstances, and set out to make the best of our situation. I myself missed the games, which, with flying, had been almost the only attractions of a service life, and was never reconciled to this sacrifice; it was too great to ask.

The cruise, which had started in May, came to an end in the last week in July, and although I had seen fine scenery and new places, nothing could have been more welcome than the sight of the familiar south coast. On a summer's day, with the carrier steaming within sight of the sun-bathed cliffs of the Isle of Wight, 822 Squadron's aircraft took off one by one, to join formation in the air and fly together across the island to Gosport; the cruise was over. Grass never looked so green in any countryside as the aerodrome at Gosport did after the monotonous grey of the carrier; it was for us a return home from a foreign country. With a great expanse of aerodrome on which to land after the tiny deck, we all made shocking landings. All seemed so different, and so nice. Nostalgia set in as I remembered "98" and those few relatively happy months. The two years which I had to serve in the Fleet Air Arm hung like lead about my neck, their weight never quite forgotten. On shore there could be no permanency, always we would be embarking and disembarking, and in the ship life was dull and uneventful, a wilderness of boredom.

Yet I was to have some good luck to cheer me. There had been an over-production of pilots for the Air Arm, consequently there were at any rate for a few months, no vacancies in carriers. To meet such a situation a "pool" at Gosport had already been established where pilots could keep in flying practice while awaiting posting. I was to spend six months there. Although it was only temporary, my stay in the pool meant, for a few months at least, a return to a normal RAF life.

The Flight which actually ran the pool had all the Fleet Air Arm types of aircraft and several others as well, and flying them was very much to one's own arrangements. There were occasional specific jobs to be done, some fetching and carrying, ferrying of new aircraft from the maker's aerodrome, or perhaps some demonstration to Army Units, but more usually I could fly when I wanted. Time hung heavily on my hands during working hours, and I often visited friends at other aerodromes, to fill in time. The flying was not new, but it was varied. I was adding new types to the few already in my log book, putting in flying hours and gaining experience.

Inevitably an end came to this pleasant aimless life of flying freedom, as I knew it must. A vacancy occurred in 821 Squadron in the *Courageous*, to which I was promptly posted. I was by then the oldest inhabitant in the pool, and had known that the sands of my good fortune were running out, so this posting came as no surprise. Life in the pool had been pleasant but devoid of purpose, to make me weary of marking time there. My allegiance to an easy life was temporary, now I wanted to advance. I knew these happy months were borrowed from carrier life; I could not hope for more miracles, such had my stay ashore seemed and resolved to take a long view in making the best of my naval life. I repeated the words "only two years", trying to make the time seem short, but it never seemed less than a lifetime to me.

I went to the *Courageous* as a Flying Officer, for I had passed my promotion examination and had been promoted in March, an "automatic" promotion based on time of service; it was 1938, and a year and a half since I had left Cranwell. Promotion to all ranks up to Squadron Leader depended on time of service only, but after that it was by selection. This rise in rank did not really mean very much, and affected me only by the increase in pay, which was more than welcome.

The two junior ranks of the service are nearly always classed together, and few appointments distinguish between a Pilot Officer and a Flying Officer. It is not until Flight Lieutenant is reached that the benefits of promotion are felt in a real increase in responsibility and authority. Pilot Officers are the "boys" of a squadron, who may be called on indiscriminately for any job, and Flying Officers are in a class only imperceptibly higher, but at Flight Lieutenant the situation changes, and one is assumed to have experience and knowledge.

The *Courageous* was almost identical with the *Furious*, and 821 Squadron little different from 822. This squadron was also equipped with the faithful Swordfish, and still composed half of naval pilots, half of RAF, but there was one small but subtle distinction: it was not a training squadron, but fully fledged. It was good at last to have finished with so much training, and to look back on my days as a pupil at Leuchars, Calshot, Gosport and in the *Furious*. Now that I was once more in a real squadron I was hoping for a little permanency, at least I would try and make the best of the life, as I had resolved to do.

Of the other six Pilot Officers who had met that first day at Leuchars and trained together for a year, all were now posted. Eddie, Fishy and I, the three ex-cadets, had actually been together with only a few months' break ever since leaving Cranwell, and amazingly we were to turn up together in a few years' time, posted to the same wartime squadron. But now we were separated, split up between the three carriers, the *Eagle* in the Far East, the *Glorious* in the Mediterranean and the *Courageous* at home. It had been a good flying year together, and when we met each other later, as occasionally happened, talk always centred on "those" days. The naval officers are not less remembered, but they have been obscured from view in their own, and now independent, service, yet I have come across three of them during wartime, one amazingly in RAF uniform with Flight Lieutenant's rank.

Courageous life I found little different from that in the *Furious*; it was one of boredom only relieved by occasional flying or weekends in strange harbours. But at least I was glad to have thrown off the shackles of training, for it had seemed ignominious to have remained a pupil for over a year since leaving Cranwell, particularly when I would receive from 98 Squadron or friends of my term tantalizing news of new developments at their RAF stations, where I would now have taken quite a senior place and been considered experienced. The expansion which had once appeared to me as a bane to the service now took on a new significance. I ceased to look backwards but gazed ahead.

Letters brought me news from the distant service of more and more interesting flying, of new and revolutionary monoplanes to fly, of vast and well-equipped new aerodromes springing up, of rapid promotion under a new scheme which granted acting rank, of the increase in night flying, of a hundred and one different things which were new, and belonged to the RAF.

If I had watched the passing of the old Air Force with regret, my viewpoint was now changed. From the Air Arm I was looking on the RAF from without, whereas previously I had judged her from within. From where I now stood, the RAF appeared a growing child of infinite promise. I saw it from behind my ship's prison-bars as a beggar sees through a window a steaming dish of food; it was desirable, but very, very remote.

I had not been in 821 Squadron for more than four months, when

I was reprieved and posted back to the RAF. The carrier had cruised during the mid-summer months in Scottish waters, in the Channel and off Cornwall, while the squadron had done no flying of note, only routine flying and practice torpedo attacks; deck-landing was now taken for granted. I had settled down as I had determined I should, and was planning for the next cruise an assault on the excess leisure problem, which I could see must be solved by some other occupation than sleep! At the end of the cruise in August the squadrons disembarked at Southampton aerodrome, which now held a small RAF station, and we dissolved, according to custom, on a fortnight's leave, which was always granted three times a year between cruises.

Leave was more welcome than ever, for in the Air Arm it was not as plentiful as in the RAF, and there were none of those frequent weekend leaves which we had come to look on as our right. No less dearly missed than this regular leave at weekends were the odd days and afternoons "off" which would be granted when a fog came up to make flying impossible, or when all the flight's aircraft were unserviceable. You could not slip off a carrier for an afternoon's golf on the ocean.

That August I was on leave in Cornwall, delightfully on leave, that is to say my leave had just begun, and I had no doubt been telling my parents of the delights of the Air Arm, without coming near to hiding from them my disappointment at being absent from the growing RAF when a telegram arrived which gave me back to the service again. It was a repetition of a posting signal which said: "Post F/O P. Gibbs from 821 Squadron to Torpedo Training Unit, Gosport, for flying duties". There was a most considerate addition by my Squadron Adjutant stating: "Report on completion of leave". Never has leave seemed sweeter than after receiving this unexpected good news, which meant that I had escaped prematurely from the Fleet Air Arm and was to be an instructor in the unit in which only a year ago I had been a pupil. I knew that I was outrageously lucky.

If I had wanted permanency, now at last I was to have it, for I remained in one unit and in one place for two whole years, but again I was to pass from contentment with my lot to dissatisfaction, but not before I had spent many happy months at Gosport. Instructing in Training Unit did not mean dual flying instruction: the pupils, who had already been to flying training school, were beyond that stage, and came to us to learn the specialized torpedo work. An instructor's work was restricted to supervision of pupils' flying, the leading of practice attacks, and some lectures.

At first this work appealed strongly to me on account of its creative nature. In squadrons every effort was directed from within to rise to and maintain a high standard of efficiency both on the ground and in the air, an effort which had an aspect of selfishness. Nor was the productive side of such effort then obvious; its object, to meet war in full readiness, was in those days a seemingly remote one. The continual desultory squadron routine could not adequately fill either time or minds, and the spirit of enthusiasm might easily die for want of an objective to sustain it. Here in Training Unit I felt that the work was immediately creative. Young pupils came, learnt from us and departed to squadrons with increased knowledge and experience. For the first year, at least, it appeared to me as valuable productive work, and I enjoyed it.

But as course of pupils followed course and the months passed by, this first idealistic impression of training did not remain; my original attitude to the work of an instructor underwent a change, and gratitude for my release from the Fleet Air Arm was forgotten. I was becoming restless again and dissatisfied, in spite of all that good fortune had done for me. As pupils came and went with mechanical regularity, Training Unit began to appear as nothing more than a mill which ground out pupils, continually and unimaginatively, who at first had been interesting, each as an individual, but soon became just another course, no different from the last. I was restless when by all accounts I should have been settled and happy in work which suited me.

This desire for a change was not inspired by the monotony of the work, or any similar self-interested source of personal discontent; its inspiration came from without, not from within. I was hankering, and seemed continually fated to do so, after some elusive quality to make life productive, creative of I knew not what. I was always looking far ahead beyond the immediate horizon, straining to see some objective, of which I had no conception at all. It might be said with some truth that I did not know what I wanted, failed to appreciate the advantages of the life I was leading, one of interest, comfort, a great degree of freedom, and above all a life of flying, and that I wanted too much.

Yet there was much to want at this time in the RAF and also much to be had. These were the expansion years, with Bomber Command equipping its squadrons with modern and still more modern aircraft. Fighter Command, always attractive, became more desirable than ever as its squadrons received the new Hurricanes and Spitfires. Yet, sadly, little happened in Coastal Command, which seemed in these years to be the Cinderella of the Air Force. There were so many gaps to be filled that vital interests had to receive first attention. The country's defence and attack had priority, and sea reconnaissance had to wait.

News of a growing new Air Force, abounding in opportunities for the young officer, had reached me in carriers, when the inadequate description in an occasional letter failed entirely to paint even a small part of the inspiring picture of the expanding Air Force. Now that I was actually back in the service, with my feet firmly planted on the dry land of one of its own aerodromes, the news which I had received seemed positively untrue in its underestimation. A flood of plenty had descended on the RAF; only money could equip and train a formidable modern Air Force, and that money was at last forthcoming from an anxious country. I could see now the evidence of expansion with my own eyes and hear for myself the impressive story: of the speed and wonderful equipment of the new monoplane aircraft, the spaciousness of the new aerodromes and stations, and of the increased responsibility entrusted to junior officers. In every way the new service seemed a paradise of new flying, and one in which Coastal Command was not yet included. I longed for the opportunities which the expansion offered, coveting not a mere advance in rank, but the new, entirely new, flying which was dawning. The river was in flood; I wanted to be in the swim and dreaded to be left behind.

If Coastal was the Cinderella among the RAF Commands, torpedo bombing was equally the neglected child of Coastal. This neglect on the part of Coastal was understandable, for her main function in wartime is to watch over the seas which surround our island and protect our ships and shores. Protection and reconnaissance were her primary role, and to take the offensive by attack was subsidiary to her chief work. Consequently, when Coastal was at last able to take her turn in expanding, all her newly gained resources were thrown into her true function of general reconnaissance. These squadrons were the submarine chasers and convoy protectors, co-operating generally with the Navy in the protection of shipping, and it was to these squadrons that Coastal was bound to give first consideration. The expansion had been late in reaching her, and she had quickly to prepare her frontier where it would first meet attack; her minor role of anti-shipping offensive would have to wait its turn. So it happened that when war broke out, Coastal Command was virtually without a torpedo-striking force at all, for the Vildebeeste aircraft with which her few torpedo squadrons were equipped had been in service for nearly ten years. It was actually a biplane and outrageously out of date.

I had mentally writhed in agony at being outside the benefits of the great expansion of Bomber and Fighter Commands, now I was to

suffer equal pangs of envy as I witnessed the reconnaissance squadrons
of Coastal Command receive preferential treatment. They were re-
equipped with modern aircraft, and equipped again with still more
modern aircraft, while the torpedo squadrons retained without change
their ten-year-old biplanes. The reconnaissance squadrons multiplied
and occupied new aerodromes and stations, and still the number of
torpedo squadrons remained the same.

I was not alone in my discontent at Gosport. Other torpedo pilots
felt the neglect which their branch was receiving, and were no less
frustrated than I to see a sky full of attractive flying available to some
but withheld from us, not by any fault of our own, but by ill-fortune.
There were no squadrons stationed at Gosport, only a few odd units
such as mine; the Torpedo Training School; the pool, shortly to move
to one of the new Naval Air Stations; and an experimental section
called Torpedo Development Unit.

Eddie, a contemporary of mine at Cranwell and in the Fleet Air
Arm, was instructing with me in Training Unit, while Victor Darling,
another ex-cadet of the same term as ours, was a pilot in the flight
which dropped experimental torpedoes for Development Unit. Not
only did we three belong to the same term at Cranwell, where our
rooms had been in the same corridor, but we had been together intermittently ever since, with Gosport our station. Often we would sit late
into the night discussing desperately and intolerantly the service,
which we persistently accused of forgetting us. Each one of us wanted
to be not in any odd unit, but in a real squadron, and above all to be
flying the new aircraft. We were being kept behind, we complained,
and not really without justification when it is remembered that 1939
was approaching to find us still flying biplanes and without a single
modern type in our log books! It was exasperating to know that the
youngest Pilot Officer in a squadron was superior to us in modern
flying experience, and with him we would willingly have changed
places rank and all. The total of flying hours in our log books was dead
flying of a past epoch, and five hours in a new monoplane would have
given us more experience than five hundred hours of biplane flying.
Changes were being made in flying technique, and we were out of
touch with modern developments, slowly and surely getting left
behind, wondering if we should ever make up the lost ground. Soundly
we cursed the necessarily neglected miscellaneous unit in which we
found ourselves. Midnight intolerance abounded in these complaining
conversations, but no solution emerged.

Yet to some extent the enjoyment of a shore life compensated for
these disappointments. The relief with which I settled in a comfortable

room in a spacious Mess after my few cramped months of itinerant life in aircraft carriers was very real. Life became normal once more, with free evenings for games, occasional weekend leave, and more rarely a long leave of a fortnight or perhaps even a month. Most pilots went home for leave, even for weekends, and to this rule I was no exception. With the increasing frequency of visits to my home and the passing from my memory of those days in carriers, there appeared anew in me a rising dissatisfaction with Mess life, which could now be compared side by side with the comfort begotten of permanency in a home, for during these years a revival in shipping was painting Cardiff once more in the comfortable colours of a mild prosperity.

But just when I was beginning to feel dangerously restless, bored with the monotony of instruction and the aimlessness of service life, activity in Training Unit increased. The number of pupils was raised, their period of training shortened, and this meant more work for the instructors.

Munich had seen the pirates' flag of skull and cross-bones hoisted brazenly to the mast of Hitler's ship to be heeded by all. Time was short, the expansion of the RAF was still incomplete, and mountains remained to be moved before a semblance of readiness could be achieved. But the warning flag of piracy had at last been seen, to inspire a feverish activity throughout the RAF and the aircraft industry, spurred on by an anxious Government. Yet all the while I myself was oblivious of all around me pointing a finger at War, for let it be whispered, then forgotten, I was preoccupied with a love-affair.

War spoiled my leave. During the crisis which preceded war I was at home, which I had visited quite often since the death of my father over a year before. He had spent his last few winters in Switzerland, but the discovery of his illness had been made too late for a cure to be effected. Nevertheless, he had lived to see a firm return of the shipping business to prosperity. The threat of war blew no ill wind either to the heavy industries or to shipping, which is so dependent on them, and he had seen the firm pay a dividend in 1938, the first for nearly ten heart-breaking years, when shipping must almost have forgotten that its reason for existence in a competitive age was not philanthropic, but to make a profit. The race with time had been won; we were now to reap the benefit of Father's insistence in sacrificing all to keep the firm going and his capital invested in it intact through the depression years. Our house and garden looked more lovely than ever during those few days of my last peace-time leave, and my family, freed now from worry, were contented in the mild, and I think deserved, prosperity. I recalled Father's wager against time, made to preserve the business he loved, and which I had spurned. It seemed now not by any means to have been a gambler's wager, but a sportsman's action; and, of course, that is what it really was.

I had completed ten of my twenty-one days of leave when I was recalled to my station by a peremptory telegram. It was mid-August, in whose fine weather I was enjoying myself and naturally I was annoyed at this interruption, very annoyed indeed, but far from alarmed. To say I had confidence in the conservation of peace would be an understatement, I knew that my recall was only a false alarm! As I got into my car to drive back to my station, I said that I would soon be returning to complete the remainder of my leave. To my generation, who had not seen a war, the repetition of crisis after crisis made each seem nothing more serious than a temporary nuisance to be quickly forgotten. To my mother, who had seen peace turn into war in a previous generation, the course of present events must have appeared inevitably to lead to another catastrophe.

I drove through a peaceful countryside on my return to duty. An occasional aircraft high in the air on a hot August day of blue sky and white cloud called to mind no more sinister reflections that the sight of a mighty battleship ploughing its furrow through peace-time waters. War was to me essentially remote from flying, which seemed to soar above mundane conflicts, and so it must have appeared to many other pilots whose eyes could not see beyond the near horizon of flying, and whose imagination was so filled by sensations of the air that no room remained for worldy thoughts of politics, differences and wars. They had joined the service to fly, with fighting far removed from their thoughts. A battleship's sixteen-inch guns appeared no more than a miracle of engineering; we were all born too late to remember earth scarred by shell craters and strewn with shattered limbs.

Realization was wishfully concealed in peace-time in the hope that recognition of the power of force might never be needed. War was nothing more than a word without meaning to the Air Force, for it was very young. Notwithstanding the panic of expansion, life in the service had continued its normal tenure; little had been left undone materially that time had permitted to be undertaken, only minds were unprepared. There was a complete absence among pilots of a comprehension of the meaning of war; realization could not be conveyed in feeble words, only by cold fear.

The journey was a long one; I was driving alone and had time to ponder. I was much disturbed by a suggestion I had just received from my uncle, one which had been recurring constantly since Father died, that I should enter the firm to fill the vacancy caused by his death.

My uncle, who had been older than my father by some years, was now by no means a young man, and the only active partner in the firm. The business was a family tradition, and the appeal from this quarter of its associations was very strong, for I did not want to see it pass into other hands, a feeling shared by the whole family. Here was a fine business, now with good years stretching before it, which was lacking in youth and needed me, and might one day need me badly, for there were no other sons or nephews yet old enough to carry on.

The business had suddenly changed its character for me; the recent pitiful years of depression were already less remembered in the new and long-promised prosperity which was now assured. If I had once turned a blind eye to the careless post-war years of plenty, memories of less happy times were now blotted out in a like manner. The firm began to hold a new romantic interest, and shipping appeared almost legendary in its appeal. Cardiff was filling out its skeleton, starved for ten lean years, and a new atmosphere reigned there. Docks bustled with activity as ships loaded cargoes, the stabbing of riveters could be heard in dry docks, and sirens sounded impatiently outside the port. Prosperity was good to look upon, and to feel. The invitation to join this world was doubly attractive to me; it was a new world and I was tired of my own world of flying. The word "new" was a star I should follow ... for how long?

Aircraft flew overhead, to remind me of my allegiance to flying. The rush of air past the cockpit, the response of an aircraft to the touch, cloudscapes of cotton-wool against a sky of blue material and the earth unreal below, a map beyond cartographers' invention of colours and shadows. Power over the earth by presence in the air; the exhilaration of speed and its mastery, the independence of ownership of the sky, the unreality of a presence in the air above an unreal world. A free spirit in a free body, loving the air, at one with the air, always to have access to flying in the earth's sky.

Could flying alone sustain me indefinitely in a service life? I looked ahead into my future in the service, when flying must be abandoned for an office chair, and the cheerful aerodrome life of the Flight Office, roaring aero engines and good company, would give place to a staff appointment remote from flying, in which the only contact with aircraft and their pilots was in the uneventful typewritten word. Such a life was emphatically one which I did not desire, and the realization of this laid flying more bare than ever as the only tie which held me to the service. Would flying always be attractive for me, would that single tie remain to sustain me? I felt that I was growing away from flying, now that its novelty had worn thin, yet the old enthusiasm would return on occasions, little lessened by time. But when the time came to abandon flying and to work in an office, I would be left detached and uninterested in the intangible paper work so remote from the air.

Service life was too aimless to attract me, companionship and opportunities for games were its chief assets, but the excess of leisure was a liability; I wanted to be more fully employed in my work. Above all, I wanted the permanency which the service never offered, for at any time I might be posted to the ends of the earth, and I wanted to settle, not to move. The home life I had just tasted seemed so superior to that in the Mess, that I wondered why I had ever wanted to leave home. Time, bringing with it experience, had been at work to change my youthful fancies. The desire for independence, which five years before had been so powerful a force in driving me from home, was now spent. Many of the conceptions I then held were now revised, and the importance of an independent life was diminished. Home life seemed infinitely desirable, and only love of flying still remained constant to bind me to the service. I saw that I had joined the RAF, regarding it as nothing more than a Flying Club, without realization of all that the word "service" implied. I was aware suddenly of a fact which had escaped me: that a service life must be accepted uncondi-tionally at its own value, or else rejected completely. I had made reservations and so failed to embrace the life. I could not help thinking that I had made a young mistake in my selection of a career, for the choice had been mine alone. I accused myself of unfounded discontent and restlessness, of being a failure in my career. Yet it could not be truthfully said that I had failed, certainly not by service standards; if I were defeated at all, it was by my own vague demands of life, seemingly never to be satisfied.

The fact that these thoughts were revolving in my mind as I returned to duty that day is an eloquent witness to my unpreparedness for war. Although any recall from leave was a rare occurrence, and a general recall, such as this, without precedent in my service experience, my confidence in the continuation of peace was still unshaken. War was completely absent from my mind, in which I was unhurriedly consider-ing the question of my future as I drove along in what I imagined to be a peaceful direction. A decision of rejection or acceptance of service life had to be made, and I was gradually reaching a decision to break with the RAF balancing the wasted years against increased experience, and deciding to enter the firm, as tradition demanded. A victory was being won of loyalty to the family business over love of flying, with not a little selfish fighting on the part of restlessness. Yet the final decision was not to leave the RAF but to remain with it, and the question was to be decided for me.

All the time my car, unknowing, sped towards war. Green hedges were dusty from sun-baked roads, a haze of summer heat hung in the air, a promise of continued fine weather. The countryside, luxurious in its green, reminded me of a similar August day, just three years ago, when I had driven to Hucknall to join my first squadron. All had been peaceful then, and seemed no less so now. I had been expectant then of the future before me, and now looked again into the years ahead for a star to guide me. I did not know that the future held high before me, not peace, but a sword.

CHAPTER VI

AT LONG LAST

WAR brought a purpose to the Air Force with a vengeance. My accusations of aimlessness against the peace-time service had now to be withdrawn in the face of the demonstration of purpose to fight and to win which was displayed on all sides. If its pilots were unprepared to fight, the enemy were soon to learn that they were by no means unwilling. The RAF at war was inspiring, and I thanked fortune that I was still in it, and cursed fortune that I could not immediately take up the sword and fight.

On my return to Gosport after my recall from leave, some of my complete assurance was at first lost in contact with the general pessimism of the Mess, where particularly the older officers thought war inevitable. As the days passed, strangely filled with tension unrelieved by any definite news, I began once more to think that yet another crisis would blow over, like so many before, and that war would be averted. This conjecture was the outcome of blindness born of ignorance, which made me the cheerful foolish optimist, hoping aimlessly for the best. Yet one attitude seemed as callow as any other in its complete impotence. An onlooker was helpless, and when news came that it was to be war at last, the feeling was almost one of relief at a merciful release from further indecision. It was almost as if the declaration of war was welcomed! The future was no longer just a matter of abstract and endless thinking and talking, but of actually doing.

Since there were no squadrons at Gosport, the effects of war were not immediately felt, and there was nothing of feverish last-minute activity which must have occurred on operational stations. Inevitably the rate of training of pilots was now speeded up, and Training Unit was sent more pupils and given less time in which to train them, work which we set out now to do. Working hours were lengthened to include every hour of daylight, and the programme of instruction was pruned of inessentials. War did not require frills in a pupil's flying, or mere theoretical knowledge, but a sound practical grounding and as much actual flying experience as could be crammed into the short span of his course.

I was instructing both naval pilots for the Air Arm and RAF pilots for the Coastal Command torpedo squadrons. Course after course passed through our hands to meet the anticipated heavy casualties in squadrons. Yet Christmas was to follow summer, and spring break in its turn on unsuspecting armies, before the RAF was really to go to war, its bombers roll out in earnest at night and fighters fill the daylight sky with stubborn defence.

I longed to take my part in the fight, but tried hard to become resigned to instructing and to convince myself, when feelings of frustration were uppermost, that the work which I was doing was important and productive. There was more work to be got through than ever before, as an endless procession of pupils came, learnt, and left us for one of the squadrons. Still, I could not help envying their good luck, a feeling shared by all the instructors. We pined for a squadron posting, knowing all the time it was impossible, for instructors were needed and there were none to replace us. We were trapped in a backwater, and wondered if we would ever get the chance to sail out into the open and fight.

It was hard to be aloof from the fight in those first uneventful six months of war, which saw little real fighting, but we had the comforting knowledge that many first-line squadrons were inactive and waiting impatiently for the offensive, while we were at least busy with instruction. But if we groaned then in our backwater at the misery of our lot, our moans were to be silent sobs compared with the wail of complaint which arose in the months after Dunkirk. It was agonizing that instruction should continue in its undisturbed monotony when the Air Force was an eruption of fighting activity, yet in our hearts we knew it must be so.

In the last war, experienced flying instructors had been allowed to go in their hundreds to first-line squadrons, there to be lost for ever to the flying schools, in which they were irreplaceable. These schools, lacking any but amateur instructors, allowed the standard of flying to fall to a sadly low level, eventually adversely affecting the fighting squadrons' efficiency. The same error was not to be made a second time, the lesson was remembered, and as the service mustered its resources as if to face a long and determined siege, it was to the training side that she was to give first attention.

Flying Training Command expanded unbelievably in the first year of war. Vast training schemes were brought into operation in the Empire, which are even now incomplete. The instructor was too valuable to be sent to war, for his experience could fashion many pilots of his own kind to strike his blow at the enemy. It was a wise policy thus to conserve the energies of training, and justified today by the high standard of flying which is being uniformly maintained. Today no front-line squadron finds its operations restricted by inadequacy in training of pilots and crews.

While in the peace-time Air Force short-service officers had out-numbered by far the handful of "permanent" officers, wartime was to see them in their turn vastly outnumbered by Volunteer Reservists, the temporary pilot who was called up or volunteered for flying training. Just as a cadet's long training had really made him no superior to a short-service officer in the air or on the ground, so now the "VR" pilot's wartime training seemed to produce results identical with those of peace-time. He is by no means a despised amateur, for his work has been wonderfully successful, and he takes his place with ex-cadet and short-service officer, flying no less skilfully and fighting on equal terms. It is, in fact, the wartime-trained "VR" pilot who is now bearing the brunt of air operations. He is in the ascendancy, and his majority must inevitably increase as the war continues, to make others seem as rare as the Cranwell officer in the peace-time service. Always there is a waiting list of applicants for training as pilots, flying is no less attractive than ever, and never before has it been within the reach of so many.

Our pupils in Training Unit were now nearly all "VR" pilots, both officers and sergeants, who were naturally drawn from every kind of civilian occupation, but appeared remarkably at home in the service after only a few months' training at flying schools, which, like our unit, had shortened their instruction for war. As course followed course I was impressed with the fact that there was no lowering of the standard of flying among our pupils, which remained at much the same level as in peace-time. Training assumed a new importance for me, and I enjoyed instructing more than ever before, for my efforts now had an obvious purpose: to impart to pupils as much of my experience as possible, for it might stand them in good stead in action. As pupils passed quickly through my hands I wished them luck and hoped to hear news of their exploits, for it seemed as if that might be my nearest contact with the war of fighting.

In spite of the increased rate of training, the tide of expansion had not yet turned materially towards the torpedo squadrons, which were confined during the first months of the war by the general obsolescence of their old biplanes to the uninspiring role of waiting for a ship-borne invasion. Even in such an event they would have fared badly in the face of air opposition on account of their slow maximum speed of only 130 knots! Their Vildebeestes were certainly the most old-fashioned type remaining in any operational squadron at home at the outbreak of war, and not surprisingly they would only have been called on in an emergency. However, there was a rumour of a new mono-plane type on the drawing-board destined for the torpedo squadrons, and until its arrival activity in the torpedo world remained static.

On the other hand, the Fleet Air Arm Swordfish, although a biplane, was doing magnificent work both from aircraft carriers and shore aerodromes, but it was by no means as old-fashioned as the Vildebeeste; on the contrary, it was remarkably well adapted to carrier operation, which imposes some formidable limitations on design on account of the small space available for taking off and landing.

So while in Training Unit we considered our naval courses of great importance, the work of instructing the RAF pilots appeared unproductive. They were unlikely to go into action until the advent of the new aircraft, and then would not benefit by what we had taught them. The tactics which we taught were applicable to biplanes only. A torpedo-carrying monoplane had never before been used, and it seemed likely that its advent would revolutionize former conceptions of a torpedo attack.

A torpedo is not comparable with a bomb, for there are no points of similarity between them. There were no difficulties in the way of progress in design of bombing aircraft, for the bomb imposed no limitations. On the other hand, the torpedo restricted design considerably. It could not be thrown off the aircraft at any speed, height and altitude like a bomb, for it was filled with delicate mechanisms easily damaged, necessitating a smooth entry into the water. In biplanes this careful drop, ideally at 60 feet and 130 knots, had easily been achieved, for the aircraft were easy to handle at slow speeds and releasing the torpedo within the limitations of speed and height above the water presented no difficulty. But the use of a monoplane was likely to present problems, for it would virtually be impossible to handle near the speeds at which a torpedo had previously been dropped. Its design aimed at speed, which after all was essential, and sacrificed control at low speeds to obtain good handling character-istics at high speeds. Also, compared with biplanes, monoplanes lacked the manoeuvrability upon which the present tactics depended.

Altogether there were many obstacles to be overcome before a monoplane could be utilized for torpedo dropping, and the instructors were worried for its future. The torpedo world was in a stagnation of old-fashioned types and thoughts, and we were aching to launch it out into waters moving with the times, a desire which could not be achieved until the advent of the new aircraft. We waited and we worried. Our branch appeared an island on which we were not only stranded and condemned to live, but one not even fed from the world outside; it was passed by and forgotten. Meanwhile we could do nothing but wait for the promised new aircraft, so long overdue, fearing that it might never be possible to harness a modern aircraft to the requirements of torpedo dropping, and wondering what would happen to us then.

However, the technical side of the problem was to receive immediate attention, even if the tactics were still unresolved, for there arrived at Gosport for Development Flight's use a Wellesley aircraft especially fitted to carry a torpedo. At last there was a new type on the station, whose biplanes looked like relics from a former war, for the Wellesley was a monoplane, with a retractable undercarriage, landing flaps and variable pitch propeller. It was in fact a typical modern aircraft.

How old-fashioned it made our Swordfish appear, and how we envied Development Flight's pilots who were to fly it! Eventually I contrived to borrow it for a short flight, and was surprised to find it easy to fly in spite of the formidable array of instruments, indicators and levers which filled its cockpit, the first enclosed cockpit in which I had flown. The Wellesley had all the attraction of something new, although flying it was only a variation of the fundamental flying I had learnt at Cranwell on Tutors and Harts.

From the Wellesley it was possible to drop torpedoes at higher speeds than a biplane could achieve, thus enabling the technical experts to experiment and anticipate the difficulties of dropping from the new aircraft, which rumour claimed to be no longer on the drawing-board but in the production stage. Stories were related of fantastic speeds attained by the prototype in the hands of the factory's test pilot, and anticipation was great for the day on which it should first be seen. It was now definitely known to be a twin-engined aircraft, yet another departure from previous torpedo-carrying types, and our doubts about employing the present tactics were increased; opinion was unanimous that it could not be done.

This new type, called the Beaufort and built by Bristols, failed to make an appearance before March, but in December both Development Flight and Training Unit received the first few off the production line of the Blackburn Botha. Now at last we had a modern aircraft to fly, but there at once arose a snag: none of us could fly a twin-engined aircraft. Our CO asked for a dual aircraft and instructor, and for days we waited impatiently for someone to come and teach us, not without a great deal of exploring inside this great monster, for so it appeared in our hangar beside the small Swordfish. But no instructor came, and in desperation we took a Botha out and taught ourselves. Again basic flying proved its value, for although the difference between the Botha and the aircraft to which we were accustomed was as wide as possible between types, no one experienced any difficulty in flying it.

The Botha was no plaything, but a business-like machine of war. There were good facilities for navigation, a chart table at which a navigator could work out his problems, a spacious wireless compartment, and a twin-gun power-operated turret for defence. We had never possessed anything like this before; the Botha was the sort of modern aircraft of which news had come years before from luckier units, and while our aerodrome had often been visited by new aircraft such as this, an opportunity to fly them had never occurred for us.

It is a practice in the service for pilots to fly their new type to a friend's aerodrome and exchange with him the new aircraft for a flight in one of his, in this way extending the list of types in one's log book and at the same time keeping in touch with new features of design. I had not been too lucky in such exchanges, as no one wanted to fly Swordfish (they had flown Tutors, they rudely said) and also pilots were unwilling to trust an old biplane pilot with their modern aircraft. Most of the new types were twin-engined, and to fly a "twin" was said to require special instruction, a theory to which my unit gave the lie.

But we were not too lucky with the Botha. Like many other new aircraft first coming into service, it suffered from all sorts of initial technical failures, "teething" troubles always present in a new type, and our hopes of many flying hours in Bothas were not realized. Instead we would gaze disconsolately at our toy, persistently decorating the interior of the hangar for weeks on end, as airmen worked on one petty fault after another with continual delays for spare parts. I shall always remember the Botha as an indoor aircraft, and not with affection, for it handled poorly.

However, in spite of this I did manage over a period of winter months to put in more than forty hours in the Botha, a large proportion of which were taken up in some petrol consumption tests which the unit had to carry out. For this purpose I made several six-hour flights, covering a large part of the country at cruising speeds almost double that of a Swordfish. I was not one of the lucky instructors chosen to go on leave that first wartime Christmas, and actually flew in the Botha on Christmas Day itself on a triangular flight to Anglesey, returning via Lands End. This was an uneventful but cold flight, for the test had to be made at 10,000 feet; and the countryside below was white with frost under a cloudless sky. Flying the new type was very different and quite demanding. If a twin is less manoeuvrable than a single-engined aircraft, there are compensations for being unable to throw it about in aerobatics. The technical side of the flying is considerable, and navigation of greater importance, and if this seemed more of a business than the former game of flying, it could nevertheless be equally absorbing.

During these winter months Development Unit perfected the actual dropping of a torpedo at high speeds from Botha and Wellesley by modifying the torpedo to allow it to be dropped both at greater speed and higher from the water than formerly. The torpedo world was now anxiously awaiting the Beaufort, which none of us had set eyes upon, but which had been reputed to be coming any day, and had been in this unarrived state for some months already. Although the technical problem was solved, no work could be carried out on the tactics until the new type arrived.

At last the promised Beaufort landed at Gosport, just when we were ready to believe its very existence was mythical, so long had we waited, but now the months of delay seemed amply justified. The usual critical band of onlookers from the tarmac became an admiring crowd for some days to come whenever the Beaufort flew. Unfortunately it had been allotted not to us but to Development Unit, which was to carry out experimental torpedo dropping to confirm the results achieved with Botha and Wellesley. One of their pilots had already been to the Central Flying School for special dual instruction on the new type, which was felt to be a necessary precaution with what was considered rather a fierce piece of machinery. Certainly the roar of its powerful Taurus engines was impressive as it sped over the ground to take off, and the fast landing speed made the approach to the aerodrome appear very tricky. But most impressive of all was its speed in flight, and as it flashed over the aerodrome envy and admiration was expressed by all of us. I climbed all over this first Beaufort on the ground, examining every detail of its cockpit, and later I was given a flight as a passenger which made me long to fly it myself.

Now at last there was no longer stagnation but movement, and soon after the arrival of this single Beaufort to inspire interest on the aerodrome, news came that the first of the Vildebeeste squadrons was to re-form with Beauforts and had actually received its aircraft. Torpedo drops made from Development Flight's Beaufort had been satis-factory, but I still wondered at the neglect of the tactical side, and how the squadron would adapt the characteristics of the first monoplane and twin ever to carry out a torpedo to an actual attack.

Our Fleet Air Arm training continued to be productive. We even received occasional news from a former pupil of how he was getting on in carriers, and it was heartening to hear he was still flying Sword-fish and still practised all we had taught in Training Unit.

The first hint that Training Unit was to receive Beauforts was contained in a signal demanding two instructors to be sent to the Central Flying School for a "conversion course to medium twins". Naturally this signal caused no little excitement, and rivalry ran high as to which two out of the ten instructors should be sent. I believe the CO decided by drawing the names from a hat, but whatever the method used, I was one of the lucky chosen, and went off with great expectation to learn to fly a Beaufort.

At the Central Flying School I was first given some dual instruction in Blenheims, in order to master the technique of twin-engined flying on an easy type. I found a Blenheim delightful to handle, and put in several hours of solo flying in one before going on to Beauforts. Although a Beaufort is the logical successor of the Blenheim, for both are made by Bristols and are similar in appearance, there was no comparison in their flying, and I was thankful for my experience in the Botha, which had been my introduction to twin-engined flying.

The Beaufort, although completely without vices, was something of a handful and demanded respect. By this I mean that it was not docile like some aircraft which will almost fly by themselves with little guidance from the pilot, but demanded constant and vigilant super-vision. Although twin-engined flying was strange, for I had come to it from years spent in flying a totally different and remarkably easy aircraft, the Swordfish (now very "old and faithful"), this first impression that a Beaufort required always to be consciously flown and never left to its own devices, particularly near the ground, is one which I have never since found reason to modify. It is by no means a difficult aircraft to fly, but to treat it with contempt inspiring neglect is to court disaster. I know, because I did so.

The reason for this characteristic, best described not as fierce but "fiery", is the alliance in the Beaufort of high-powered engines and wings of small area, both features contributing to high speed, with, at the same time, considerable weight. It is by no means a large aircraft, but the fuselage is spacious to carry the crew of four, petrol for several hours' flying, and of course the heavy torpedo.

After several hours' solo flying on Beauforts, my instructor deemed me competent to fly medium twins, and I returned to Gosport and to the old Swordfish. It was now only a matter of waiting again, this time for Training Unit to be re-equipped with Beauforts. The naval instruction was becoming independent, since the flight had acquired a number of experienced naval pilots, now appropriately to teach their own pupils. The RAF flight, I felt, would be dead until instruction started on the monoplane aircraft. However, to show that the activity in the torpedo world was continuing, news arrived that there were six Beauforts ready for our collecting from the makers, and, as can be imagined, no time was lost before they were on our aerodrome. The authorities now decided to discontinue training while the instructors learnt to fly the new aircraft. The rate of training had been excessive during the war months and out of all proportion to the wastage in squadrons, which, on account of their initial inactivity and present re-equipment period, had suffered few casualties. With relief we completed the instruction of our last course in June, and thankfully handed over our Swordfish to the naval flight which left us shortly afterwards for their own aerodrome. Now we were a Beaufort flight at last.

Meanwhile more Beauforts were delivered by ferry pilots; hardly a day passed without a new aircraft arriving, until finally the unit had at least thirty to provide a paradise of flying, brand new and exciting flying, to the long-suffering instructors to whom it had been denied. The day which had dawned for most other units years before, dawned now on ours which had been neglected and forgotten. Our feelings were those of other pilots on receiving their new aircraft two, three, and even four years ago, but if the moment had been long delayed, it was now infinitely sweet. We looked out from our hangar at the new grey aircraft dispersed along the aerodrome boundary with feelings of pride and relief no longer to be labelled old-fashioned. These were our aircraft and we flew them: Beauforts.

The Battle of Britain followed the evacuation of Dunkirk, to find me still in Training Unit and still aching for a chance to fight. The wireless news related each evening stories of successively more glorious days of aerial fighting, and more personal accounts came in letters from friends telling of the feats of their squadrons and more sadly of the death of other friends, yet always omitting personal reference, which I could fill in by reading between the lines. It was impossible to remain contented and still be absent from the struggle.

The knowledge that I was young and an experienced pilot, the feeling that to fight was my vocation, and that to couple fighting with flying might supply the missing quality for which I had been searching—all these thoughts revolved in my mind through that sun-baked summer, Hitler's Blitzkrieg summer, so hot, so fine, that a true description in time to come would be disbelieved.

I was flying Beauforts nearly every day, and growing to like them more with every flying hour. Mechanical "teething" troubles were again considerable and restricted our flying, but we had so many aircraft that it was always possible to produce at least one when required. Beaufort flying did not seem the kind of which I might tire after the novelty had worn thin. The aircraft had to be flown right from the start of the take-off until it had actually stopped running at the end of the landing run. The powerful engines pulled it through the air at speeds not even registered on the airspeed indicator of a Swordfish. So clean in design was the Beaufort that with undercarriage retracted and tail wheel tucked up it seemed to slip through the air like skating on ice, not ploughing through it like the old biplanes. To enter a gentle shallow dive was to see the needle of the airspeed indicator rapidly cover the 200-knot scale, pass the 300 mark and still continue upwards.

How long had I waited for such an aircraft, and how rewarded the wait now seemed. Hardly a day passed without one of us finding some new point in the flying of a Beaufort to discuss, to make it seem like Cranwell days and first flying enthusiasm all over again, for the other instructors were equally keen on the aircraft which they too had awaited, perhaps with rather more patience than I had.

The flying was now all that I had hoped for, but we were not occupied fully, for training had not yet restarted and was still waiting for the squadron's decision on the question of new tactics. Even if there had been pupils and work to do in Training Unit, I would not now have been satisfied; my ambition was to take a Beaufort to war. In June the first torpedo squadron to be equipped with Beauforts had completed training on the new type and taken its place in the front line. Vague rumours of its first operations came to us, which made us long to take part in the work we knew so well and have our say in the formulating of new tactics. For this squadron was to decide, after some trials, how a torpedo attack could best be launched using Beauforts, and then make its demands accordingly on Training Unit for the necessary instruction of pilots, who would then go out to squadrons ready to drop a torpedo in action and take part in the current attack. My forecast that previous tactics would have to be modified out of all recognition was to prove accurate, but it was made from no stroke of genius, merely from common sense.

It looked as if the squadron might take some time to evolve tactics, and I thought that the lull in training activity might meanwhile be utilized as a lever by which to obtain a posting. I determined to try the effect of pleading that I was superfluous to requirements in my present appointment, and so get myself posted to a squadron. But I was not the only instructor to seize on the situation for his own ends, for I found that all the other instructors were secretly trying to get posted to squadrons, thinking their efforts went undetected. For one instructor to escape might be possible, but for a whole flock to be allowed to leave was unimaginable. The personnel staff officer at Group Headquarters must have been at first surprised, then annoyed, as he was approached one after another by Training Unit's instructors, who singly and confidingly presented their own particular reason why they should be posted. This approach proved fruitless. "Instructors are valuable, and must be preserved" was the reply, and no posting followed.

In the end I benefited by a more subtle method. I got a Squadron Commander to ask for me. In July Squadron Leader Donald Francis, "Fanny", one of Development Flight's pilots, who had also been in the *Courageous* with me, after a long agitation in which he had eventually proved he was superfluous in his present appointment, had got himself posted to the Beaufort squadron. This triumph of perseverance, for Fanny had been moving heaven and earth for several months for this very posting, gave us all new heart. As I saw him off from the Mess, I said half jestingly, "Tell your CO I want to join his squadron", and afterwards thought little more about it, particularly as July passed into August and September came, still without news of a posting.

I was becoming resigned to the situation, this resignation only occasionally to be cast off by news, not from remote bomber or fighter squadrons far removed from our world, but from the Beaufort squadron so filled with our former pupils that we had a proprietary feeling of ownership, as if it were our child. Now came news of its doings, of daylight torpedo attacks on ships in the Channel, bombing of Dutch oil-refineries and incredible stories of a torpedo attack in a French harbour at night. Resignation could not reign long in this kingdom of reported achievement. After only a few months in the line the squadron was already making a reputation for its work; even fighter pilots, usually confined within their own outlook, were heard to express admiration for this Beaufort squadron, and this I could not help thinking was praise indeed.

I had not been so ambitious as to try and obtain a posting to a fighter squadron, but this did not mean I had outgrown my hankering after fighters, merely that I knew such a posting was outside my reach. A posting to any squadron would be welcome, and to continue the work in war which I had learnt in peace-time seemed logical. I wanted now to reach the Beaufort squadron, to the exclusion of all other desires.

In the end I was lucky, the first lucky one among all the instructors, who nevertheless were all to leave and take their place in squadrons within the next few months, for I was posted. In the last week in September I received a signal, rivalled in acceptability only by the one which at a word had removed me from the Fleet Air Arm. It told me, "F/Lt P. Gibbs to report to No 22 Squadron forthwith for flying duties". As I passed the signal round among the other envious instructors I blessed the initiative of Fanny, who I knew must have been instrumental in fixing my posting, for it was to his squadron that I was now going.

This conclusion of two years in Training Unit had none of the sad good-byes and reluctant parting of a similar occasion in peace-time. I wanted to leave, as did all the others, and could not conceal my desire. My wish for settlement and permanency had been completely obscured by a determination to fight, no matter what the cost might be. Petty considerations of personal comfort seemed inconsiderable in wartime. I felt no inconsistency when I made every effort to leave the previously desired settled existence for a life in which there was no pretence at permanency. These had become little more than trivialities which must wait until another day. My objective, hitherto nebulous and varying, was now fixed before me. It was to fight.

CHAPTER VII

THE SWORD IN MY HAND

I ARRIVED at the aerodrome on which my squadron was based by air in one of Training Unit's Beauforts, bringing with me another pilot to fly the aircraft back. My departure had been delayed for several days due to bad weather, and although the "forthwith" of my posting signal was elastic, I thought I should telephone and let the squadron Adjutant know when to expect me. I heard clearly, in spite of the considerable distance, and was given a remarkable first impression by the voice which answered me: "Yes, old boy, it will be quite all right, old boy. Yes, I'll tell the CO, old boy, we're looking forward to seeing you, dear old laddie!" This remote telephone welcome was as cheering as its manner of address was unconventional. I was to find that Alec Gammon, the squadron Adjutant, addressed everybody in this fashion, from officers to the most insignificant airman, who might even be known by his Christian name! But the CO was addressed with a punctilious "Sir".

I now met the owner of this voice in person, as I reported to the Adjutant's Office to signify my arrival, where I was greeted with a positive fusillade of "dear olds" for which my Christian name was substituted as soon as it was read from the arrival form I had just filled in. I was later to find that behind this flippant façade lay a very considerable efficiency and no mean capability of maintaining discipline. Alec was to remain the one constant in the squadron; new pilots came, crews were posted away or became casualties, but Alec remained, a selfless servant, invaluable in wartime to maintain the spirit of a squadron and its continuity.

He was now a Flight Lieutenant in the administrative branch, and a Volunteer Reservist who had joined the RAF for the war. In the last war, after being wounded in France, he had been seconded to an RFC training wing, and so was no stranger to a flying service. He did not believe that squadron spirit was an abstract quality whose presence was desirable and hoped for; he absolutely personified such spirit by untiring work on the squadron's behalf, knowing each of the officers and 500-odd airmen intimately and ever willing to make any sacrifice for them. If I am ever lucky enough to command a squadron, my efforts to seduce Alec from his first love, to be my Adjutant, will place in insignificance the efforts to obtain my own posting from Training Unit.

He told me now that the CO, Wing Commander Braithwaite, was away for the day at a conference but had left instructions that I was to join some other pilots from the squadron who were at an aerodrome in Bircham Newton for some night flying training. The CO had rightly assumed that I had no night flying experience on Beauforts, but I imagined he little knew that I had not flown at night for nearly four years and had only three hours' night flying in my log book. However, I knew that the sooner I was qualified to fly at night, the sooner I could start operating, and so welcomed this opportunity of dual instruction.

Before leaving I had lunch in the Mess and met the squadron's officers, all of whom I had known before, either as my contemporaries in the Fleet Air Arm or as pupils in Training Unit, a situation which alleviated the "stranger in our midst" feeling usually present on joining a new unit. To my surprise, the Mess seemed filled with naval uniforms, their owners belonging to a Fleet Air Arm squadron which shared the aerodrome with the Beaufort squadron. Several of these pilots had been our pupils, and their squadron was now lent to the RAF until completion of a new carrier, for which they were destined.

Here was an amusing reversal of a previous situation, my arrival at Leuchars, but the majority of the naval pilots seemed glad to be ashore, whereas we had never been resigned to being afloat. Certainly they did magnificent work, almost entirely devoted to laying mines in enemy waters at night, when the aircraft's slow speed was no disadvantage. The way in which they overcame the lack of good navigational and wireless facilities in their Swordfish was remarkable, and it earned genuine respect and admiration from the RAF pilots. When this squadron left the aerodrome for its carrier some months later it was much missed, and everyone was pleased when a few weeks later their CO received a well-deserved DFC.

The pilots of our squadron told me there had been a lull in operations recently due to bad weather. However, I heard quite a lot of general information on what sort of work the squadron undertook, which revealed that it was something of a "Jack of all trades", for the Beaufort is not only a torpedo carrier but a general purpose aircraft capable of carrying also either a load of bombs or a mine. Consequently odd jobs were given to the squadron, which normally kept it fully occupied, as there was at this time only one other Beaufort squadron to share such work, operating from a Scottish aerodrome and something of a rival of ours.

It appeared that very few targets had been presented for a torpedo attack, but six aircraft had dropped torpedoes within the harbour at Cherbourg by moonlight, encountering fierce opposition but wreaking havoc among ships anchored there. The squadron had also been laying mines regularly in enemy waters—not a very popular operation, as the actual result of a pilot's work was never seen; although he might hear later from Intelligence that a ship had sunk in a minefield to which he had contributed several mines, by the time the news reached him the flight would be long forgotten. Some bombing of land targets had been carried out as well, and a raid on some oil-refineries at Ghent had been particularly successful.

Altogether the impression of the squadron's role which I took away with me that afternoon was a most favourable one on account of its variety and interest. Always the squadron was striking, and often at something new and in a different way, torpedoes for ships, bombs for ports, and mines in ship-infested waters. I had never doubted that I should like squadron life; now I could feel the edge of an atmosphere of keenness which would have sent even the most hesitant away with a desire to fight. It made the days which I had now to spend in night flying training seem like so much lost time. The present would not have been too soon to start operating.

As in those first few deck-landings, so with Beaufort night flying, I was not completely confident in my ability. I had quite forgotten the experience of those few hours' night flying of years ago. To add to my misgiving, I recalled that those hours had been flown in the pre-black-out era of lighted towns and naked headlamps, indeed of light everywhere to help a night-flying pilot. It had all now to be learnt anew with the Beaufort, which, if commanding respect in its handling by day, would certainly require very careful attention at night. I felt ashamed that with Flight Lieutenant's rank and nearly a thousand hours' flying in my log book I was still virtually a complete beginner at night flying, and little comforted by the knowledge that I was not myself to blame for this state of affairs. It was the result of the era in which I was trained, which had ignored night flying, as had the Air

Arm and Training Unit in which I had the misfortune to spend vital years. I was later to pay rather dearly for this neglect, which had been quite outside my control. No one could have wanted to be in the swim of modern flying from its first days more than I, nor could anyone have felt more apprehension at being withheld from it all these years. Anxiety for the future had been powerless to avoid the situation which now arose. That future was now the present, and I was a night-flying pupil.

Night flying in black-out conditions means instrument flying. This generalization is not without its exceptions, for on bright moon-light nights the horizon is often well enough defined for a pilot to fly by ordinary visual means, but such nights are rare and a large proportion of night hours will always be spent entirely in instrument gazing. It was to this type of flying I referred when I suggested that it was to become less of an art and more of a science, for the secret of instrument flying is conscientiousness; flair will be of no avail.

The flying instruments show a pilot within the cockpit all that he can see in daytime by looking outside at the horizon or the ground. One instrument reproduces the attitude of the aircraft, indicating whether it is climbing, diving, banking or turning. Speed, height and direction are all revealed to a pilot by his flying instruments, six in number and mounted directly in front of him on a panel specially insulated from vibration. In exactly the same place in every service aircraft is an identical instrument panel; it is the pilot's bible, to be read continually, and essential to modern flying.

I had at least been able to practise instrument flying both in Botha and Beaufort, and felt confident that I would have little difficulty with night flying once the aircraft was actually in the air, only taking off and landing would present real problems. It was not with instrument flying that I was to have trouble at night; indeed, initially I found no difficulty at all. My instructor gave me half an hour's instruction in a Beaufort specially fitted with a duplicate set of controls, and after he had made one circuit and landing to demonstrate the procedure I flew unaided, with few corrections from him.

Across the aerodrome stretches the flare path, a long line of lights, spaced at intervals, pointing into wind. A floodlight at the up-wind end of the flare path illuminates the ground on which the aircraft will actually touch down, but its use is restricted to the last part of the approach only, for the bright light might reveal the presence of the aerodrome to the enemy intruders high above. The end of the landing run and obstructions are indicated by an occasional red light, combining with the coloured navigation lights of the aircraft to make a gay show of lights dotted in the blackness all around.

Sitting beside my instructor at the dual set of controls, I watched him take off. Throttles are opened for the aircraft to move forward, gathering speed as it runs down the line of lights to rise into the air before reaching the end of the flare path, and the light on the boundary vanishes beneath us. Now nothing can be seen ahead but utter blackness. All the lights of the aerodrome are behind us, and although it is a cloudless night with a starry sky, no horizon is discernible. My instructor has been flying from the moment the aircraft left the ground entirely by the instruments, illuminated by a dim light shining directly on to their panel.

Much the trickiest part of a night take-off is the transition from visual flying to instrument flying, which must be made immediately the aircraft becomes airborne, a time when it is still near the ground and without much flying speed. The period of transition is one of slight tension but nevertheless momentary, for the aircraft accelerates rapidly away from the ground once its undercarriage begins to retract, and both height and speed are increased within a few seconds to safe figures on the dials of their respective instruments. The sensation of a night take-off, particularly in a heavily loaded aircraft, cannot be classed as a thrill; the whole procedure requires too much concentration to be regarded so lightly.

Reaching a safe height of a thousand feet, my instructor raises the flaps which have been used to shorten the take-off run, adjusts the running of his engines and settles down to fly comfortably by instruments. He turns the cockpit lights down to their dimmest, which improves my vision of the sky outside, previously appearing so dark in comparison with the bright light within the cockpit. Now it is possible to distinguish very faintly a blurred line which is the meeting point of earth and sky, the night horizon.

My instructor, who has flown straight since leaving the flare path, turns round through one hundred and eighty degrees, indicated on his gyro compass, and the aircraft is pointing back at the aerodrome, whose lights soon come into sight ahead. Soon he is flying down-wind past the aerodrome, preparing to make an approach and land. Lowering his undercarriage, he turns again through one hundred and eighty degrees, and the flare path is now straight ahead, its line of lights stretching before us. Flaps are lowered to aid control at low speeds, and we descend steadily at a normal speed of approach. Suddenly the floodlight is switched on to shed a pool of light on the ground to the right of the flare path, indicating where we must land. We approach the floodlit path rapidly, and individual blades of grass can almost be distinguished as we rush into the light itself, my instructor holding the aircraft just off the ground until it finally touches down, running from the floodlight up the line of lights into the darkness, coming to rest before the last light is reached. We are down, and this is night flying.

Swordfish night flying was play in comparison with this, which was a business not to be lightly undertaken. Nothing could illustrate better the change which flying has undergone in the last decade than the difference between pre-black-out Swordfish night flying and this present Beaufort flying. I was a biplane pilot trying hard to adapt myself quickly to modern practice, an adaptation which should really have been spread over a period of weeks. In some squadrons the transition to modern flying had taken place during years in which re-equipment with first one and then another new type of aircraft at long intervals made easy stepping-stones to final acceptance of the changes of half a decade. In such cases conversion would have been a matter of course, with each step so small that it could be taken in the stride. The new order came so gradually that its advance passed unnoticed. To me the transition was no mere step, but had grown into a cliff during the neglected years, which I had now to scale. I encouraged myself with the thought that I had learnt to fly the Botha without instruction and had no difficulty with the Beaufort by daylight. I could and I would teach myself modern night flying.

I made two circuits upon which my instructor had little to comment, except to criticize the rather flat angle of my approach. However, he considered that I was flying safely enough to go off solo, and I made half a dozen uneventful landings in an hour's flying, during which the moon came up to make the horizon easily discernible. I went to bed that night with a feeling of satisfaction at having laid a ghost. The fear that I might be left behind by modern flying vanished into oblivion. I was flying a modern aircraft, no less, indeed probably rather more, difficult to fly than most types in service, and flying it passably by day and now at last by night. The cliff, now appearing no more formidable than some common hill, was scaled to gain equality with those fortunate enough to have taken a round-about path. The past did not matter now; bacon and eggs at four o'clock in the morning was followed by sleep, and that sleep was good.

Night flying makes greater demands on the weather than daylight flying. Weather conditions in which an aircraft can fly safely in the daytime may often be dangerous at night; low cloud can be very treacherous and limited visibility is accentuated by darkness. In this way I was kept away from the squadron for ten days by unsuitable night flying weather, for it was now October and summer nights had given way to winter. At the end of this time I had flown for three hours at night and made several circuits and landings without any incidents occurring.

I returned to my squadron, in what was euphemistically termed a "fully trained" state, a designation I took liberty to question. I could fly a Beaufort by day, and I could manage to take it into the sky and return it to earth again at night, but I would have liked many more hours of practice in this, of which war cheated me. The instructor had been asked to return us as soon as we could fly at night with confidence, and there was a minimum of three hours' solo set, which I had just, but only just, achieved.

An operational squadron has little breathing space in which to train her crews and attend to her aircraft; the preparation for and carrying out of operations, even at a rate which appears unbelievably slow, is sufficient to extend all her resources. So pilots and aircraft were urgently wanted back as soon as our training was finished, and I was first to return. Later I was to wish that I had insisted on putting in some more hours of practice night flying, and was to curse my weakness in not doing so. But I knew that further training might take long to accomplish, since suitable night flying weather might be awaited for weeks. Desire to start operating overcame my discretion, and I returned to my squadron trained in name only.

North Coates, the station at which my squadron was based, had an aerodrome typical of Coastal Command, situated right on the Lincolnshire coast. The country stretched flat for miles around almost at sealevel; indeed, there was a bank of earth raised along the aerodrome's coastal boundary to protect it from the inroads of the sea. Surprisingly, the aerodrome surface, although not blessed with concrete runways, was never during the whole winter put out of action by softness from heavy rains.

The Lincolnshire flatness of the country surrounding the aerodrome, for all the coastline is cliffless from Skegness to Grimsby, held distinct advantages for flying, not the least being that sea-level, indicated by zero feet on the altimeter, was synonymous here with ground-level. This meant that a pilot coming in from sea at night or in bad weather knew that he was clearing land by the height actually indicated on his altimeter, without having to worry lest he was over an unexpected mountain, as might happen at some inland stations. While the aerodrome was not as large as one would have liked, the approaches were excellent and unobstructed by virtue of the flat surroundings. This featureless coastline of land merging into grey North Sea from Wash to Humber might fail to please in peace-time, but it now appeared as desirable a situation for an aerodrome as could possibly be imagined.

The Mess at North Coates was an old-fashioned single-storeyed building, but our squadron had the use of a modern house, formerly used by the Station Commander, in which most of our officers slept, although we still messed together in the station Mess. A room had been found for me in the house, where I deposited my very few belongings, for on leaving Training Unit I had decided to travel as light as possible and, not without regret, sent home all the personal effects I had gathered around me in my record two years of settlement. I had been in two minds whether to dispense with my car or not, but since petrol could be obtained for leave I decided to have it with me and arranged for a friend to drive it up from Gosport. It did in fact prove useful, for we were in a remote spot.

On meeting the CO I took the opportunity to thank him for asking for me to be posted to his squadron, and he explained that there had luckily been a vacancy when Fanny had put forward my name, and I was now to command one of the flights. Although he was a Wing Commander, as are the CO's of most twin-engined squadrons, he appeared quite young, an impression which was deepened by the enthusiasm with which he recounted to me the squadron's past history and his hopes for its future. He was reputed to be an excellent pilot, but at this time was just recovering from a night flying accident which had occurred while landing on his return from a raid. In all probability this crash was merely caused by bad luck, but a healing scar on his face bore witness to it. All the squadron's officers were referred to by their Christian names, a habit striking a friendly touch and often to be found in squadrons, where only the CO himself is always "Sir" and the Flight Commanders "Sir" just occasionally. Inessentials have a habit of disappearing in the face of real work, and in the squadron there was less formal discipline yet more efficiency than I had found elsewhere.

Wing Commander Braithwaite showed me with some relish his leave scheme, a monster chart which showed the squadron's crews divided up into sections and indicated in calendar form when each section was to go on leave. There were periods of forty-eight hours and three days' leave alternating every fortnight, and a long leave of twelve days every quarter. This scheme was the CO's pet child, and I was to find that he would make any sacrifice to maintain the schedule and give a crew the leave they anticipated. To the uninformed it often may have seemed that the Wing Commander's object was to send crews on leave, not on operations! But there was sound purpose behind this fanaticism for leave, and it was no mere personal idio-syncrasy. He knew that an operational crew needs regular and frequent rest to relieve the strain of flying and fighting, and was determined that leave should go on in all but the most extenuating circumstances, when crews could definitely not be spared.

After digesting the leave scheme and making appropriate comment, I was taken down to my flight, which occupied a hangar looking on to the aerodrome, and left to my own devices, to meet my flight sergeant and examine my aircraft. I sat in the first Flight Office I could call my own, and felt immediately at home.

Although I had been a Flight Lieutenant since March I had never before commanded a flight, as somehow there had always been a senior instructor above me in Training Unit, where I had only occasionally run a flight during the temporary absences of its real owner. The squadron consisted of three flights, all run by Flight Lieutenants: Fanny (my saviour) in "A" Flight, Flight Lieutenant Dick Beauman in "B", and myself now installed in "C". Command of a flight meant that I had, coupled with flying, a full-time job to occupy the whole of working hours, for the first time in my service career. Seven Beauforts were in my charge; I had a hangar in which to put them for repair or overhaul, about eighty airmen to work on them, and a flight sergeant to supervise their work. No less important were half a dozen pilots, some officers, some sergeants, all of whom had been recent pupils in Training Unit, and their crews of navigators, wireless operators and air-gunners. I could not be otherwise but happy among people I knew, with a modern aircraft to fly and real work to do. At last, I thought—this is the service.

Very little flying is possible in a squadron except on actual opera-tions, for every hour an aircraft spends in the air necessitates its presence on the ground for many more hours of maintenance. The effort required to keep even a small proportion of our Beauforts always ready to take the air was an exhausting one, needing many hours of work on unserviceable aircraft through day and night.

The complexity of the modern aircraft and its considerable equip-ment can hardly be appreciated by the layman, who may regard the preparation of an aircraft for an operation as no more exacting than that of his car before a long run. Only if he could take the place of a Flight Commander, the garage owner of seven Beauforts, would he realize the inadequacy of his comparison. An aircraft today is a highly complicated piece of machinery, far removed from the simplicity of former biplanes, which even in their turn were never really compar-able with a car.

Every day and all day I was trying to speed up work on my aircraft. Airmen swarmed over dismantled Beauforts in the hangar, and the flight sergeant would always promise completion of the work, yet always fail in his estimate of the time it would take. Work which was beyond the capabilities of a flight was carried out by a central maintenance section, run by the squadron Engineer Officer, who would take an aircraft from a Flight Commander's hands and return it to him on completion of the work.

Maintenance of aircraft proceeds endlessly. There is so much to go wrong and so much which does go wrong, yet everything for an operational sortie must be right, absolutely right. All instruments must be operational, all cockpit lights serviceable, wireless working, engines functioning correctly, hydraulic mechanism working, and gun turrets in order. The list continues endlessly; this is but a selection of the points checked and tested daily by maintenance crews before an aircraft may leave the ground.

A Beaufort is a complicated aircraft, no more or less than any other twin-engined aircraft in service, for it is in the vast increase in complication that the price of an advance in speed and fighting power has been paid. At the end of my time in the squadron I was to be tired and weary, not of operations and their attendant risks, nor of flying itself and the strain of concentration, but of the struggle to produce serviceable aircraft and supervise maintenance work which proceeded continuously yet was never completed.

I wish outsiders could pass through the hangars of any operational station to see not the flying on the aerodrome outside, but the mechanical activity within. Aircraft are dismantled, engines are being changed, a turret's guns are being fitted, a wireless is being removed, an airman is painting a letter on the side of a fuselage; a wing is being camouflaged in greens and browns. There is the hum of machinery, the hiss of paint sprays squirting their coloured mist at metal; drills revolve and hydraulic pumps chug. This is a factory with a purpose, where work has a meaning.

"When will *E* be ready?" "I can promise it for midday tomorrow, Pat." "Good, if you ring me up when she's ready I'll test her, we'd like to use her on Ops tomorrow night."

Here are Engineer Officer and Flight Commander; one wears wings, the other is without them; one publicized by press and wireless as the knight of modern times, with the aircraft his steed, the other remains unnoticed in an unromantic background, and being of the earth not of the air, he is forgotten by an uninformed and unappreciative crowd whose attention is directed skywards and whose eyes look indiscriminately for wings.

This maintenance work is the very essence of the Air Force. Without its great efforts aircraft would be wingless and tied to the earth. It is to these men, to the engineers and mechanics, the airmen who are fitters, riggers, electricians, welders, wireless mechanics, armourers; it is to all airmen of the skilled trades who work on aircraft that much, very much, is owed. Their work is unspectacular and its great importance unpublicized. Night shifts and day shifts airmen work endlessly on aircraft. Aircraft returning from operations riddled with bullet holes and those hit by exploding shells, aircraft crashed on their return and aircraft which never start but crash on take-off. Airmen are continually working on aircraft, carrying out routine overhauls or repairing damage, and often hours of painstaking work are spent on aircraft which fly out, sadly never to return. Always airmen are working to produce the aircraft for pilots to fly.

The conversation between Flight Commander and Engineer Officer touched on two features of squadron life, telephones and test flights. The pairing may appear unconnected, but these two often walk hand in hand. Some pilot is always wanting to make a test flight, and the telephone is invariably the means of its arrangement. Every office owns a telephone and every station has its own exchange, a ready means of communication at once convenient for facetious conversations with one's friends and necessary for business purposes. All RAF stations have also a broadcasting system which is only used for general or urgent announcements, but at any time a loud-speaker may blare into your ear some vital piece of news, usually telling you that you are wanted urgently somewhere else.

If telephones rang continuously, as they invariably did, their ringing was not infrequently the prelude to a conversation about test flights. "Is *A* ready for test yet, we want it for to-night?" "What aircraft are serviceable in your flight?" And very often, "No, *B for Butter* won't be ready for another day", a statement which might be repeated daily for a whole week. To take an aircraft up on a test was almost the only means of putting in some flying except when actually taking part in an operation; consequently pilots were always finding a reason for testing their aircraft, not once, but often two and three times during the day. As a rule, all the serviceable aircraft were given an airing at least once daily, and a pilot always gave the aircraft which he was to fly on an operation a thorough test beforehand. On such a flight the aircraft is taken out to sea, where all the guns are fired to ensure they are in working order, engines are very carefully checked both by their instruments and their behaviour, wireless is tested by an exchange of signals with the ground station, and the working of the blind flying instruments is examined for any fault.

Every pilot, not without reason, took great trouble over these test flights, and hardly ever did an aircraft land from one without requiring some small adjustment. Occasionally a major fault would be found, to result in the aircraft being pushed into the hangar, making one less available for whatever operations the day might bring. A Beaufort had an unfortunate habit of becoming unserviceable directly a pilot turned his back on it. One would be left at its dispersal point after a test flight in a perfectly serviceable state, yet on being flown a few hours later it would be found unaccountably to have developed a fault during the short time it had been idle on the ground.

In truth, there were so many minor things which could so easily go wrong, the whole machine was so complicated, that very rarely everything worked without exception. Pilots learnt to concentrate on necessities, and if some inessential gauge failed, the fact was noted for attention at the next periodical inspection, for there was much equipment which, although useful, could be dispensed with without endangering the safety of the aircraft. It was only by this method that we could hope to have available the number of aircraft we desired.

Working hours now had a meaning: from half-past eight in the morning until five o'clock in the evening, and often much later, I was to be found in my Flight Office, in the maintenance hangar, bargaining for a time of completion of one of my aircraft being overhauled there, or in the Operations Room. There was also much visiting of other squadron offices, those of the CO, the Adjutant and the other two Flight Commanders, the squadron armament and signals officers.

Not only were such visits an opportunity for pleasant gossip, which turned inevitably round flying, maintenance and operations, but equally an occasion for business, and decisions would be made sitting on the desk in a Flight Office, cup of tea in hand, to the accompaniment of a roar of engines outside and the intermittent ringing of the telephone bell within. There was work to do, and no more congenial or effective way of doing it.

Wherever a pilot might be, there was always the chance of the telephone ringing to herald the announcement of an impending operation. "The weather's all right, the Wing Commander has fixed it with Group, it's Dick, you and I in *J, L* and *G, with Y* as a reserve— no, plenty of time, 11 o'clock take-off, see you in the Ops Room." A typewritten order was distributed throughout the squadron each morning, detailing the pilots for any operation which might occur, together with the aircraft to which they were allotted and the armament to be used, bombs or torpedoes. Operations were taken by all the pilots in rotation, except in the event of an important target appearing, when the most experienced pilots would be sent.

During the first few months of the squadron's operational life its sorties were originated by the Group Headquarters under which North Coates operated. This group ordered the operations in a broad manner, requiring a certain number of Beauforts to attack a specified target with a certain bomb load. The method of attack and often the detailed timing of it were left entirely to the Squadron Commander's own arrangements. This system was excellent for previously planned operations, such as bombing of land targets or mining, but these were operations to which the squadron had no wish to be restricted. It was essentially an anti-shipping squadron, yet in those first months few ships had been found for it to attack, a situation which was making its pilots impatient. Although the squadron had undertaken some interesting bombing missions, and many less liked mine-laying operations, its pilots, who were all torpedo-trained, were not unnaturally clamouring for a chance to attack ships.

At this time there were very few squadrons operating at all by daylight, with the exception of fighters, and even they were employed only defensively over our territory. In general the RAF was on the defensive in the daytime, confining its offensive operations to night bombing sorties, and shipping went unattacked.

It was Dick who changed this state of affairs by flying up the Dutch and German coasts to see what he could find, an occupation he found more enlivening than a routine sortie. He did this on several moonlight nights on which he found it possible to pick out ships silhouetted in a moonbeam. After he had found and attacked several ships in this manner it was realized that there was "something in it". The result was that our aircraft were now sent out on moonlight nights with complete freedom to fly anywhere over a large area of coastline searching for ships. Torpedoes were used as well as bombs, and ships continued to be found and sunk.

Not satisfied with inventing this freelance operation, which became known as a "Moonlight Rover" (really a very good description of Dick himself), Dick urged that it would be quite feasible to rove on the enemy coasts by daylight, providing certain weather conditions prevailed. The Authorities were immediately agreeable; if darkness was a cover under which it was safe to operate, so equally was bad weather. In this way the "Daylight Rover" entered the squadron's repertoire of operations and soon became extremely popular.

Obviously the success of this daylight operation depended on the presence of bad weather, and Group left the decision on the conditions to the Wing Commander's discretion, with the result that there were always inquiring pilots in and out of the Meteorological Office throughout the day searching for some part of the coast which might have cloud over it. Anybody finding suitable weather would urge the Wing Commander to ask Group if we could operate. In this way operations were actually initiated from the squadron, when the CO rang up Group suggesting that conditions were suitable and asking to send some aircraft, a request that always drew assent unless there was a more important operation pending for which we must be reserved.

The Wing Commander had a good eye for Rover weather, of which the requirements were that there should be extensive cloud with its base not higher than a thousand feet. Ideal conditions were given by a cloud-base of about three hundred feet accompanied by limited visibility of three or four miles, and even by slight rain. Patchy high cloud was useless, for it could never be reached in time to escape from attacking fighters.

The necessity for the presence of a cloud on daylight operations was entirely due to the menace of enemy fighters, which were infinitely superior to our Beauforts in speed and manoeuvrability, and with whom it was folly to attempt engagement. Enemy shipping rarely sailed further than ten miles from the coast, more often much nearer, and so it was always in a position to receive fighter protection. It was therefore essential to have cloud close enough at hand to be quickly reached by a roving aircraft should fighters be sighted. The menace of enemy fighters was a real one, and by no means overestimated, for a Beaufort in open sky would be powerless in face of the numbers which might be sent to intercept it. Cloud was our ally, and for Rovers we had strict orders to return if insufficient cloud cover was found, a provision it was wise to comply with.

While Rovers were nearly always initiated by the squadron and subsequently vetoed or approved by Group, other operations originated in Group and orders came for them through the station Operations Room, where first word of an impending operation would be heard. Nearly always we received notice to operate early in the day, enabling preparations to be carried out in advance. Aircraft would be loaded and tested by their crews, and details of the target, weather forecasts and route would be studied carefully beforehand. These were usually night operations consisting of dropping bombs on some coastal harbour or the laying of mines in enemy waters.

Group might also order a number of aircraft to carry out night

Rovers in the moon period only, and it would be left to the Wing Commander to decide where his aircraft should go, a decision which he in his turn often left to the pilot. Each pilot had his own ideas where ships were to be found, and the competition which these freelance day and night operations aroused often resulted in two hundred miles of coastline being covered in search of a target. Rarely did a pilot return until shortage of petrol demanded it.

In every case the decision as to whether conditions were suitable for the operation which Group ordered rested with the Wing Commander, who was excellent in his judgement of the weather and rarely made an error, a fact we all learned to appreciate. An operation might be cancelled night after night on account of unsuitable weather, but whenever it was possible to operate, night sorties usually went according to plan and Rovers were productive. It was always wise to wait for the weather. Of course Group might override a decision to cancel, but this was never known to happen, for the importance of a particular operation was always taken into consideration when making a decision on the weather.

For the first time in my flying life the importance of meterology was now brought home to me. In the past I had often telephoned the Met Station to inquire if the weather was suitable for a cross-country flight, and on rare occasions when a decision was in doubt had gone around to the section to discuss it with the Met Officer and see the situation on the weather chart. Now I visited the Met Office frequently, often looking for cloud, and spent much time conferring with the Met Officer before an operation, a precaution which was always repaid.

Equally often visited was the operations block, a bomb-proof building which housed the Operations Room (always abbreviated to Ops—the word was used so often), the Intelligence Section and the ground wireless station. In Ops Room are a battery of telephones, a number of busy people and a map. Of the telephones, some are connected to the station exchange and are the means of contacting CO's, Flight Commanders and other office-owners; others are tie lines, direct private lines connecting Ops Room with that at Group Headquarters. It is by these lines that orders to operate are communicated to the Controller and subsequently confirmed in writing by signal received on a teleprinter.

The busy people are the Controller himself, who is the link between Group and the squadrons on the aerodrome, telephone operators, clerks, tea-brewers, navigators and plotters, the last two dealing with the map. This map stands vertically at a convenient distance from the Controller's desk, and, being some twelve feet square, necessitates the use of steps to reach its northern boundary. On it is drawn in broad outline the part of the world in which the station's aircraft operate, with aerodromes and a few towns indicated to relieve its bare appearance. When an operation is arranged, tapes are pinned to the map, joining the aerodrome to the target by the route selected, thus representing the path of our aircraft. Enemy and our own naval forces are indicated by symbols, together with any strange phenomena such as a balloon broken loose from its moorings or a friendly whale!

From a glance at the map it is possible to gain an immediate impression of what is happening in the air, and this information is supplemented by times of take-off and return of aircraft, detailed by their letter written on a specially arranged blackboard, also opposite the Controller's desk and near the map. Signals received by the wireless station from aircraft in the air are passed immediately to the Controller, and the situation on the map is adjusted according to the news.

Glance at the map, read the blackboard, look through the incoming signals, and without asking a question the complete story of the operation in progress is told. It may be the exciting story of a ship attacked and left sinking: "One merchant vessel, 5000 tons, position ten miles west of Terschelling lighthouse, estimate one hit", reads an incoming signal from *W* out on a Rover. Or sadly the blackboard is seen to list the times of return some hours ago of all aircraft but one; Beaufort *L* has not yet returned, and a glance at its time of take-off reveals that its petrol must be exhausted. It is overdue, shortly to become missing.

There is an ever-changing situation in Ops Room. Tapes on the map join the aerodrome with new targets to be visited; ships are found in unexpected waters; times of take-off against letters of aircraft on the blackboard show that an operation is in progress; a signal brings news. Always there is something new, a continual variation on the endless theme of aircraft attacking the enemy, by day and by night, succeeding or failing. The Operations Room on a Coastal Command Station records the progress of aircraft going out and coming back, but it cannot be said to control them. It is not the nerve-centre of operations like a Fighter Operations Room, where the Controller chats continually by radio-telephony with pilots in the air, and puppets representing the enemy and our own aircraft are moved rapidly over a horizontal map, from which the Controller sizes up the situation and directs the aircraft accordingly. Here contact with aircraft in the air is more remote, distances are greater and duration of flights longer, and communication with aircraft made by the slow wireless telegraphy made slower still by the necessity of coding messages. Operations Room holds up a mirror to a situation over which its control is small. Its aircraft are far away, equipped to fend for themselves, and from those aircraft and their movements, the decisions and problems of their pilots, a Coastal Operations Room is remote. All depends on the pilot.

If the pilot is admitted to be his own controller (and certainly nobody controlled Dick on a Rover), then the Intelligence Section is the star by which he is guided. "Intelligence" is information about the enemy's doings; where he is placing his flak, what ships he has in certain harbours, where his aerodromes are and what aircraft are on them. There is nothing about the enemy in which the Intelligence Section are not interested. However insignificant a piece of information may appear, it may be the key to a discovery of importance.

So if this section is full of information vital to a pilot, it is equally concerned with obtaining detailed information from him on his return from a sortie. What flak he has seen and where, any unusual lights on the coastline, a description of any aircraft seen or ships encountered. A crew report to the Intelligence Office immediately on returning from an operation, sit down in comfortable chairs and drink tea, while the pilot and his observer recount every detail of their flight from memory aided by reference to the observer's log. All the time pieces of information are added by wireless operator and air-gunner, and the Intelligence Officer interrogates to make clear certain points in the narrative. At the end of the interview a detailed picture is pieced together and a report in writing sent to Group by teleprinter. In Intelligence Section are files containing the essence of such reports collected from every operating unit throughout the Air Force, and enlarged by secret service information.

Here is news about the enemy, up-to-date news, constantly being added to, corrected or withdrawn according to changing circumstances. Here is information a pilot must have, if he, as captain of his aircraft, is to be able to make his decisions to the best advantage. To neglect this news is to endanger the success of any sortie. Pilots would spend half an hour each day reading the files and chatting with the Intelligence Officers about new occurrences on what we were beginning to call "our" coastline, a designation comprising the German, Dutch and French coasts from Kiel to Boulogne. Only by keeping up to date with this intelligence would a pilot find shipping on his Rovers and come back to tell the tale.

For attacking specific targets, Intelligence was no less necessary than for Rovers; and when such an operation was ordered, information of the latest flak concentrations, together with detailed maps and aerial photographs of the target, would be displayed in Intelligence Section and absorbed by the crews at their leisure.

Aerial photographs can often tell the Intelligence Officer much more than a pilot's description, and our pilots always tried to bring back photographs of what they had seen on Rovers. Not only were these valuable from an information point of view, but to return with good photographs brought a feeling of pride, almost of bringing back a trophy, and to produce one which showed a sinking ship was every pilot's ambition.

Dick's observer, Paddy, would often return with twenty exposures, for Dick was particular in his choice of target and would examine many ships in his rove along the coast before finding a target to his taste. Paddy would photograph everything within range, and often returned with a selection of views of beaches and sandbanks.

Here was a fighting organization. Twenty Beauforts to take bombs, torpedoes or mines to the enemy's shore, a pilot to fly the aircraft, an observer to navigate, and a wireless operator to help him, and an air-gunner alert in the turret to repel attack. An Intelligence Section to guide the pilot and observer, strangers in a foreign land of war, and an Operations Room staff to watch over their progress from departure to return. A Squadron Commander to decide, lead and guide the twenty crews under his hand, and a workshop with three hundred airmen to prepare the aircraft and, whether pilots fly or are idle, to continue their endless work. An Adjutant to maintain contact with both air and earth, the air-crews and the airmen, to remain in continuity the personification of the squadron. Finally, an album of photographs, taken by daylight from the squadron's Beauforts, showing ships sinking, ships sailing, harbours, aerodromes and towns on the enemy coast. Here was my station and my squadron: North Coates, October 1940.

CHAPTER VIII

NOT DEAD, BUT ALIVE

MY first operational flight was a daylight Rover on which I followed Dick. The squadron had previously been sending aircraft out singly on Rovers, but ships had often been missed by the one torpedo which a single Beaufort carried, and experiments were now being made in the use of formations of two or three aircraft to attack a target simultaneously. It was certainly an excellent idea that a newcomer to operations should follow an experienced pilot, and I looked forward to following Dick, with whom I discussed all details of the proposed tactics before taking off.

The weather at our aerodrome was bad by ordinary flying standards. Cloud was low and visibility only a few miles, conditions which the Met Officer had forecast as extending across the North Sea to the enemy coast. My feelings as I taxied out behind Dick's Beaufort before take-off were predominantly of excitement, much greater, I would think, than that of a player before an important game or a boxer before a fight. This was a skin game of high play, and if the stake was greater, so was the possibility of reward: the striking of a real blow at the enemy. If this excitement was the keynote of anticipation, nervousness was no less present—not that which produces a shaking hand or chattering teeth, but a nervous apprehension of the unknown, a feeling of tension. Excited, I felt elated with my good fortune to be operating at last; nervous, I wondered exactly what this operation held in store for me. Years of training, years of unconscious anticipation must have been behind these contrary sensations, which were always to be reproduced in a lesser degree before take-off on an operation, and always to become diminished when once I was actually in the air and flying.

Dick crossed the North Sea flying at a few hundred feet, as was usual to avoid detection by radar, making for Den Helder, which apparently he always visited, not with the intention of attacking ships, for the water was too shallow to launch a torpedo, but because he liked to see if there were any targets there likely to come out into the open sea. For Paddy also this little port was a favourite photographic subject. The weather appeared likely to remain ideal, the sky murky with thick low cloud, and the water grey as only North Sea can be. I flew on the right of my leader, a few spans away, a distance near enough to see Dick grinning encouragingly at me through the perspex surrounding his cockpit and to discern Paddy busy among the paraphernalia of navigation, the maps and charts, rulers, pencils and dividers.

There is something comforting about being one of several aircraft flying in company, a feeling of security as of two children walking hand-in-hand in a dark wood. Whether following or leading, I was always to prefer being one of a formation to flying singly and alone; nor was predilection for company a mere abstract fancy, for a number of aircraft close together lend each other mutual protection from fighter attacks by concentrated fire from their turrets. For a formation to stand united is strength and to be divided often is to be irretrievably lost.

One hour passed thus, the two Beauforts flying together over the sea and under weather which still remained ideal cover. Clouds were low enough to be reached quickly should fighter opposition be encountered, and visibility low enough to make the operation of fighters extremely difficult, yet sufficient to offer good chances of sighting any ships there might be on the shipping route. Consulting with my navigator, I found that it would not be long before land was sighted, and tension increased with the passing of minutes as mile after mile was covered to bring us nearer the enemy. When the coastline at last appeared ahead, the sight of it came as an anticlimax; it looked so friendly and peaceful, a seaside for children to play on. I do not know quite what I had expected; if to be met by a barrage of fire or chased by several squadrons of Messerschmitts had been in my mind, it was a picture of imagination far removed from actuality. Dick crossed the coastline of one of the Dutch islands at a height of 100 feet with as much nonchalance as if he had been flying over Brighton beach, and I followed, not exactly feeling that this was the most natural thing in the world, but at least unquestioningly.

The weather was ideal. I doubted if fighters could ever have found us in the visibility of only three or four miles, conditions which inspired a feeling of safety coupled now with one of curiosity, as of an explorer in a strange land. I could see a gesticulating conversation in progress between Dick and Paddy, indicating that they were differing in their opinions as to where we were. Meanwhile we ran along a line of beach behind which sandhills stretched inland, where there were no signs of life of any sort, much less of military activity. My navigator thought that Dick was east of his intended landfall, a surmise soon proved correct, for when Dick and Paddy had settled their differences, we turned round over the land and flew back westwards.

Den Helder was on the easterly point of the Dutch mainland, and it appeared that Dick had definite ideas on how to reach it, since we now crossed over sandhills and a wilderness of low-lying grassland to a stretch of sheltered water actually between the islands and the mainland, down which we proceeded to fly. Dutch fishing vessels and small villages came out of the mist and were passed by in a flash, looking like toys on a nursery floor to a grown-up person, and the living people and animals trespassers there in a miniature world.

I was beginning to think that this was not the best place to search for shipping, when we turned sharply towards what was appearing ahead as a harbour with quays and wharves alongside which were ships. A small town arose behind the port itself, while other ships were at anchor in a sheltered basin outside the harbour.

We crossed the town at a few hundred feet under a cloud-base little higher, and turned to circle. A camera kept pointing from Dick's aircraft at every ship we passed, and he seemed oblivious of the fact that a stream of tracer bullets had started to play from a shore battery, shortly to be followed by further firing from all sides, not least from the ships themselves. This was no nursery floor, but reality; my disappointment at the initial lack of interest in our presence shown by the enemy now changed to respect for his preparedness.

I was beginning to think that our continual circling under fire was asking too much of Providence, when Paddy's photographic inclinations must have been satisfied, for Dick left the area, flying eastwards and coastwise, followed by the bursting of shells around us until we vanished from sight. Cooling in the comparative peace after this rather hot reception, I tried to analyse exactly how Dick had managed to come upon the place apparently without warning being given, and realized that we had approached it from the back, the inland side, a direction from which the enemy might expect their own aircraft to appear, but certainly not ours.

The few seconds of copious but not very accurate fire had been lively. The intermittent lines made by tracer shells had rarely been dangerously near to us, and Dick had certainly done a lot of twisting and turning which I had only just been able to follow. Now all was peaceful as the seemingly friendly beaches of successive islands were passed on the starboard side in our flight eastwards: Texel, Terschelling and Borkum, where Dick knew intimately every little village and headland on a featureless coast, indeed he almost knew the waters of the sea itself which surrounded them.

Several little harbours were visited, and occasional shore batteries in positions on the coast fired at us, but it did not seem to matter. Sometimes the tracer shells made coloured streams of red or green to vary the more common white, sometimes their bursts came near, appearing to pass over one wing, to make Dick turn away and then turn back again; he did not ignore flak, he played with it. At intervals the camera pointed from the side of his aircraft, and always there was animated conversation between pilot and navigator. They appeared to forsake the usual means of communication by microphone and intercom, preferring to make it a more personal affair of shouting at each other above the roar of the engines.

My own efforts were restricted to following blindly, by no means a sinecure, for Dick's decisions to make a turn were unpremeditated and preceded by no signal. My navigator followed our progress on his map, keeping me informed of landmarks which we passed, while neither wireless operator nor air-gunner were mere spectators, opening fire on the small ships which came within range much as a sportsman out pheasant-shooting may pick off a passing rabbit.

If this desultory coast-creeping was a harmless photographic pursuit, it was certainly not finding us any targets for the torpedoes which we carried. The waters over which we flew were shallow and I knew that shipping followed a route at least five miles out from the shore. Dick apparently was in no hurry to get down to business, spending a large part of the time roving not over water but over land. As we flew eastwards the cloud height still remained ideal, but visibility began to fall, making flying neither easy nor pleasant, and the chances of finding a ship diminished.

However, at last Dick pointed his aircraft seawards, to make me wonder at first if he were making for home on account of bad weather, a question soon answered by a change of course followed at intervals by more changes. Land had disappeared behind us, and according to my navigator we were now flying in a general easterly direction between five and ten miles out from the shore. Sky merged into sea to make formating on the leading Beaufort a difficult task, not lessened by the presence on the windscreen of a fine rain beginning to fall. I was just falling back a little to simplify the task of following, when I saw the wings of the leading aircraft rock slowly from side to side. My heart missed two beats, then started thumping, for this was the pre-arranged signal to attack; but to attack what? I searched the sea around frantically but uselessly for the expected target.

It later appeared that Dick had circled some ships which I had failed to see in the mist and rain, being fully occupied in trying not to lose my leader. Now I could do nothing but follow at a respectable distance, trusting that I would be led to the invisible target. Accordingly, I had fallen back further and was following more blindly than ever with some apprehension, when ahead loomed up first two and then more ships, riding peacefully at anchor. Dick made straight for the largest target of about 2000 tons, and following about two hundred yards behind I saw his torpedo drop into the water, the splash leaving a pool of white foam from which a track of bubbles started towards the target. So sudden was the attack that I had now no feelings at all of fear or excitement, but went through the aiming procedure like an automaton, and passing over the spot where Dick's torpedo had entered, I pressed my release, then began, as he had done, a turn away to the right.

The few seconds which had separated our drops were nearly to become the time between life and death. Our arrival was unheralded; until the first torpedo was seen to enter the water we had probably been taken for friendly aircraft, but by the time I came in to attack our hostility was recognized and it seemed as if every gun on every ship was pointing at me. As I turned away, white flashes from the guns were followed by continuous silver lines passing in front of me to burst in dark puffs of smoke far beyond, and miniature waterspouts showed evidence of shells bursting in the water all around. I had dropped the torpedo before this pyrotechnical storm had really started, but as I turned steeply away from the target there was a simultaneous rending of metal and three explosions in my aircraft which shuddered under the concussion. We were poised less than a hundred feet above the surface of the water, my cockpit was filled with smoke, my navigator and air-gunner wounded, and the aircraft out of control.

The Beaufort flew us away into the mist, with ships and shells disappearing from sight behind it. I have no remembrance of how we came through, how the turn was completed or how the smoke cleared from the cockpit to reveal a scene of blood and wreckage. To me that aircraft and its crew are still at the bottom of the sea off Borkum, and mutual congratulations are being passed from German ship to German ship: "Congratulations, your bird I think, Captain; good shooting."

From the German wireless that evening came the news: "One Beaufort aircraft was shot down by our naval forces and another driven off." By the time I heard this statement I was past caring, but as for poor Dick, they maligned their man. He was never driven off, I only wish he could have been.

German tracer is light flak, produced by guns firing 37-mm shells set to explode either at a predetermined range or on impact. In my port wing half-way between engine and wing tip was a large hole made by such a shell, a hole which worried me not at all, for the port engine was running correctly and in any case there were more immediate troubles to make this hole seem just a hole and nothing more.

My air-gunner was hit and badly wounded; a shell had come through the side of the fuselage and exploded in the turret, seriously injuring his right leg and thigh. I had heard his voice cry "I'm hit"; words which were meaningless, for at the time I was busy trying to control the aircraft, which was reeling drunkenly, when an explosion had occurred almost in my face. A third shell had pierced the perspex in the nose, bursting near the face of my navigator, who was standing just beside me. Blood flowed, smoke obscured my vision, and destruction abounded everywhere.

Yet none of these things was a reality to me. Broken glass and pools of blood seemed insignificant in the face of my discovery that something was seriously wrong with the aircraft. A Beaufort was flying me and I had not control of it. A fraction of a second elapsed before I realized that the elevator control cables had been cut by the shell which burst in the turret, and a little longer before I realized that it did not in the least matter. Between these two realizations a voice monotonous and dreary, a very soulless fiend of a voice, repeated in my ear: "Shot down on your first operation!" "Shot down on your first time out." And there was devilish mocking laughter, an accompaniment to the chant now whispered, now shouted in my ear to the roar of the engines. Grey sea merged into grey sky, while rain fell. "Shot down on your first operation", chanted the voice, followed by the crackle of hollow laughter. There was nothing in my heart, no answer in the chaos of shattered instruments, white maps spattered with red blood, white overalls soaked in oil. A fountain of blood from my navigator's wound mingled with the moans of pain from my gunner in the turret, sounds which seemed to come from another world. Between the realization that my elevator control wires were cut and the discovery that it would take more than that trivial misfortune to defeat us was a timeless period lasting not more than half a second by a clock in this world, but long enough to live a lifetime in the devilish world of disappointment.

"We're quite all right", I said in reply to the ghostly voice; then, to make my answer more convincing, shouted in a new steady voice I had just found, "We're quite all right". This was not a statement to which I expected an answer, certainly from no earthly source, but one came over the intercom from my wireless operator: "He's not quite all right, but he's not too bad." Oblivious of what had been happening in the front cockpit, he had been occupied in the rear in getting the air-gunner out of the turret, and was now making him as comfortable as possible in the passageway.

This practical attitude to our plight brought a new sense of responsibility to the front cockpit. I moved the control column backwards and forwards to its full extent without altering one whit the attitude of the aircraft, but a trial revealed that rudder and aileron control was still normal. In what direction we were flying I could not tell, for the gyro compass was rotating mockingly, indicating every direction in turn, and I could not trust the magnetic compass, which was probably shocked by the explosion. Slowly time was returning to normal, and responsibility took charge as I checked the unbroken instruments and examined the essentials of the cockpit to see if they could be made to work. Meanwhile my navigator was endeavouring to stanch the flow of blood which issued from a cut in his cheek. Moving the control column loosely backwards and forwards, I tried to show him that all was not as serene as it seemed, but the lack of control appeared not to surprise him at all.

My feeling of disappointment at being shot down was now replaced by one of elation at still being in the air. The precariousness of our position was forgotten in the face of the fact itself: we were still flying. This elation I passed to my navigator by grinning; here was a joke, something very, very funny, an incident to be laughed at; we had been shot down, yet were still up. It was enough to make one grin, and I grinned, pointing to the shattered glass and bent metal all round us. My navigator grinned back, a grin through blood; he was grinning now with red amusement at the control column being moved freely backwards and forwards without in the least influencing the aircraft's behaviour. I turned in my seat to look backwards down the passage extending to the turret and engaged in some dumb conversation with my wireless operator, who was kneeling over the injured gunner stretched out on the floor. The answer to my inquiring look was an uplifted thumb and an understandingly ghastly grin, for the gunner had no superficial blood-spurting cut but some serious jagged wounds. Wounded is not dead, to be flying is not to have been shot down, nor is the air an ocean-bed: we were alive and still flying.

An aircraft has trimming tabs, miniature control surfaces adjusted by a wheel in the cockpit by which the aircraft can be "trimmed" to fly straight and level without movement of rudder, aileron or elevator control. This adjustment, being intended to compensate for distribution of load, has only a very limited effect, but nevertheless it is effective over a small range and completely independent of the normal control system. This meant that my elevator trimming tab was worked by different wires from those which I knew to be cut. Immediately I found the elevator control producing no response, in desperation—but quite automatically—I tried the elevator trimmer, and found to my relief that it still worked. A small adjustment by hand on the wheel, up came the nose of the aircraft, and we climbed; a turn of the wheel in the other direction, and down went the nose for the aircraft to start a gentle dive. Control was limited, nevertheless it was effective.

This was a momentous discovery, which I immediately demonstrated to my navigator, who only nodded laconically as if this was the most natural way of flying imaginable. He was more interested in his shrapnel-pierced charts, over which he showered blood enough to make more red territory than ever appeared in any Imperial atlas. Eventually, after some calculation, he handed me a message which read: "Steer 265° Magnetic", which I countered with a cry of "No compass" and some further explanation to show that I wanted him to check my compass with that on the bombsight. Luckily they agreed, indicating that my compass was still sound, and I started to turn gingerly on to 265°, exercising great caution, since my limited control would be inadequate to counteract any violent manoeuvre. Slowly the nose came round, pointing continually at the junction of mist and sea which was the horizon, until it reached 265°, the way which led to home.

Two hundred miles of flying over the North Sea allowed time for much to be done, and soon we were flying comfortably and serenely, waiting to make a landfall. Pilot Officer Macfadden ("Mac"), my air-gunner, was in good heart but in great pain, nevertheless taking a lively interest in where we were going and what was happening, for from his recumbent position he could not see out. Jim Coulson, the wireless operator, had been busy at his set, letting our base know that we were returning and helping the observer by obtaining navigational information. The latter was giving me alterations of course as if lines on a chart were always ruled in blood. I, myself, was thinking very hard about the difficulties of landing.

Luck had kept us in the air at a critical time; afterwards presence of mind had taken charge from luck to start us on our journey, and now an all-round effort was bringing us home. But I was worried about the problem of making a landing with such limited control, and as we neared the coast I became no less worried about the weather. We had been flying under a cloud-base of about 300 feet, with visibility gradually decreasing, and I feared that our aerodrome might be closed down completely by bad weather. After making a good landfall south of the aerodrome, which resulted in an exchange of thumbs up with the crew, we ran northwards up the coast with the visibility deteriorating, until it was only just possible to see far enough ahead to fly in safety. I blessed the flatness off the coastline, for had an obstacle appeared ahead I could not have turned on account of the poor control, nor could I have climbed to enter cloud and fly blind, for the instruments were a forlorn drunken collection, indicating everything but the truth.

In these conditions it was not surprising that we flew straight over the aerodrome before realizing we had reached it. One boundary came out of the mist just ahead, we shot across the aerodrome surface and the far boundary vanished behind us, leaving a tantalizing memory of hangars and Mess which had passed in a flash. I knew that a landing here was impossible; the state of the aircraft demanded a long straight approach, and to approach an aerodrome which I could not see in an aircraft I could only just control was not my intention.

We turned, an impatient turn which brought us more consciously nearer to disaster that at any other time during the whole flight. Not only was the crippled Beaufort a liability, but the weather was against us, and the trimmer very nearly failed to bring the aircraft out of a dive in which the ground came up towards us at a sickening rate; for a split second I saw the whole struggle availing nothing, then all was well. Disconsolately I flew back again down the coast, where I knew conditions improved, trying to decide where I should land and cursing the weather, which some hours before had been our ally and was now a bitter enemy. We were all tired; Mac was moaning again, cold and very weak from loss of blood. Jim came up to tell me he thought Mac was becoming exhausted. The observer too was disheartened; he had achieved his end in navigating us safely back to the aerodrome, and his efforts were now spent.

As for myself, the ghost of a landing which should by now have been settled walked again before me. I was weary enough to make every field we passed in the flight down the coast appear an attractive resting-place for a tired Beaufort, yet I knew that to attempt a landing in such restricted space was to court disaster; we must land on an aerodrome.

It was my intention to land at the Norfolk aerodrome where I had been night flying only a few nights ago, but on reaching the south side of the Wash the weather inland looked worse than ever, and I turned to fly along the coast westwards, not now looking at fields merely with a feeling of remote longing to be down, but with the firm intention of landing in one of them. However, I still had plenty of petrol and I kept postponing a decision, hoping for an improvement in the weather, a hope which was to be realized. As we flew westwards down the Wash visibility improved to open our prison door and let us out into safety once more. Fields became regarded again as no more than green fields, and aerodromes became the only place for an aircraft to land.

I knew an aerodrome near by in the Lincolnshire fens, to which we now made our way in visibility increasing to a luxurious ten miles compared with the few thousands of yards in which we had been flying. As the hangars came into sight, landing problems were forgotten amid the general excitement at the approaching end of our journey.

Making a wide circuit of the aerodrome, turning this time not impatiently but steadily, I ended with the aircraft pointing from a distance into wind and towards the aerodrome, and lowering the flaps, started a long low approach at a speed only slightly above stalling speed. The normal hydraulic method of undercarriage operation was out of action, so when it appeared certain that the aerodrome would be reached, I lowered the wheels by an emergency lever. After just clearing the boundary I throttled back the engines and switched them off completely together with the petrol, a precaution against fire if we should crash. To flatten out for landing was impossible, since the trimmer was ineffective at slow speeds, but owing to the low approach the Beaufort's attitude was not too abnormal. It struck the ground wheels first, bounding into the air and leaping across the aerodrome in great strides which I was powerless to control, finally coming to rest with a screaming of brakes just before the far boundary.

This curious arrival of a strange aircraft had not passed unnoticed, and an ambulance came up immediately to take the wounded away, while Jim and I helped them out. As the ambulance drove slowly across the aerodrome we watched without words a tractor towing our Beaufort away to a hangar, a dead aircraft. This had been a flight, and it was over; the earth upon which we stood was solid and the North Sea no deeper, no wider than a mill pond: we were safely down at last. I went to sick-quarters to see the wounded before they were taken to hospital, and found my observer was not too badly cut in face and arm, but Mac's leg was seriously injured by shrapnel and some bones were broken. Jim and I were unscathed, and looking at the wounded, we wondered silently what damage we had inflicted on the enemy in return.

An aircraft came from the squadron to fetch us, and we returned just before nightfall to North Coates, where Dick was waiting on the tarmac to greet me. No grin could have been broader as he told me that the ship had been a mine-laying vessel which both our torpedoes had missed by half a length. He had seen me flying in the rain of flak coming from the surrounding E boats, small heavily armed vessels, and guessed that I would be hit, but lost sight of my aircraft as it vanished in the mist. "I laughed the whole way back," said Dick, "and Paddy kept telling me to shut up and show some reverence for the dead!"

With cans of beer in our hands at an hour well past midnight, mutual recriminations became lazily incoherent. When finally we made our way unsteadily to the squadron's house, all else was forgotten in our efforts to explain why we had missed a stationary target. Alone in my room, I suddenly knew I did not care, that I had been lucky, my crew capable and brave, and that now I was tired, very tired, with bones aching and heavy head on my pillow; at last.

No other operational flight was to be quite like the first one. Rovers continued, but often uneventfully. There were not always ships to be found, and those actually encountered could often be taken completely by surprise and the attack made without a shot fired. These operations were very dependent on weather, which rarely gave the required conditions; sometimes two days in a week might promise suitable cloud cover, a promise not always realized. Pilots might go out only to return with their mission uncompleted owing to lack of cloud, or they might find cloud but no shipping, bringing back as trophies photographs of harbours and ships too small to be attacked with a torpedo.

Occasionally we carried bombs, enabling us to attack inland targets if no shipping was found. Aerodromes, gun emplacements and harbours were often the recipients of bombs originally intended for ships at sea. It was a wonderful freelance role, that of our Beauforts in these months. The reward of perhaps several sorties might be the discovery and sinking of no mean ship. The penalty of ignoring absence of cloud cover or of rashness was to be shot down by fighters or by flak.

The Rover was a clear-cut game with well-defined rules of conduct for the safety of aircraft and crew, a game which must have been tantalizing to the enemy, who could never know quite when aircraft might descend on his shipping or his shore. Eventually he was to build up an organization to counter this type of raid, bringing with it continually changing conditions to this operation. Always the enemy was increasing his defences, always it was necessary to modify our tactics accordingly; to ignore change was to court disaster. The wise pilot listened carefully to the reports of others, sifted the Intelligence information and drew his own conclusions; this was a skin game, and to leave a loophole of ignorance which might have been closed was to invite failure. Aircraft flying out under cover of bad weather, searching the enemy coastline in daylight for ships to attack and sink: this is the bare frame of an ever-variable picture, that of the Rover, the most demanding operation in individual effort, the most satisfying in achievement, the most thrilling in action.

The exacting requirements of weather conditions made Rovers rare treats, for often when cloud was low on the enemy coast the weather at our base was too bad for aircraft to take off. Conditions had to be just right, and they rarely were so. Other more organized sorties were the squadron's staple employment, and my next flight, which took place a week later, was a mission by night to a port in north-west Germany. My first daylight operation was over, and now my first night show was before me.

During the afternoon the whole crew came up with me to test the aircraft and get accustomed to working together, for my wounded navigator and air-gunner were now replaced by two newcomers, only Jim remaining with me as wireless operator. After the test, on which all went well, my new observer and I spent over an hour in Intelligence Section deciding how best we could attack our target, which was the docks at Bremerhaven. Intelligence revealed that the liners *Bremen* and *Europa* were alongside one of the wharves there, information which recalled to me their frequent presence in the peaceful Solent in Gosport days. We then went to consult with the Met Officer, who promised a clear sky over the target, but warned us of an intervening bank of clouds. Since the barrage at Bremerhaven was reputed to be intense, we decided to fly over the cloud-layer, since the height so gained could be maintained over the target, enabling us to make a steady bombing run undisturbed by fear of flak. The attack was timed for the early hours of the morning, when the moon would be at its highest, an arrangement necessitating a midnight take-off. Six of our aircraft were to attack the same target.

As we taxied out over the aerodrome, the moon was just rising out of the sea to light up the cloud-bank about which we had been warned. Take-off was made straight towards the rising moon, for the wind was easterly, and my last view of the ground, before leaving the lights of the flare path and turning my whole attention to the instruments, was the sea rippling in a silver ladder of moonlight, looking unpleasantly near. Now I could look out no longer, my eyes were concentrating on my instrument panel, and only when a safe height of 1000 feet was reached did I release my vigilance. Cockpit lights were then turned out completely, to leave me facing the rows of luminous painted figures and pointers which were the instruments. A circuit of the flare path allowed time to adjust the running of the engines and for the crew to settle down, then we turned towards the moon, flying eastwards and climbing higher over the bank of clouds which separated sea and stars. We were on our way.

We climbed gradually as the cloud mounted before us, until with an hour passed we were at 10,000 feet, and still climbing over a cloud-ceiling which still rose. The moon was rising in the night sky of stars to make clear the horizon and illuminate the mountainous cloudy surface below. Bright flashes of white light and streams of tracer of several colours revealed activity far away on our right. These were guns from the Dutch Islands, where I had been on my last flight, now stirred to life and firing blindly at I knew not whom, for we were far out of range. Searchlights too shone up through the cloud to make silver coins on the cotton-wool floor in the distance. We were remote from this fairy display of shimmering deadly rain and steadily searching beams. The engines droned healthily and ceaselessly, monotony set in as we sat cold and motionless each at our station, flying high in the air, eastward.

With the passing of a second hour the cloud had ceased to rise, and stretched level before us. The moon was now higher, and its light to our accustomed eyes shone brightly as the sun. The engines turned as before, and were unnoticed by ears grown used to their continuous sound.

Monotony gave way to anticipation as the edge of the cloud-layer was approached, revealing the enemy coastline far below and on our right. Now apathy became stirred by activity as we neared our target. Searchlights played far ahead, forming pyramids with their beams in colours of electric blue and white. Sharp stabs of flame from the ground revealed the presence of batteries of heavy guns firing unavailingly into the night sky. Speeding through the darkness at a height of three miles in the air, the ground beneath seemed impotent to harm us. We, who had rarely broken the night's silence, began to talk, animated conversation about the brightness of the moonlight, the smoothness of the night sky through which we glided, the myriads of stars above us and the answering twinkling lights on earth. Flashes of less indiscriminate fire and more purposeful wanderings of the beams of light increased as we neared the target.

Searchlights begin to menace the aircraft and black smoke puffs are appearing everywhere to fill the sky around with obstructions. I twist and turn to avoid the searchlight cones, flying always towards the target, guided by my navigator peering down at the black map beneath. The earth below is alive with firing guns, flashes come not singly but continuously, flashes from guns hurling up shells to explode with the crack of a whip heard above the roar of the engines, the acompanying flash leaving behind it a pall of black smoke drifting in the light of the moon. We are at 6000 feet now, descending to see our target more clearly, and the air beneath us is intersected by streams of burning rain and pools of light. When searchlight beams light the aircraft I become momentarily blinded in the fierce brilliance of the light, only to recover and make a turn to slip out of their clutches.

The peace of the journey is now lost in the heat of the fight. We are all talking again, no longer pleasantries of sky and weather, but vital injunctions: "Flak coming up very near on the port side" from the air-gunner, and I swing away to the right. "We've got to get round a bit to starboard" from my navigator, followed almost immediately by: "Keep straight on that course, target's coming up ahead." An aching desire first to turn one way then to turn another, a reluctance to fly straight, so necessary for correct use of the bomb sight, has to be overcome. Through the forest of lights and maze of exploding shells I fly straight on, eyes looking out neither at the burning earth nor the flaming sky, but concentrating on the instruments.

After a timeless purgatory of flying on a straight course I hear my navigator say, "Bombs gone", and I turn gratefully away, to dive and twist and climb our way out of the inferno of blazing searchlights and tongues of spitting gunfire pouring out their endless tracer rain.

As we drew away to safety my gunner brought me news of a fire starting near the target. Flames, he said, were leaping upwards and clouds of black smoke filling the sky. With this I turned to look back and saw for myself a great blaze below, whose glowing light placed searchlights and gun-flashes in insignificance.

There was a happiness of success in us all as we made our way homewards. Beams of light still searched the sky and guns fired ceaselessly while the fire blazed, a candle burning in the night, until it was lost in the distance.

We flew back over the cloud-layer, the road by which we had come, now flooded with light from the moon at its highest. Conversation had died with the passing of the activity over the target, leaving all silent against the droning background of engine noise. Nearing our coast, gaps appeared in the cloud-bank through which we gradually descended until land was sighted, a blurred line in the distance. Now we were faced with the problem of identifying our landfall on the coast, for no help had been received from the wireless, which had broken down. Finding that we were over a coast of high cliffs, which could not be Lincolnshire, my navigator decided we were north of the aerodrome, and so we turned southwards to follow the coastline. Soon his position was found to be incorrect, for an inland stretch of water was recognized as a Norfolk broad, a signpost to turn us northwards and bring us to our aerodrome, where a friendly flare path was aglow. I made a careful approach and landed safely, taxi-ing through the darkness to the aerodrome boundary, where transport came out to bring in a tired crew. Five hours in the air, bombs dropped, a fire started, and my first night operation was over.

I was now very much less worried about night flying, for the flight had doubled my total of night flying hours and increased my confidence immeasurably. This night operation had been a good experience, settling any fears which the unknown darkness and enemy defences may have held for me. Other crews had seen "my fire", for I felt a proprietary interest in it, and considered it to be caused by oil-tanks ablaze, on account of the dense black smoke which had swirled upwards. They too had thought the flak fairly accurate, but the flight on the whole a pleasant one, opinions which I shared, although I had no other experiences by which to make comparison.

Only one pilot, Joe Willis, had failed to reach the target, landing in the light of dawn after a tour of the North Sea which he attributed to faulty navigation. Dick, independent as ever, had been over the target when he had seen a nearby aerodrome with flare path lit and aircraft landing, where he had been unable to resist dropping his bombs. Jimmy Hyde must have been there about the same time as I, since he had actually seen my fire start burning.

Generally we felt satisfied with the night's work; all aircraft were home safely, the target had been attacked and all crews were now tired and ready for sleep. At least a whole morning in bed was indicated, preceded by bacon and eggs and coffee. As I walked across from the Mess to our house the sun was up, to make daylight seem strange to eyes accustomed to the night's darkness, and I tried to imagine flying unshielded by its cover into the barrage of which we had been in the middle, only to dismiss the idea as merely an unpleasant thought. I did not know then that at midday in only a few weeks' time Dick would be seen for the last time entering that very barrage, never to return.

CHAPTER IX

THE FURNACE

ON my second daylight Rover I was not subject to the vagaries of
following Dick, but was myself a leader, being followed by a sergeant
pilot, Norman Hearn-Phillips always known by his initials "H-P", who
was, incidentally, a very much more experienced operational pilot
than I was. Unfortunately we ran out of cloud cover when nearing the
Dutch coast, where we found blue sky above us and not a cloud in
sight, much less within reach. I confess to taking then a foolish risk,
which experience would now forbid me, for I continued for some
twenty minutes roving in these dangerous conditions within sight of
the enemy coastline. Poor H-P, who knew the danger so much better
than I, must have been seething with something less mild than dis-
approval, but he kept following all the same when he could have been
justified in leaving me and turning for home.

All this time not only were we flying within sight of observers on
the coast, but passing several suspicious-looking small vessels which
would, in all probability, report our presence to the shore if it were
not already known. But this was my first Rover as a leader, and
although I knew that to remain near the enemy coast under a clear
sky was playing with fire, I was determined to find some target to
attack, and kept persuading myself to stay a little longer when all the
time I knew I should turn back.

Just as I was reaching a decision to abandon this foolish pursuit and
return to our base, two ships appeared steaming in line ahead and not
very close inshore. Without wasting time, for the blue sky was worry-
ing me, I signalled to H-P to attack, only to find he had anticipated
the signal by breaking formation, and we both went in to the attack
low over the water, dropping our torpedoes simultaneously. The

lesson which I had learnt from my last attack on the dangers of lagging behind the leader had not been lost on H-P, who was well up with me as I dropped, and we turned away together. Afterwards we circled out of range for a few minutes, waiting to see some result of our attack, but the leading ship, which had been our target, had turned sharply towards us as we were attacking and we now saw the tracks of our torpedoes pass harmlessly ahead of the vessel. During the attack there had been little opposition, and it was not until we were turning away that first one and then several guns had started firing. Although the water around us had been dotted with the splashes of exploding shells, nothing had come very near us, and for the first time I realized the benefits to be obtained by taking a target by surprise. We had not dallied over the attack and so had enjoyed an approach free from flak, during which we had been able to take steady aim.

As we flew back empty-handed, I felt dissatisfied with the day's work, knowing that I should not really have remained out roving in those weather conditions, and also feeling a little guilty at having wasted two valuable torpedoes on a ship which was really too small a target. For a torpedo to have a reasonable chance of a hit, the target should not be less than two hundred feet long, a length achieved by ships of about 5000 tons, while I estimated our little target at 2000 tons, and even then made a generous allowance to cover my poor choice of target. Nevertheless, the flight and the attack did constitute added experience; if I was making mistakes, at the same time I was learning, and if the mistakes were not fatal ones, I had to thank good fortune for her generosity.

These first three flights had taken place within a span of ten days, during which the squadron had continued what I came to know as its usual activities. Dick Beauman and Ian Mackie, while out together on a Rover, had met a Heinkel 115 floatplane which they had chased in and out of broken cloud for twenty minutes. Dick, after exhausting his front guns' ammunition, had poured rounds into the Heinkel from his turret guns until he had to give up the chase when it finally escaped into thick cloud. Dick had rarely enjoyed a flight so much, and not surprisingly his aircraft was found to have one or two holes in it on its return! There had also been one or two moonlight Rovers on which some inconclusive attacks on shipping were made, and an uneventful mine-laying operation by night off the Dutch coast. All these activities were typical of the variety of the squadron's work. We might be ordered to drop bombs, mines or torpedoes anywhere within our aircrafts' range, and we might be moved to operate from any aerodrome in the country at a moment's notice. In this variety, this continual novelty and uncertainty of our operations, lay the real fascination of our work.

My next few operations were a batch of three which took place within a period of one week spent at an aerodrome in Cornwall. Six of our Beauforts were ordered to move to a station called St. Eval near Padstow, where they were to be used to drop bombs on Lorient, the enemy submarine base in Western France. At this time the battle of the Atlantic was at its height, and the situation was becoming critical, with many thousands of tons of our shipping being sunk each week. These attacks in which we took part in that week in November were the prelude to incessant attacks in later months in which both Coastal and Bomber Commands joined. This regular bombing of the submarine bases of Lorient, Brest and St. Nazaire must have had a direct influence on the course of the Atlantic battle, and was in no small degree responsible for the eventual decline in our shipping losses. Now was the first time that this particular submarine stronghold had been attacked, and we had been chosen to do it.

Fanny led the formation of six aircraft down to Cornwall, each complete with its air-crew and carrying airmen to look after the machines during our indefinite stay. A Beaufort is not a spacious aircraft, and a glance down the corridor from the pilot's cockpit revealed a scene reminiscent of a London bus in the rush hour! There were suitcases, aircraft tool kits, boxes of spare plugs, thick flying suits for night use, parachutes and kit-bags, among all of which were wedged our three airmen passengers as well as the normal crew of four! Moves were always thus; there was so much that was essential to take with us and so little room in which to stow it.

We arrived at our destination in a furious rainstorm, less one of our number who had left the formation *en route* and whom we later learned had forced-landed with engine trouble, crashing his aircraft but not hurting anyone. Now the remaining five aircraft buzzed round on a circuit of a strange aerodrome in blinding rain, landing one after the other; first Fanny, the leader, then I, followed by Joe, H-P, one of the sergeant pilots, and finally Ian, who not so much landed as arrived, leaving his aircraft an upturned wreck in the middle of the aerodrome. Certainly there was an excuse for this mishap, for rain was pouring down more heavily than ever as Ian came in, the last to land, and he must have been able to see very little through his rain-covered windscreen. Luckily no one was injured, but our detachment was now two aircraft short, and Fanny signalled for two more to be sent from North Coates as soon as possible, for a force of six was needed and the work was important.

To operate from a new aerodrome was a welcome change, and we studied carefully the Intelligence about a part of the enemy coast, North-Western France and the Bay of Biscay, not before encountered. On the morning after our arrival we intended to fly around near the aerodrome to familiarize ourselves with the surrounding landmarks, and also to give practice to our wireless operators in working with a new ground station. Some of us had actually taxied out and were preparing to take off, when a red light was flashed at us from the control tower, indicating that we were wanted urgently. On arrival post-haste at Operations Room, it transpired that a large tanker had been sighted west of Brest making for the harbour, and Group required three of our aircraft to attack it with torpedoes. These were quickly loaded, and H-P and I took off to join up on each side of Fanny, who was leading the formation. This was not a roving operation depending on the presence of cloud cover, but a strike at a specified target for which we should not have to search long if the position we had been given proved at all accurate. All the same, we hoped fervently for at least some cloud, knowing the reputation of Brest peninsula as a hornets' nest of fighters and calculating that the tanker would be nearing the shore by the time we reached her.

We flew out low over the water, an aircraft close in on either side of the leader, welcoming every rainstorm through which we passed and looking askance at clear patches of blue sky, of which there were not a few. It was showery, unsettled weather, and since the month was November, we hoped always to have wintry cloud not too far away. At first luck was with us, for as we came upon the French coast it was covered in a passing storm which extended out to sea, and we flew down the coast with fair confidence, passing low between Ushant and the mainland, where guns barked ineffectually from shore batteries.

In this type of operation it is essential to waste no time in finding the specified target, for time lost in searching will be utilized by the enemy in bringing his fighters to the scene. Flak is one story, fighters are another, and a very different one; we could take our aircraft out of range of gunfire in a few seconds, but we could never hope to shake off fighters in a clear sky. As Ushant passed out of sight behind us, our cover of rain and cloud vanished also from our reach, to make the situation a critical one. On a Rover Fanny would have turned back long ago, for in truth the cloud, which we had fondly thought of as cover, was really the product of wishful imagination. It was high and far from our reach in the event of attack, while visibility beneath was excellent for fighter operations.

Now Fanny had no option but to continue, a course made no easier by the knowledge from the firing of the shore guns that our presence

was already known to the enemy. It was easy to imagine hordes of
fighters taking off from their aerodromes, and feeling among the crew
was tense as we searched the sky for a sign of the enemy, but
surprisingly nothing came. Soon our target was sighted in the expected
position dead ahead, to be greeted with the rocking of the leader's
aircraft, the signal for us to prepare to attack. As we approached we
put on speed and spread out until all three aircraft were pointing at
the target, a tanker of at least 10,000 tons, steaming sedately towards
the grey coastline. Its look-out was not slow in seeing us, and long
before we were within torpedo range several guns opened what I could
now call the "usual" tracer fire. Fanny did a lot of twisting and turning
until we came within range, when first his torpedo, then H-P's, and
finally mine entered the water within the second, and we turned away
together, following Fanny as he circled out of range.

As we looked back, the tracks of our three torpedoes could be clearly
seen on the surface of the water, intersecting less than a length behind
the target. I was sick with disappointment as I realized that we had all
underestimated the ship's speed and so missed astern. The whole
hazardous flight was in vain, three valuable torpedoes were lost, and
the best target we were ever likely to see was steaming on unharmed.
The bitterness of this failure far outweighed all thoughts of fighter
interception on our return flight; only disappointment occupied our
minds. As we formed up on either side of Fanny, thumbs down signs
took the place of the smiles of encouragement that had passed
between us on the outward flight. We were vaguely thankful to enter
a friendly rainstorm as we repassed Ushant, from which again came
feeble gunfire. Despondency increased as we neared the Cornish coast
and safety, for the story which we had to tell our waiting crews was
one of failure—of "the one that got away". It was, I found, a story
which had to be told all too frequently, and I myself was often to tell
it. Many times I was to see a ship continue on its way unharmed by
our attack, and to wish a Beaufort could carry two torpedoes to give
us a second chance.

This failure was doubly unfortunate, for the squadron's reputation
at a strange aerodrome had not been enhanced by losing two of our
aircraft on arrival, and now, by missing what had admittedly been a
sitting target, the situation was made worse than ever. However, our
two replacement aircraft arrived that afternoon with their crews to
make our force of six Beauforts complete again, and we determined
to succeed in the important work which we had been sent to carry out.

Bad weather prevented us from operating for two nights, and gave
us additional time to complete preparation. Intelligence reports were

supplemented by conversation with pilots of the St. Eval squadrons, who knew from personal experience the local conditions of operation. It was general opinion that we had been lucky to escape interception on our day show; certainly Intelligence did indicate a great many fighter aerodromes in the Brest area on which both Messerschmitts 109 and the formidable ME 110 had been seen, and there seemed to be no good reason for our immunity from attack. It was satisfying to know that the enemy could occasionally be caught napping, although this isolated failure to intercept us could not be taken as a precedent for aircraft to wander on the coast by daylight without cloud. Our requirement of cover was not born of fear of the enemy's fighters, but of knowledge of their organization and respect for their fighting qualities. For a Beaufort to be intercepted in open sky was for it to be lost.

Weather on the third night promised good conditions over the target, little cloud, with the moon rising in the early part of the evening. The attack on Lorient was to be a heavy one, for squadrons of Bomber Command were also taking part, and to avoid interference with them a time was allotted when our aircraft should be over the target. Thus Fanny was relieved of the decision as to our time of take-off, which was fixed for seven o'clock in the evening.

Two hours before this time crews gathered in Operations Room to be "briefed" by the Intelligence Officer, who, from detailed maps and aerial photographs of the target, explained the objectives of the raid and advised on a method of attack. Navigators worked out their courses and plotted them on charts, studied small-scale maps of the target area, memorized features of the coastline and, not least important, obtained details of the route home and lighting facilities at our strange aerodrome. Wireless operators, who earlier in the day had tuned their transmitters and receivers with the ground station, now collected their aircrafts' call signs and other necessary wireless information. The air gunners had no duties now, having cleaned and tested the turret guns during the afternoon, when all the crew had flown on a short test flight of their aircraft.

Meanwhile pilots supervised their crews' activities, consulting continually with their navigators and referring frequently to the Ops Room staff. For a crew to be a real team is an essential to success, and my crew were just beginning to know each other after three operations together and several test flights, on which they always flew. Sergeant Stephenson had replaced the observer wounded on my first flight, and my air-gunner was a newcomer also. Jim, my wireless operator, was now the only one remaining from the crew which had been with me on that memorable first flight. He was to become something of a mascot, flying on every operation I undertook, always keeping Steve well supplied with information received by wireless, which was invaluable for navigation back to our base after an operation. He was an excellent operator, quite fearless, and still appeared to have confidence in me despite our experiences on that first flight. He was a link without which I could not have been successful.

A roar of aero-engines rises from the darkness of the aerodrome's boundaries as pilots run their engines to check instruments and gauges. The flare path suddenly lights up as the time of take-off draws near, a row of guiding white lights ruling a line out over the blackness of the aerodrome, contrasting with the irregularity of the red obstruction lights dotted about on hangars and around the boundary. One by one Beauforts taxi out to take off in prearranged order, separated only by a few minutes, each aircraft an indistinguishable shape within the triangle of its red, green and white navigation lights, whose colours are reflected occasionally in the perspex or on the propellers. One after another they take off in succession, fairy lights and tongues of flame from the exhausts race down the flare path to the accompaniment of a roar of engines and rise slowly into the darkness. High up they turn left-handed to circle the aerodrome, then all lights are extinguished to make the Beauforts an unseen sound in the night air, diminishing to silence as they set out on their courses to the target, one after the other.

There was rain to be flown through before the fair weather was reached, which made the first part of the flight an instrument-flying exercise for me. For the best part of an hour either we were actually in cloud or the perspex was covered in rain, which made seeing out an impossibility. Later, flak was seen coming up far away on our left from what we took to be Ushant, confirming Steve's calculations of a turning-point, and we thereupon altered course a few degrees east to bring us into the Bay of Biscay. The weather improved as the flight progressed, which was in accordance with the forecast, and I felt lucky in having a moon again to light the horizon by which I could fly. After long periods, concentrating on the instrument panel within the confines of the cockpit becomes wearisome, and to fly by looking outside at a moonlit horizon is much pleasanter and less tiring.

We had decided on 3000 feet as the height at which we should fly, as the Met Section had forecast a completely clear sky above the target. Now, after more than one hour's flying, the cloud ceased to be continuous, becoming more and more broken into gaps, through which stars appeared, until eventually we flew out into the promised cloudless sky. The jagged western coastline of occupied France could now be seen clearly, with its estuaries, promontories and little islands, features by which Steve had no difficulty in identifying our landfall as a little north of the target. So brilliant was the moonlight that I was able to follow the coast southward without the necessity of flying on a compass course. There was no cloud in the sky, giving ideal conditions for night flying, and this was made easier still by the probably intentionally poor black-out of French country farms and villages, from which lights twinkled upwards in reply to the sky filled with stars.

Mine had been the second aircraft to take off, following three or four minutes after Fanny's. So it was not surprising to see very considerable flak and searchlight activity far ahead, such as I had seen previously at Bremerhaven; it signified that Fanny was near the target. With my destination thus indicated, I climbed to 5000 feet to allow sufficient height to glide in silently over the target with my engines just ticking over, a method of approach which might allow me to attack undetected. As we drew nearer, searchlight beams, which were working in groups of three, converged ahead of us and flak poured upwards through the apex of light. Both the lights and the gunfire were meeting at a point directly above the target area, forming a cone through which we had to fly to reach our objective. On all sides there appeared greater opposition than I had encountered on my first night operation. Searchlights, all with powerful violet-coloured beams, scanned the sky above the harbour in methodical fashion, and groups of three would suddenly be extinguished, only to reappear a moment later pointing to a different quarter.

There seemed no alternative but to try and jink a way through this barrage as best we could, so, pointing the aircraft over the target, I commenced to fly across the danger zone. We had hardly started the run when first one, then three, and in a moment another three searchlights had the aircraft a prisoner in their beams; blinded by the glare, neither I nor Steve could see outside the cockpit. I focussed on the instrument panel and started a dive, still held by about a dozen beams, until, with rather more speed than I like to see indicated on the dial, I pulled out of the dive and turned steeply, a manoeuvre which took us out into welcomed blackness again. It had been a most unpleasant few seconds, in which I had felt helpless, and to continue would have been foolhardy, with my aircraft illuminated and accurate flak bursting all around. It was good once more to be out of the fierce light and in the open sky, hidden under cover of darkness, with time to circle unhurriedly and confer calmly with Steve to decide what we should do.

As we flew around at a safe distance from all this activity there seemed to be no answer to the question of how we were to drop our land-mine—which we were carrying for the first time—on the target. Even if we could pass unscathed through the barrage, Steve could see nothing of the ground below in the face of glare from the searchlights, consequently he might drop the load anywhere. While we were talking over this problem, without reaching any solution, I happened to look towards the target, where I saw another of our Beauforts, held in a cone of not less than twenty searchlights and surrounded by bursting shells, flying straight through the barrage to disappear into the darkness beyond.

This was an encouraging example which decided me to try my luck again, and I set the aircraft at the target as a rider sets his horse at a formidable jump, full of determination and diving slightly to gain speed. I raced through the barrage, never taking my eyes from the instrument panel but guided entirely by Steve's enlightening commentary coming over the intercom punctuated by occasional remarks from my air-gunner on the enemy's marksmanship. Yet in the end it was all to no effect; Steve had been dazzled and saw nothing of the ground beneath, for searchlights had held us continuously from start to finish of the run across the target, and again we flew out into the safety of the night to try and decide what to do now. To return with the land-mine undelivered was unthinkable.

There was no doubt that the last attempt had been better than the first. I had been prepared for the glare and had not even started the run over the target by visual flying as I had done previously, but kept my eyes directed on the instrument panel throughout, only seeing the searchlights and flashes of bursting shells out of the corner of my eye and hearing of our progress through the telephones. Also our speed made the unpleasant period under fire much shorter than before, and the task of the defences less easy. In addition, I knew that by now several of our aircraft must be in the vicinity, which would serve to divide the enemy's attention and prevent them from concentrating on one aircraft. Steve suggested more height, I thought we should go in lower, but remembered that the land-mine produced a considerable concussion on bursting and it was not safe to drop them below some thousands of feet. So height won the day, and we climbed until we reached 7000 feet, then turned once more towards the target.

Again flying entirely by instruments, again guided by Steve, who was peering downwards from the navigator's position in the nose, we passed into the target area in a fast shallow dive, hoping that our third attempt would be lucky. The ground below was a furnace of flames belching from guns, tracer came up as inverted fiery rain and searchlights illuminated sinister black smoke puffs all around the aircraft, for we were again held within their beams. Suddenly I felt sick at heart with the task and weary with the concentration of flying. I was inclined to turn and dive away to the peacefulness of the surrounding darkness, when a violent explosion just ahead made the aircraft shudder like a ship striking a hidden rock. At the same time Steve, who had been directing me towards the target, cried, "Hell, I'm hit", followed immediately by: "Carry straight on; right a little, right a little, keep steady on that course". A timeless pause intervened, in which I knew he was taking final aim, and then I heard Steve's voice say "Land-mine gone".

Gone was the load, and I went too, diving and turning out of the furnace of fire in whose heat sweat poured down my face. Never before had I seen the instruments in front of me registering such a combination of figures and attitudes. Speed was over the 300-knot mark, height was being lost so rapidly that the altimeter needle was reeling off hundreds of feet like the second hand of a clock, and the aircraft was banked vertically in a diving turn. These vigorous manoeuvres sufficed to shake off the searchlights, and the aircraft sailed out again into the black night.

My first thoughts was for Steve, my second for damage to the aircraft. We had received what is irritatingly known as a near miss. The shell itself had not hit us, but a piece of its shrapnel had entered through the nose and embedded itself in Steve's thigh. Jim left his wireless and went up to the navigator's cockpit, while I tried each of the controls in turn and scrutinized the engine gauges for evidence of damage. With relief I saw that all appeared in order. Apparently Steve's wound, although painful, was not serious, and since it was not bleeding very much, there was little that could be done for it in the air. Steve said he could manage to navigate us back, proving his words by handing me the course to be steered for home, on to which I turned. The shorter the journey home, the sooner his wound could be properly tended, so I flew back at a fast cruising speed straight across the Brest peninsula. A welcome landfall was made at the Lizard, which seemed to be creeping out over the moonlit sea as if to justify its name. From there to St. Eval was a short hop, and as I circled the aerodrome, with the lighted flare path beneath me, it seemed as if yet another eventful flight was at an end.

I crashed on landing; I know not why. Perhaps I was tired, with resulting carelessness, perhaps I was over-anxious to get Steve down and so cut short my approach, or more likely the reason was a genuine error of judgement. Yet no excuse could obliterate the fact which remained; I crashed. It was not a serious accident such as stalling into the ground or spinning down helplessly out of control, nevertheless it was a crash, and my first in six years of flying.

I approached too fast, touching down, not level with the floodlight, but far up the flare path, and amidst a shrieking of brakes we left the last light behind, crashing in darkness through the aircraft boundary to come to rest, a wrecked aircraft, in an adjoining field. No one was injured; we all climbed out and gazed speechless at the battered wreckage that had been our Beaufort. It was a sad ending to a memorable flight, in which Steve had bravely carried on in great pain to complete the mission, and navigated us home afterwards without complaint. As we helped him into the ambulance, smiles of good-will and jokes about the flight were exchanged, but I felt I had let the crew down badly by a needless crash.

Fanny had returned before me, and had also experienced trouble on landing. His aircraft had slid down the flare path on the wet grass with its wheels locked by the brakes and the aerodrome boundary looming up ahead. Fanny thought quickly and he thought well. Opening up one engine, he swung the aircraft round in a semicircle, finishing his run sliding sideways but coming to rest with his Beaufort undamaged and still on the aerodrome. This was the action of an opportunist and typical of Fanny, for the Beaufort's undercarriage might easily have collapsed under the strain of a turn at such speed. Nevertheless it was a correct decision, and I cursed myself as a fool for not having thought of it at the time as he had. After this incident and my actual crash, we were worried about what might happen to our other pilots who would be returning at any minute, and persuaded the aerodrome control officer to keep them circling while the flare path was moved to give a longer run.

Fanny and I stood on the balcony of the control tower looking out over the aerodrome as first one Beaufort, then another, and finally a third came over flashing their identification letters. *C for Charlie* was Joe's aircraft, *L* with H-P flying it, and *G for George*. All were there circling with their navigation lights switched on and impatiently flashing their letters in a request for permission to land.

At last the flare path is ready in its new position and a green light is flashed upwards from the flare signalling the letter of the aircraft to land. Two lights approach in the darkness, the red and green navigation lights on either wing tip, level, very steady and coming gradually lower and nearer. As the aircraft approaches, the sound of its engines grows louder until it drowns the hum of the other Beauforts still circling above and waiting their turn to land. Suddenly the floodlight, always used sparingly, so as not to attract the enemy, shines out over the aerodrome for it no longer to be a hidden carpet of darkness but revealed as a real field of grass and solid earth. The eerie twin lights, which with the noise of engines alone locate the aircraft in the night, come rushing into the little pool of artificial daylight shining on good firm soil, to be transformed into the Beaufort we know and can now see before us, a glimpse of spinning propellers, shining perspex and grey fuselage. As the aircraft touches down, the floodlight is extinguished and this momentary impression is lost again as it runs up the line of lights to come safely to rest, once more just two pinpricks of coloured lights, not now ghosts in the dark sky, but real lights on firm earth.

One by one they came in and landed uneventfully, five Beauforts that had set out as six. One hour passed and then another without a sign of the missing *E* which Flight Lieutenent John Barry was flying. No sighting reports from the observer corps, no wireless messages, no news. We stood all together on the balcony of the control tower, searching the sky for the sound of distant engines or a glimpse of a navigation light which might be John's. Fanny and I, and H-P and Joe, all waiting and all with the same unspoken thought: John was lost. The effort of the night's flying was forgotten; flak and searchlights seemed poisoned torches on a distant planet, and the flight itself a witches' tempting ride through the night to a forbidden land, a journey for which the toll was now to be paid with the loss of lives. Pilots standing in the dark looking out over the blackness of the aerodrome, with ears listening up to the night sky, waiting for John to return.

And John came back. Long overdue, the missing aircraft came into sight, and before an excited audience circled and landed without incident. We all went out to the boundary to greet the crew, for whom we had almost given up hope, and crowded round the aircraft as John climbed down, grinning broadly and with a story. It appeared that everything had gone wrong for him. He had been unable to find the target in spite of searching every nook and cranny for many miles along the coastline, and in the end had given up the task and returned, only to find that the navigation was so inaccurate that his landfall on our coast could not be recognized. While flying around trying to get his bearings, he had found himself in the middle of a balloon barrage over Plymouth, and in an attempt to extricate himself he had, not surprisingly, hit a cable. Incredibly, John had managed to right the aircraft from the subsequent spin, not before it was dangerously near the ground, and he eventually flew out of the barrage with nothing more serious than some unknown damage to the Beaufort's wing.

Further perseverance in coast-creeping had eventually resulted in some point being recognized by his navigator, and afterwards to reach the aerodrome was a simple matter. All that mattered now was that they were down, we were six again and very happy.

At four o'clock in the morning six crews sit around a table with bacon and eggs and coffee before them, tired crews talking about the flight, their aircraft, the damage they had wrought, the smooth running of the engines, the initial cloud and rain, the petty worries of a few searchlights and a little flak, and their gladness to be home again. "I saw Fanny cross the target at 3000 feet—so did twenty searchlights." "I thought Met had let us down until we were nearly there; how do they do it?" "Flying through that barrage was like putting one's head into a sack of straw." "I could see the aerodrome from miles away, and did it look good!" "*C for Charlie* flew like a bird." And so it goes on, until six tired crews seek their beds as the sun rises on another day.

My crash had reduced our force to five Beauforts, and now the damage to John's machine from impact with the balloon cable was found to be considerable, bringing our number down to four. So the next night John, Ian and I, who were all without aircraft, watched Fanny and the three others take off again to attack the same target, rather with the feeling of children left behind on some treat. I was disappointed at being left out, but had only myself to blame for failure to exercise proper care on a night landing. I knew well enough that if I were approaching too fast I should open the throttles, climb up again and make another circuit. I accused myself of carelessness which might have resulted in a tragedy, and resolved to profit by the lesson so lightly learned and in future, whether fresh or tired, to take more trouble.

I had also been giving some thought in an effort to solve the problems of attacking such a well-defended target as Lorient. The cone of AA fire could easily be flown through with a fair chance of the aircraft escaping unhit, for several of our pilots had done so, yet all were agreed that little could be seen of the ground in the glare of the searchlights, which could not be shaken off. While our land-mines had fallen in the target area it could not be said whether they had hit specific targets.

This attacking of land targets, which we carried out from time to time, was to supplement forces of Bomber Command, who had many commitments and not always sufficient aircraft available to meet them. Bomber squadrons were accustomed to this sort of operation, often attacking well-defended targets and always by night, work for which we in Coastal Command were not trained, and I wondered how the bomber pilots launched their attacks. Thinking the matter over, I decided that we had done better at Bremerhaven because we had been higher, and resolved to try a height of 12,000 feet at least for my next attack, which should prevent the aircraft being held by searchlights and allow a steady run up to be made. Unfortunately I never had the opportunity of trying out these tactics, which I now know as those usually employed by bomber pilots, for I never made a night attack on a similar target again.

All four of our aircraft returned safely from the second raid; in fact, Joe returned with some engine trouble only half an hour after taking off. Such an occurrence was not infrequent, for to continue with an engine which might fail was rightly discouraged. Yet to return is often a hard decision for a pilot to make; all preparations for the flight have been made, the night take-off has been negotiated and the crew are settling down to yet another operational flight, when suddenly some gauge indicates a failing engine. Oil pressure falls, an engine splutters momentarily, only to recover and continue running smoothly as before; or perhaps the wireless cannot be persuaded to work, or the turret jams. Very sadly the pilot turns for home, his mission unaccomplished; but to return is to ensure that he fights another day, to continue may be to lose needlessly a valuable crew and aircraft. Of the other three who had set out, Fanny and H-P of course had found the target, where they had received a hot reception, but the third pilot had searched in vain for Lorient and returned with his land-mine still loaded.

Fanny and H-P were a complete contrast both as personalities and in their methods, although they achieved similar and very creditable results. Fanny was dashing, a brilliant pilot by day and by night, and above all aggressively fearless. His method of leaving the target at night after delivering his attack was to dive steeply down to within a few hundred feet of the ground, pouring tracer from his front gun into anything that might be ahead, while Flight Lieutenant Pennington, his gunner, blazed away at searchlights or gun posts with his turret guns. It this way he had extinguished a searchlight during the torpedo attack in Cherbourg harbour and made the crew of another run for cover, leaving the beam pointing skywards at a drunken angle.

Fanny was also blessed with a grand crew. Sergeant Bob Farthing his observer, had all the imperturbability of a farmer's boy, whom in fact he resembled even to his habit of sucking a piece of straw between his lips throughout a flight. At all events he was an excellent navigator, who never failed to locate a target or, equally important, to bring his aircraft to the aerodrome. Their operations always went to plan, out and home to time. It is understandable, then, that when Fanny became missing his return was still confidently awaited long after the Beaufort's petrol must have been exhausted.

Fanny was very devoted to the automatic pilot, nicknamed "George", with which some of our aircraft were fitted, and he always flew on George by day and by night, except when near the target or low down.

More experienced than Fanny, now with over forty sorties of all kinds to his credit, H-P was a very quiet and unassuming sergeant pilot, who if not brilliant, was the essence of reliability. There was no rashness about his operations, no flamboyance about his flying, but always a great steadiness in everything he undertook. For some reason he did not always have the benefit of a reliable navigator, but this was compensated by the excellence of his wireless operator, who rivalled mine in efficiency. H-P himself, self-effacing and almost mouse-like, would never have been taken for a lion-hearted pilot who had been with the squadron since its first operation, yet both he and his wireless operator were later awarded Distinguished Flying Medals for their work. After the Cherbourg raid he had found that the hydraulic pipe lines on his aircraft had been shot through and so neither the under-carriage nor flaps would work, yet he made a perfect night approach and belly-landing, hardly damaging the aircraft at all. Before leaving the squadron he completed over fifty operations, and all were characterized by great determination allied with reasonable care. I think he was the ideal operational pilot, though lacking perhaps the powers of leadership which Fanny possessed. Fanny inspired a terrific fighting spirit and led the way in aggression, while H-P was content to follow with an experienced and cautious eye the feats of his leader, and perhaps to admire them also. But there was room for both Fanny and H-P in the squadron; indeed, we would have liked more of both types.

The next night we were reduced to three aircraft, for Joe's Beaufort, *C for Charlie*, which had returned on the previous night with engine trouble, could not be made ready in time. Fanny decided to give a rest to one of the crews who had flown on two nights in succession, so I persuaded him to let me borrow Ian's navigator and have another attempt at the target which had given me so much trouble last time.

As the evening approached it looked as if the weather was going to be against us, and when six o'clock came without the Met Officer being able to hold out any hope of improvement, Fanny decided to cancel, a decision which the Bomber Command squadrons had already made. However, after supper the situation changed, for Met promised improved conditions over the target in the early hours of the morning, and after a telephone conversation with the Group Controller, Fanny obtained permission for us to attack at first light the next day.

This was an operation requiring very careful timing. The moon went down soon after midnight, so to arrive early over the target would be to see nothing in the complete darkness. Conversely, a late arrival would result in our aircraft being easy daylight interceptions by enemy fighters. It was essential to find sufficient light from the dawn to see our target, yet at the same time for the sky to be dark enough to hide our aircraft from the enemy and make the task of their fighters difficult. Our navigators set to work, and after juggling with the wind speed, the Beaufort's cruising speed, with the time of sunrise and other variables, in the end produced from their calculations a time of take-off for ten minutes past four in the morning. With all preparations made, we went to bed early that night with the unpleasant knowledge that we were to have a three o'clock call on a dark, and probably wet, winter's morning.

Lorient at dawn was not the same target that had given us such an unpleasant reception at night on our last visit. Searchlight beams were impotent in the half-light in which we arrived exactly according to plan and within a minute of our estimated time of reaching the target. As we drew near to the harbour, approaching from the east towards the growing light, we were flying in the true half-light before a grey dawn, in which we could see but could not be seen.

From the considerable gunfire around the target I guessed that Fanny was making his low getaway after the attack, for the tracer trajectories seemed very flat, and I benefited by this distracted attention in being able to pass over the harbour without a shot being fired at me. Only as I dived away towards the west, after the land-mine had been dropped, must my aircraft have become visible from the ground, for we were followed out to sea by numerous shell-bursts, all falling behind and not really menacing us.

I think the defences must have been taken by surprise, thinking that they had been spared a night attack due to bad weather and not expecting a raid to take place in the light of morning. In comparison with the previous night few guns seemed to fire, or perhaps their flashes and tracer lines had appeared more formidable against a background of darkness than in the rapidly growing light of dawn. But I was most thankful of all for the absence of searchlight beams. They had been switched on when the attack started, but their light had appeared feeble when challenged by the light of day, and they had soon been extinguished as useless.

The return home was a pleasant daylight flight, first westwards to take us quickly from a hostile coast, then northwards for home. Hardly had we left the target than the sun rose red before us to herald a stormy November day, and we flew back through occasional rainstorms, under grey clouds and above a rough sea, making a landfall at Lands End, a finger of rock pointing westward.

Thence we followed the Cornish coast northwards and eastwards, past the Longships lighthouse, St. Ives and Carbis Bay, all of which I had known since childhood, when I had played on their sands and bathed in their sea. Later I had played golf each summer in Cornwall, and now caught glimpses of the courses which had been scenes of peace-time holidays, Lelant, Constantine and St. Enedoc. We passed Perranporth and Newquay, with its five sea-swept beaches, then Treyarnon and St. Merryn, recalling peaceful picnics and bathing on hot days, when the blue sky matched the sea. Those were lazy summer beach days of a past age, and I longed for them to return.

Yet Cornwall and peace-time were not remote dim memories on that November morning. It seemed that only yesterday I had left home, recalled from leave by a silly threat of war, and had driven through undisturbed countryside with thoughts of the future occupying my mind. Peace-time recalled my childhood on these very sands. The Atlantic rollers breaking on the beaches came from the same sea on which our ships had then sailed profitlessly, when after a former war money had flowed as soft sand did then through our childish fingers. Those were careless days of careless years, yet they did not seem to matter now. I looked back on those unworrying times in which I had grown up, time passing slowly and summers spent here in Cornwall, separated from each other by a long year of real time. As I flew along this lovely coast I knew so well, waking solitary and peaceful in the early morning, I looked forward through the disturbed present to peace once more. I knew that although my personal future was undecided, such a decision was remote now, and I felt that I could find contentment in whatever the future could offer, particularly here in Cornwall.

Our work at St. Eval was now completed, for the three raids on Lorient were all that was required of us, and we prepared to leave the next day. That evening should really have been spent in resting, for we were all tired after our early morning operation, but the call to celebrate the success of our stay was too great, and the evening we spent was to say the least a convivial one.

It was the general opinion that the raids had been successful. Certainly the submarine base must have received a hammering, since

Top: Aerial view of Cranwell College, North Aerodrome and Mess (in the foreground), circa 1932-3. (RAF College, Cranwell)

Above: Cranwell College Rugby XV, 1935, from left to right:
Standing. Pilot-Offr. J. R. A. Embling. F./C. H. E. Bufton. F/C. Sergt. F. R. Foster.
Pilot-Offr. B. J. R. Roberts. F./C. J. M. N. Pike. F./C. G. V. W. Kettlewell.
F./C. P. E. Warcup. F./C. Cpl. W. I. Rowbottom. F./C. J. A. Pitcairn-Hill.

Seated. F/C. G. S. ff. Powell. F/C. R. P. M. Gibbs. F/C. P. B. Chamberlain.
F/C. Sergt. T. S. Rivett-Carnac (capt.). F/C. M. G. Stevenson. Pilot Offr. D. M. H. Craven.
F/C. F. H. Lynch-Blosse. *(RAF College, Cranwell)*

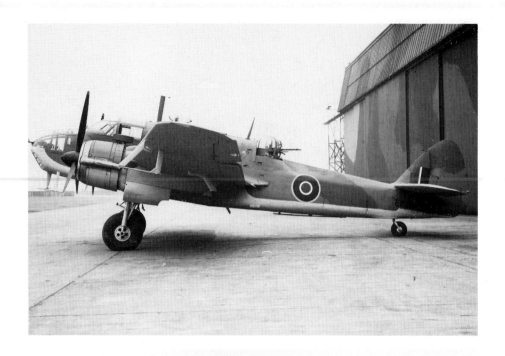

Top: A recently manufactured Beaufort photographed in early 1941 before delivery to an active squadron. (*N Franks*)

Above: Tony Gadd survived this spectacular crash landing at St.Eval on 6 April 1941, after W6537 was set upon by enemy fighters. (*A Gadd via R Hayward*)

Far right top: Repaired after its crash-landing the Beaufort W6537 has become OA:F and has now been fitted with a single gun in nose. (*C H Barnes via R Hayward*)

Far right middle: Flt Lt 'Fanny' Francis (standing, second from right) with his crew and ground crew in front of N1151 OA:I 'Popeye' at North Coates. As with many Beauforts flying 'Moonlight Rovers' the under surface is painted black. (*A Gadd via R Hayward*)

Far right bottom: The 2100 - ton *Hans Broge* torpedoed and sunk off Texel by the author on 15 June 1941. (*R Hayward*)

Top: Avro Tutors flying in formation, with leader inverted (*J J Halley*).

Above: Passing-out Term, Summer 1936, from left to right:
Back Row. – F./C. J. W. Fordham.   F./C. A. M. K. Phillips.   F./C. C. D. S. Smith.
F./C. P. M. Astley.   F./C. J. B. Tait.   F./C. H. R. Goodman.
F./C. D. A. Kerr.   F./C. E. Culverwell.
Middle Row.– F/C. Cpl. R. P. M. Gibbs.   F/C. Cpl. P. S. Jolliffe.   F/C. R. J. M. Bangay.
F/C. Cpl. W. I. C. Inness.   F/C. O. J. M. Barron.   F./C. Mehar Singh.   F./C. G. Burges
F./C. Cpl. W. H. Ingle.   F./C. Cpl. W. P. Shand.
Front Row.– F./C. Sergt. V. C. Darling.   F./C. Sergt. J. R. Fishwick.
F./C. Sergt. M. G. Stevenson.   F./C. U./O. D. Greville-Bell.   F./C. U./O. P. B. Chamberlain.
F./C. U./O. A. M. Bentley.   F./C. Sergt. P. E. Warcup.   F./C. Sergt. R. P. R. Powell.
F./C. Sergt O. Godfrey.
Absent. – F./C. A. A. T. Bulloch.   F./C. Cpl J. H. Humphris.   *(RAF College, Cranwell)*

Top: Hawker Hart, K5864 (*J J Halley*)

Middle: Probably the whole stock of torpedoes at North Coates in front of Beaufort L4516 OA:W, in late 1940. (*Public Archives of Canada via R Hayward*)

Bottom: Beaufort I L4510 of the Torpedo Development Unit, Gosport dropping a torpedo and discharging a smoke canister during trials in Stokes Bay, early 1940. (*A Gadd via R Hayward*)

Top: Squadron Leader Norman Hearn-Phillips having the last laugh? (*N Hearn-Phillips*)

Above: Two Beauforts of 22 Squadron out on a Rover. The nearer aircraft with its code painted in red is OA:R W6491, while OA:M is X8922. (*R Hayward*)

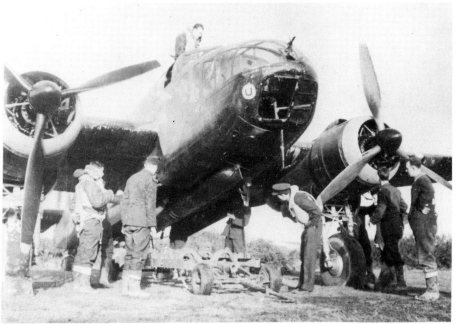

Top: Johnny Lander, who went on to command 22 Squadron in Burma, with his crew on AW201 OA:D. (*R Hayward*)

Above: Preparing for the next strike. The pilot checking the torpedo on N1000 OA:U is thought to be Flg Officer White (*C H Barnes via R Hayward*)

Right: The view from the rear gun position following an attack on enemy shipping. (*N Franks*)

Below: Portrait of Pat Gibbs by Eric Kennington. (*N Franks*)

we alone had dropped several land-mines in the target area, and our force was small compared with that of Bomber Command. Fanny and H-P, true to form, had flown on every operation, three night shows and the torpedo attack, while I had missed one. Our failure to hit the large tanker on the first day after our arrival still rankled, and I felt guilty at having to return to the squadron without my observer or my aircraft. Steve had been taken to hospital at Truro, where quite a large piece of shrapnel was removed from his leg, but he was now comfortably on the road to recovery. However, it would be many weeks before I could expect him back in my crew, and for the time being I would have to find another observer. I felt not a little guilty that in six operations I had lost two aircraft, two observers and an air-gunner, and although the Beauforts would be replaced and the wounded would recover, this was a poor record. However, my excuse was that I was gaining experience.

To have these six operations behind me, three night and three day, increased my confidence immeasurably, and I felt I could hold my own in any kind of sortie. These first few operations are always a stiff jump, which when successfully cleared may leave an open field of achievement ahead. Of the crews that are lost, many become casualties on one of their earlier operations through some mistake made in ignorance of real fighting conditions. These can never be impressed on pilots by Intelligence reports or even by personal advice, but are only learned in the hard school of actual experience. To listen and to read may be great aids to a new pilot, but for him to go and see for himself is for true realization to be born. Shells and bullets are real harbingers of death, not the harmless fireworks of childhood days. The enemy is a formidable foe, ever watchful by day and night, and ever ready to intercept a raiding aircraft. He is well equipped, and prepared to defend his important bases tenaciously and viciously. Only by personal experience will a pilot learn these things, only by fighting will he know the meaning of war.

To underestimate danger, even to be completely unaware of its presence or ignorant of its meaning, is the fatal error of many brave young crews, who, aggressive, and with undeterable courage, sail in where equally brave but more experienced men tread warily. The aircraft is valuable, and its crew transcend the value of mere money; operations are planned with the safety of both very much in mind, and it is only luck which cannot be taken into account. It is an unwise pilot who ranges avoidable dangers up against him in company with rare misfortune. Bad luck dogs some pilots' steps whenever they fly, but I believe good luck has been my companion on many flights. The vagaries of fortune are unpredictable, but luck seems to come to those who court her, and the careful pilot is often a lucky one. Yet I was hardly careful, and luck has flown its full share of hours with me.

Fanny, H-P and I flew back from St. Eval to North Coates in formation. I managed to find a crew who were willing to stay a few days and have a seaside holiday while one of the other aircraft was being repaired, and so I took their Beaufort. As we took off, a westerly gale was blowing a great sea in from the Atlantic, whose waves were dashing themselves against the headlands and splitting upwards into pillars of foam. Far out to sea vast waves were forming, to roll shorewards and break thunderously on the beach, whipping the sand into a fury of beaten spray. White horses stretched along the whole coastline to give Cornwall a wide lace collar of white surf between her cliffs and the open sea. I had never seen a November sea here before, either from land or air, and it made a contrast with the phlegmatic North Sea which was the squadron's playground. It was a wonderful sight beneath us as we rose peacefully above the turmoil to join formation and fly away, eastwards.

Fanny set his automatic pilot to fly the first course home, and leaving it in sole charge and quite unattended, vanished down the corridor, only to appear at the back of the aircraft, making facetious signs at me from the open door. He soon tired of this wordless converse, and after a talk with Penny in the turret made his way forward again, where I could see him sitting on the navigation table, cup in hand, drinking tea with Bob.

Thermos flasks of tea were always carried on operational flights and moves between aerodromes, and the aerial tea-parties which took place were no less a feature of squadron life than their counterpart on the ground, the flight tea swindle, with the advantage that the tea was supplied gratis by a grateful Government. One of the delights of the return flight from some far-off target was the opening of a flask and handing round of cups of hot tea, usually accompanied by slabs of chocolate.

On the ground tea promotes conversation, and in the air is no exception. By the arrival of tea-time the crew usually had some witty remark to make about the attack, and gems of understatement were the usual fare at these sessions, or appropriate reference to some forgotten incident of a previous flight. A typical remark was made by my air-gunner about the shell-burst which wounded Steve: "A lot too near this end of the cab for my liking".

There is no lack of humour in the air, particularly on the return journey after a successful show. The purpose of an outward flight to the target is not conducive to idle talk, and conversation is restricted to the job in hand. However, the crew are often elated on the return flight, just as travellers returning home from a foreign country. Much will have happened over the target, and many strange sights will have been seen, all of which are discussed over a cup of tea when comparative safety is reached and the aircraft is well on its way home.

But sometimes amusing comments are made impromptu during really vital incidents. When John had hit the balloon cable and was struggling to gain control of his aircraft, he heard the voice of his navigator saying in an injured tone: "I wish you'd keep on a steady course", to which John was far too busy to make an adequate reply. A similar incident occurred to another pilot of the squadron, whose instrument flying left something to be desired. Control had been lost in some thick cloud at night, and the Beaufort was spinning unpleasantly firmly towards the earth with the wretched pilot making every effort to change this state of affairs, when his observer handed him a message slip on which was neatly written: "Keep a steady course on 250° *Please*." In the end the spin was mastered, which was no mean feat, for a twin-engined aircraft spins very viciously, and the pilot still keeps that message slip as a reminder of an unpleasant incident. He says that the fact that he still flies with the same observer bears witness to his sense of humour.

On our return to North Coates, the Wing Commander was not unnaturally anxious to hear about the doings of his squadron's detachment, and particularly why our aircraft had been simulating the ten little nigger boys in the daily reduction in their numbers. Six Beauforts had started out, two more had been sent to replace those that had fallen by the wayside, yet only three had now returned, although two more would soon be ready and were only awaiting spare parts.

Over some cans of beer before lunch Fanny told the whole story, stressing the difficulties of operating away from our own workshops and attributing the accidents entirely to ill-fortune. We had together made out a report on the week's work, which laid much emphasis on the success of the attacks on Lorient and belittled the accidents as incidental to such work at a strange aerodrome. The writing of official reports produces a result not unlike a work of Chinese philosophy. Superficially little can be stated but bare facts, but actually there runs throughout the report a wealth of innuendo, expressing opinion. We did not say that my accident was caused by the flare path being too short, or that Ian's crash was due to an inaccurate Met forecast; we left these inferences to be drawn.

In any case, Fanny had received a signal from the AOC congratulating him personally on his own four sorties and on the work of the detachment generally, and this was produced after the report, with the air of playing a trump card. In truth, the Wing Commander had both a sense of humour and of proportion, and knew that the work which had been done far outweighed the incidental mishaps, although, like us, he was disappointed at the failure of the attack on the tanker. We were above all a torpedo squadron, and could only justify the high cost of these weapons by success. He was especially pleased that there had been no casualties, for a crew might easily have been lost on such work, and congratulated Fanny deservedly for his good organization. I think the Wing Commander felt that the squadron had acquitted itself well at a strange aerodrome, and was more pleased at this than at anything else, for to maintain a high reputation for his squadron is every CO's desire. On our part we were all glad to be back. Cornwall and the West Coast of France had been a change, but North Coates and the North Sea were our home, and to return home is always welcome.

CHAPTER X

OPERATIONAL MILL

SHORTLY after our return from St. Eval two notable events occurred, one happy, the other sad: my turn for leave came round, and afterwards a crew was killed in an accident. The previous week had seen several new pilots posted to the squadron, among them Squadron Leader Robinson, formerly my Flight Commander in Training Unit. Now he in his turn had escaped from training to an operational squadron, and came to us as Second-in-command, a newly promoted Squadron Leader. With him came another instructor from Training Unit and also Victor Darling, who was not only an old Gosport friend but a contemporary of mine at Cranwell. Since our names were adjacent on the leave scheme, our forty-eight hours' leave came at the same time, and we decided to spend it together.

There are three main requirements, often conflicting, of wartime leave from an operating squadron. Air-crews naturally want to see their families as often as possible, sometimes want and invariably need a few days of complete rest, and above all, and not surprisingly, they want a "good time". Generally the latter choice prevails over all other considerations. A family may live far away, only to be visited when long leave is available, and to "waste time" by spending a quiet leave, and so taking a rest, is rarely the decision of the young pilot or his equally energetic crew. The good time leave is the choice of the majority.

Quite what the expression a good time implies is much dependent on the individual and circumstances, and must be left to the imagination, but such a leave is usually connected with the familiar formula of beer and good company. The two- and three-day periods of leave were hard to fill, for journeys to join family or friends were ruled out by the difficulties of wartime travelling and the short time available. On the whole, I think our crews were wonderfully lucky in the amount of leave they received, and generally successful in the arrangements they made for spending it.

But whatever form leave may take, a crew at least has the benefit of a change of atmosphere. The liability of being called from their beds at night for an unexpected operation, the waiting for friends to return from a sortie, the continual noise of aero-engines and bustle of service activity; it is from this unsettling atmosphere that they escape. From the few days of complete change given by an occasional leave, however and wherever they may be spent, the crew returns fresh to the grim task of fighting, which they take so lightly that the adjective seems almost out of place. But in reality the task is grim, and the strain much greater than is generally imagined. If air-crews appear to be on leave often, it is with good reason. Whether they have been on many raids or have been idle, whether they themselves feel they want leave or would prefer to be operating, they still need regular rest and they are rightly made to take it.

Victor and I chose the "peace and quiet" type of leave, partly because I was a little weary, partly because Victor was just married and this was the sort of holiday his wife wanted. At all events, the three of us spent in Lincoln two of the quietest days imaginable. Not the least pleasant part of the leave was the journey by car, for driving through the countryside was a pleasure made rare by petrol rationing, and I felt it had been worthwhile to have my car with me at North Coates if only to use it for leave.

Two undisturbed nights, spent at an hotel high up in old Lincoln near the cathedral, were rest indeed after the early rising and late bedtime of the week spent in Cornwall. At the end of the forty-eight hours I returned to North Coates anxious to increase my number of operations and get on with the business of fighting, at which I considered myself no longer a complete amateur. Yet my total of six operational flights appeared negligible compared with those of Dick and H-P, which were in the forties. Even Fanny, a comparative new-comer, had completed his twentieth operation at St. Eval. All the same, I had at least made a start, and was now anxious to hasten the time when my total should reach double figures.

A few nights after our return from leave, a sergeant pilot who had not been long in the squadron crashed after a night take-off, and all the crew were killed instantly. They had been setting out on a moon-light Rover and their aircraft had appeared steady enough on take-off and during the climb, until, reaching a fair height, it had begun a turn to make the usual circuit of the aerodrome before setting course for the objective, when for no apparent reason it dived straight into the shallow water near the shore. Fanny and others who had been watching waded out to the aircraft, which they found so completely wrecked that nothing could be done until daylight. From this curious and inexplicable accident it was not easy to draw any conclusions, except to attribute it to the most likely reason, an instrument-flying error. It had been a dark night, with no moon and the stars covered by cloud, and the only explanation was that the pilot had been looking outside to see the flare path below rather than at his instruments.

Such a happening was a rare and sad occurrence. The hazards laid by the enemy to ensnare a raiding aircraft are sufficient odds, and for a crew to be caught in the trap of a flying accident before the real enemy is reached is tragic. Yet I realized that even a misfortune could teach a lesson, and this accident shouted loud for all pilots to hear: "Believe what your instruments tell you".

It is almost unknown for the blind flying instruments to fail completely, for of the six which are of vital importance, some are driven independently of others, and if one fails, it can be dispensed with quite easily. Not only can one or two of these instruments fail without preventing the pilot from continuing to fly "blind", but the source of power to the blind flying panel is duplicated, so if one engine fails the instruments still continue to function. Many an aircraft has been flown home through cloud on one engine.

When in doubt, a pilot must fly solely by his instruments and leave all looking out to his observer. Peering optimistically into the thicket of darkness outside the cockpit will avail the pilot nothing, for while he is doing so the aircraft may be diving into the ground or climbing up to a stall. A pilot's intuition as to the aircraft's attitude is completely unreliable; only the instruments can be trusted, and they must be trusted always. They are good friends and tell the truth.

On Thursday, the 15th November, there was a full moon. This was the night of the devastating raid on Coventry by huge forces of German bombers operating largely from aerodromes in Northern France. On the next night our squadron was ordered to take steps to restrict the activity on these enemy aerodromes and so prevent a repetition of the catastrophe of the previous night. Six of our Beauforts were to visit various aerodromes in the Cambrai, Amiens and Lille district, and bomb flare paths and hangars to prevent night flying from taking place. If the enemy aircraft were on the ground they would be unable to take off, if in the air they could not land, for at the first sign of aircraft lights we would drop bombs and cause the lights to be extinguished in the general panic.

This type of operation, which has since been carried out regularly by night fighters and is called an "Intruder", was at this time completely new, not only to the squadron but to the Air Force. We had never attacked aerodromes at night before, and anticipated no little difficulty in finding them, since they are nearly always situated in the open country without river, coast or railway to guide a pilot to them. To simplify the matter, it was decided that a single aircraft should go over at last light, which would ensure that the target was found, and drop a load of incendiaries on aerodrome buildings to start a guiding fire for succeeding aircraft.

Dick and I were both keen to have this job of fire-raising, so the Wing Commander tossed a coin between us as to who should go first, and I was in luck. This again was an operation as dependent on good timing as our early morning attack on Lorient; to arrive early would mean that I should find myself flying in broad daylight in the Calais-Dieppe area, which, like the Brest peninsula, was a hotbed of enemy fighters, yet to arrive late and in complete darkness would defeat the whole object of the flight. My new navigator and I worked out the time of take-off very carefully, and since our target was sixty miles from the sea, arranged a route which took us inland at an innocuous part of the coast, the little seaside town of Berck-sur-Mer.

Years of day flying had made me somewhat conservative in my views on night flying, and although it now held no terrors for me, I still preferred to fly by the light of day. I was prepared to accept the chance of being seen by the enemy, and if necessary to do battle with him, provided I myself could also see. The outward flight to France that evening was therefore extremely pleasant for me, for it was made in the pale light of evening. Leaving the Lincolnshire coast and the Wash behind, we crossed Norfolk and then the Thames estuary, to fly along the coast of Kent to the North Foreland. The sun was just vanishing below a sea horizon as we flew out into mid-Channel, where we could see the little harbour of Boulogne in the distance and a few ships at anchor within the shelter of its jetties. Here we altered course, running down the French coast some ten miles out, past Le Touquet eastwards to Berck-sur-Mer, which my navigator easily recognized from afar.

We had reached our turning-point and were still flying in virtually broad daylight, making the run in to Cambrai a hazardous undertaking, when luckily there appeared above us a long bank of cloud through which I climbed on my last course, southwards. This cloud-bank was a layer of white cumulus, dead level on the top and only 4000 feet high. This was wonderful and unhoped-for protection, but I could not tell if the cloud would break before reaching Cambrai, or if I would have to descend through it to find our position.

However, before going into cloud my observer had made a note of the time of passing over Berck-sur-Mer, and since he knew our speed and course, our position at the end of the short time taken to cover the last sixty miles should be accurate from his calculations. He arranged to let me know when only three minutes remained before our time of arrival, in order to give me time to descend through the cloud-layer, under which the aerodrome should appear dead ahead. As the seconds passed for this was an affair of seconds not minutes, the daylight was disappearing rapidly and the eastern sky was becoming filled with darkness. I was beginning to think that we were already late and had miscalculated the flight, when the edge of the cloud-layer appeared ahead, under which was Cambrai itself.

This was both a fine piece of navigation and a piece of good luck. We had benefited by the cloud when we had needed its cover, and were now able to discard it when darkness made cover superfluous. Not only could I now see the town of Cambrai quite clearly, but also a very bright flare path to the west of the town, and near by the usual hangars and aerodrome buildings.

There was now no time to lose, for in another few minutes the remaining twilight would have completely faded, so, without waiting, I dived towards the hangars, telling my observer to select the bombs and at the same time opening the bomb doors. At my approach the flare path was suddenly extinguished, but the red boundary lights remained burning and the hangars were still clearly visible. Realizing that the enemy were uncertain of the Beaufort's identity, I switched on our navigation lights, to which the enemy immediately responded by relighting their flare path; we were thought to be a friendly aircraft! That misconception must have been short-lived, for immediately afterwards I let go all my incendiaries at 1000 feet in a fast shallow dive, climbing up to turn and dive down again, releasing my high-explosive bombs on the flames which were already leaping up. The incendiaries were doing their work, and the destruction of the high-explosive bombs would add fuel to the fire. I had switched off my navigation lights as I let go the first bombs, for once they had recognized us as hostile the enemy's defences were not slow in coming into action. Again the usual tracer lines crossed the sky, not concentrated, but coming up from widely separated points around the aerodrome, and the ubiquitous searchlights began to play their blue-white beams.

I very much wanted to circle round at a safe height and watch the progress of the fire, which was now in full blaze, for the sight of a hangar and the surrounding wooden buildings in flames was a cheering one, but I could not find a safe piece of sky anywhere. Searchlights were not working in the usual cones of three, but nevertheless they were chasing me effectively, while the flak was being "hose-piped" round the sky very liberally and coming up rather too accurately in my direction.

In these circumstances I thought it wiser not to stay, and reluctantly we turned our backs on the glowing fire to make for home by the route we had come, still receiving plenty of attention from the ground until the Cambrai area was finally left behind. This part of France consists of open country, but it seemed there was at least one gun and search-light in every field, and although the defence was not as concentrated as that of ports such as Lorient or Bremerhaven, it did appear that the enemy was prepared for attack on his aerodromes. On the flight to the coast I was amazed at the beams from cars' headlights which were visible on the straight French roads, at the poor black-out, and at the many strange lights, flashing and rotating aerial beacons to guide the German airmen home and dummy flare paths to hoodwink attacks such as our own.

As we repassed the North Foreland a balloon from a nearby barrage could be seen falling in flames, a descending light inferior to an enormous and bright full moon which was just rising out of the eastern sky. We returned coast-wise, as my navigator, who was making his first night flight, was not quite confident of the position of some balloons along the Thames estuary. To follow the Norfolk coast by the light of that moon was a simple matter, and after crossing the Wash we flew up the straight Lincolnshire coast to see our aerodrome lights from far away. Night flying under these conditions was easy and navigation presented no problems. Exercising great care, I made a deliberate and slow approach followed by a safe landing, the aircraft coming to rest only half-way down the flare path. I did not forget the lesson of my last night landing at St. Eval and was determined not to make another careless mistake.

Our five other aircraft had gone at half-hourly intervals, in order to spread the raid over the best part of the night—Dick, Joe, and H-P, Flying Officer Ken Campbell, who was on his first operation, with Jimmy Hyde making the sixth. First to take off, I was first to land, and after making my report to the Intelligence Officer I waited in Operations Room with the Wing Commander to hear the varying stories told by the other crews on their return.

H-P had been guided by my fire, which was dying down when he arrived to rekindle it. Dick had found an aerodrome of his own around which he had played for half an hour, dropping his bombs singly whenever a light appeared. Joe had covered most of Northern France, doubtless creating air-raid warnings everywhere, but without seeing a single aerodrome, and in the end had dropped his bombs very low indeed over Ostend, where he had been given a hot reception. It transpired that he had thought he was crossing the coast at a quiet spot when he was suddenly enveloped in such fierce activity that he realized he was over a target, and attacked it accordingly. Ken told much the same story, but he had taken Boulogne as his alternative target, which he had attacked from 500 feet through a typical barrage of flak and searchlight cones. For a first operation this showed some initiative, which was later found to be a characteristic of Ken's flying. He was aggressive and full of determination.

To all of us the night's work was very satisfying. Everybody had dropped their bomb load, and if aerodromes had not always been the target, harbours were no less important. Aerodromes in darkness are hard to find, and for an aircraft to be in their vicinity prevents the enemy operating from them no less than an actual attack. Our six Beauforts were continuously over the Northern French aerodromes until the early hours of the morning, and the success of the whole operation was reflected in the enemy's inactivity that night. Although the weather was perfect and the full moon was up, hardly any enemy aircraft came over, and certainly they made no attack comparable with that of the previous night on Coventry. Looking back through my log book, I single this out as my most successful operation, for it went completely to plan.

The very next day Met promised Rover weather around the Frisian Islands, and as it was our turn to operate, Dick and I were once more paired together. Dick was leading as before, but this time I followed knowing what to expect. He had been out of luck recently, having inexplicably missed an easy target off Texel when we were at St. Eval and now he was thirsting for a ship and success. A few days earlier, news had come through that H-P had been awarded the DFM, largely on account of the part he had played in the Cherbourg attack of some months ago, when he had brought his crippled aircraft back to the aerodrome and made a skilful crash-landing without the use of under-carriage or flaps. This was the first award of a decoration to anyone in the squadron, and was thoroughly deserved for fine steady work. We thought it could now only be a matter of days before Dick would get a DFC, for he had been doing outstanding work which could hardly pass unnoticed; indeed, his decoration seemed already overdue.

The subject of decorations is a vexing one. A "gong" is an incentive to great efforts, and a just award can do much to inspire a squadron, in addition to rewarding an individual, but an unearned decoration is likely to cause dissension. No pilot ever engages in a pursuit of medal ribbons; they are normally far from his thoughts, which are directed not on selfish personal gain but towards the common task of destroying the enemy. Nevertheless, a pilot is human, and recognition is appreciated. An action medal is not only a reward for bravery, but also for skill and devotion to duty, and recognition of this is implicit in a decoration. It is a mark of appreciation, the country's "thank you" for a gift, that of fighting well for her. There was still nothing to distinguish Dick from any other pilot on the squadron save his reputation, which elsewhere might be unknown, yet he was undoubtedly head and shoulders above the rest of us, and we all hoped that another ship would fall to his aim and so make his decoration certain.

We crossed the North Sea under gradually lowering cloud, to make our landfall in ideal Rover weather. As I followed Dick over the same sandhills, beaches and islands which we had passed on that first flight together, all seemed familiar, as if we had never left the scene. According to Dick's custom, we paid a visit to Den Helder harbour, then flew up the coast to Borkum, a German seaside resort like a little Brighton, with its hotels along the front and bathing-beaches, and passed the lonely Terschelling lighthouse, flying eastwards.

As the German coast replaced the Dutch the weather became thicker, visibility decreased and the cloud lowered to range the elements not on our side as cover, but against us as obstruction through which we had to fly. Following Dick became increasingly difficult, and to make the task no easier my port engine was giving trouble. There was nothing seriously wrong, but it was inclined to lag when I opened the throttles to keep up in formation. The result of this was to make formating hard work, aggravated by the rain, which was now covering the perspex, and Dick's turning first this way, then that, always without warning. He was again spending most of the time in roving over land, but where we went did not in the least worry me, for the enemy would never have expected raiding aircraft to come over in such weather, and could certainly not have intercepted us. Had it not been for the engine trouble which persisted, I would have been enjoying the experience of following Dick; only to see him and Paddy gesticulating was worth the flight!

I had a suspicion that we were heading for the north of the Elbe and the estuary leading to the ports of Wilhelmshaven and Bremer-haven, which were favourite hunting-grounds of Dick's. Once, when visiting Coastal Command Headquarters, he had been shown an aerial reconnaissance photograph showing the liners *Bremen* and *Europa* alongside a wharf at Bremerhaven, surrounded by protecting barges and anti-torpedo nets. A staff officer had remarked casually as he handed Dick the photograph: "There's a target you'd give anything to see!" Little did he know the man whom he was addressing or the seed which this suggestion planted in Dick's mind.

From that time Dick had taken every opportunity to rove up to Bremerhaven and take a look of desire at these two ships, which I had so often seen riding at anchor in the Solent in peace-time. At tea sessions in the Flight Office he would often draw a plan of the estuary and indicate where he thought a torpedo could be dropped with a chance of success, and I would try to dissuade him by saying I thought the scheme not only suicidal but impractical. Nevertheless, on one occasion he nearly succeeded in launching an attack, when, attracted by these two 40,000 ton ships, he had utilized a moonlight Rover to pay a visit to Bremerhaven. The scene was vividly described to me by his observer, on whom it left an unforgettable impression of dis-approval, for Paddy, although just as stout-hearted, did not share his pilot's rashness.

They had flown up the mouth of the river very low over the moonlit water, horizontal tracers from the river-banks making a bridge under which their aircraft passed. At first, searchlights had not been very effective, being unable to follow the fast-moving aircraft which was so close to them, and the guns had not been able to depress sufficiently to be a menace. But, negotiating a bend in the river, Dick found him-self faced by a complete bedlam of fire and held in a pool of light, out of which the giant liners loomed up straight ahead. To attack was impossible, for hardly had he seen the ships than he had to climb steeply to avoid actually ramming them.

Paddy told how he had crouched on the floor of the Beaufort, where he had an excellent view of Dick's demoniacal expression in the light of the searchlight beams. With eyes concentrating on the instruments flying with one hand on the stick, the other arm raised above his head as a shield against any shrapnel that might come in, Dick had made his way out of what Paddy described as "Dante's dress rehearsal". Then a lively discussion had ensued between them over Dick's proposal to make another attempt, a course from which Paddy managed to dissuade him. Yet the episode was not forgotten, and Dick's thoughts often returned to that night at Bremerhaven and that momentary glimpse of the whale which, when almost on his hook, had got away.

After an hour of hard work in nursing my troublesome engine and craning my neck to see through the open window, for the perspex in front was opaque from the rain, I gave up the struggle of trying to follow. Visibility was now reduced to less than two miles, the very lowest in which it is possible to fly visually, and as I turned for home I glanced back to catch a last sight of Dick's Beaufort being swallowed up in the rain and mist. To break formation had been a difficult decision, but one virtually made for me by the fact that I literally could not stick to Dick any longer, and to continue alone with a doubtful engine seemed foolish.

Arriving back at the aerodrome after an uneventful return flight, I was surprised to see Dick's Beaufort already on the ground outside his flight and surrounded by a knot of people. On landing there awaited me a most bitter disappointment. Only two minutes after I had broken formation, Dick had come across a convoy at anchor in the mouth of the Elbe and had aimed his torpedo at a large tanker, which had been left sinking and in flames.

This feat was the subject of wild congratulations for Dick, for here was the ultimate success to crown his past achievements which we had all hoped for. The sinking was proved by one of the finest action photographs Paddy ever took, showing a close-up view of the tanker belching clouds of thick black smoke and with its deck aflame from stem to stern. To add to this picture, Dick had indulged in an action which was typical of him, flying past the bow after the attack in order to read the ship's name, by which she was later recognized as a well-known tanker of over 7000 tons. I was inclined to reproach myself for not having stayed longer in formation, but the decision to leave had been made and was now in the past; in any case, another torpedo could not have damaged that tanker any more.

We were all pleased when the show was given deserved publicity in the wireless news that evening, for we always listened for reference to the squadron's operations, and being mostly daylight shows, they usually made good stories. There was always a gathering of pilots in the Mess at news-time on such occasions, and as the announcer recounted some exploit which was our day's work, smiles of success would be exchanged and cans of beer called for to drink the successful pilot's health. Achievement was very sweet.

In sad contrast to these scenes of success was the aftermath of failure. When one of the squadron's aircraft had been lost, one or two of us would sit quietly in the CO's private sitting-room, listening unwillingly through the German announcements in English in the hope of hearing a claim of prisoners taken. However, it was more often the bare statement: "Enemy aircraft attacked our shipping, one was shot down by our defences". To know how an aircraft had been lost was to learn a lesson almost as valuable as one of personal experience; we always tried to picture the circumstances of a loss of one of our aircraft and take steps to avoid a similar danger to ourselves in some future operation.

Not only was Dick's success featured heavily in the wireless news, but the action photograph was released by the Air Ministry for publication in the press, and the blazing tanker burning like a fired oil-well, which in fact it was, could be seen that week featured in all the newspapers. I suppose these reports were to us like favourable criticism to an author or a good notice to an actor appearing in a new play. Publicity was not sought, but recognition was welcome, for it increased the squadron's reputation. A turn came to most of us in due course to hear such accounts of our own shows, with the announcer talking about the ships and fires we referred to as our own, but to receive recognition of successive exploits in the form of a decoration was the good luck of the very few who survived: to become missing was the fate of so many.

The weather was being kind to us at this time, for, being November, cloud was plentiful, and since our force was not required for any specific work, Rovers flourished. Two days later, after the excitement of the squadron sinking another ship, I was again out roving, this time leading Victor Darling on his first operation. The cover which the Met had forecast on the enemy coast was certainly present—not in the form of the desired low cloud, but as thick fog. I tried to plough through it, but finding the task impossible I climbed up, flying on instruments to a few thousand feet, where I came out above a layer of stratus cloud, with Victor's aircraft nowhere to be seen.

There were no gaps in the cloud-layer through which we could see land to establish our position, which we only knew approximately from calculation. However, we continued southwards and westwards, hoping for the cloud to break and the coast to appear below. It was no departure from normal practice to rove southwards down the Dutch coast towards the Channel, although the eastern beat along the Frisian Islands was more favoured as the scene of most of the squadron's successful attacks. We were determined to give the weather a thorough test, for although conditions appeared unsuitable they were at least quite safe, with excellent cover close at hand; the only disadvantage of flying along the top of the cloud-layer was that the enemy would be aware of our presence.

Our usual Rover tactics were to search low down near the surface of the water, where a Beaufort is both difficult to see and hear. In this way we would operate almost as superfast motor torpedo boats speeding over the surface, and could often take our target completely unawares. To fly directly beneath a cloud-layer would seem superficially to be safer than low down, but it was known that the enemy had detectors which were accurate in locating aircraft flying high, but quite ineffective to deal with low-flying raiders. In addition, a Beaufort could be easily seen in the open sky, and had in any case eventually to come down to drop the torpedo, when it must inevitably be seen bridging the gap between the cloud-base and the water.

Height held no advantages for us; we habitually flew over the water no higher than 50 feet, to avoid detection by enemy radar, ready to climb to the cloud above us only in the event of fighter attack. Cloud was our refuge in an emergency only, the sea was our real cover, and we stayed near it, our drab aircraft merging into its changcable colouring. Thus had the old biplane tactics, of diving to an attack from a height, which I had taught and questioned in Training Unit, been superseded. A Beaufort's characteristics and actual fighting conditions had swept aside old theories, and the new tactics were developed by our squadron from hard experience.

While it was quite safe to fly along the mountainous range of rising cloud as I was then flying, it was also quite useless. My Beaufort carried a torpedo to be dropped near the surface of the water, and now we were not only high up in the sky but in all probability flying over land, not sea. This last suggestion was soon shown to be correct by a timely gap in the cloud, which revealed a stretch of canal and road-intersected Holland—only a passing view, but my observer identified our position as near Leyden. As if to prove his words, breaks in the cloud became more frequent, and map-like Holland spread itself below in pieces like a jig-saw puzzle, a pattern of straight ruled waterways, traditional fairy windmills and dykes, with the old university town of Leyden itself coming into view, a picture framed by banks of white cumulus cloud.

Below me was a lovely view of green countryside, old buildings and apparent peace, but it was superfluous to the work in hand, of which I was rudely reminded by a pretty stream of red and blue tracer shells coming up towards me, just wide enough of their mark to seem not lethal liquid fire but a delightful shower of coloured rain. That the enemy's detection system was effective seemed proved by this prompt action from the ground defences. The equivalent of our own air raid "red" alarm must have prevailed all the time I was flying innocuously above the cloud. Now I wished that I carried bombs with which to attack the gun batteries which fired upwards ineffectively as I crossed from cloud to cloud. On reaching the Hook of Holland we were greeted by green tracer from the coast, an addition to the day's colours, but this fire was more accurate than before and rather less pleasant, for the cloud was becoming decidedly thin. I could see from Amsterdam along the coast to Ostend, and almost to England, for eastwards the sky stretched cloudless.

My first intention was to return along the coast beneath the cloud layer above which I had been flying, but on descending I found the cloud-base too high to offer cover for a flight at sea-level, and I realized that to fly directly underneath it would be to silhouette the dark shape of my Beaufort against a white screen of cloud. As our presence had already been detected, it seemed unwise to continue aimlessly roving in these unsuitable conditions, and I turned for home from another fruitless flight with a little more experience gained, which might perhaps be used to good effect another day.

I reached North Coates just before dusk, to find Victor's Beaufort also on the aerodrome circuit at the same time as mine. He had run into similar conditions, but had turned northwards after we had separated, finding no real cover but enjoying his first sight of enemy territory and some harmless firing from the ground.

It had been an uneventful, fruitless but enjoyable flight, on which new territory had been explored. Holland looked green and peaceful that day, little different in appearance from our own Lincolnshire, but in fact so changed under the conqueror's feet. I still remember grey old Leyden framed in white clouds, and more brightly coloured streams of tracer: red and green and blue.

CHAPTER XI

A SHIP GOES DOWN

DURING the following week there were few operations, and my turn to operate did not come round. Instead, I was engaged in the endless Flight Commander's pursuit of chasing the demon "serviceability", for most of my Flight's aircraft were in the hangar either being repaired or overhauled. A small hole had been found in the wing of my own aircraft, *K for Kitty*, after the Cambrai show, which must have been caused by a piece of shrapnel. Quite when this happened I could not say, for nothing had appeared to come very near us. At all events, my aircraft was temporarily out of action and in the hangar, so I took the opportunity to have an automatic pilot fitted. I had already tried the automatic pilot on Fanny's aircraft and found it very much to my liking. Its advantages for night flying appeared considerable, for it could take charge and leave the pilot free to look out or confer with his crew. Its use seemed to have special applications at aerial tea-time!

It was not possible for each pilot to have a personal aircraft which he alone flew on every operation, for this aircraft might be unserviceable when it was his turn to operate. So we made a compromise by allotting aircraft to pilots and coupling them together whenever possible. In this way, if *L for Leather* was Jimmy's aircraft and it was his turn to operate, he would fly *L* if it were serviceable; if not, he would take an aircraft belonging to somebody who was on leave. This proved a satisfactory arrangement, by which a pilot flew his own Beaufort on nine operations out of ten.

While we all disliked having to fly somebody else's aircraft, this dislike was surpassed by a hatred at another pilot flying our own. Everyone had his own chosen cruising speed, a certain "boost" pressure and speed at which he ran his engines, a special method of "running them up", and even a certain procedure in switching them off. Every pilot differed in these small but important details, and to see somebody mishandling one's own engines was agonizing.

We treated our engines as a mother looks after her children, and for the same reason; we wanted them to live and grow up to a safe old age of many hundreds of flying hours. A reliable pair of engines are worth all the guns and armour-plate, automatic pilots, frills and fancies which may be added to an aircraft; an engine failure is very rare, but usually results in disaster. The Taurus engines of the Beaufort were singularly responsive to careful treatment. Flying to and from the target we nursed them like babies, but when danger demanded we never hesitated to flog them like cattle. They always responded to a call for speed, pulling the sleek Beaufort through the air faster than any aircraft in service at this time outside Fighter Command.

Naturally everyone suspected everyone else of maltreating their aircraft. "It has never been the same since Ken was chased by 109's", Jimmy would complain bitterly, and indeed I do not suppose his Beaufort ever was! But it was never necessary for anyone to fly on an operation in a doubtful aircraft. The air test should reveal any fault, and on rare occasions a pilot might test two or even three aircraft before he was satisfied. Faulty engines would be changed for brand-new ones by the hard-working Maintenance Section, and within a few days somebody's favourite Beaufort would be itself once more. They were wonderful aircraft with fine engines, and we loved them.

Flight Commanders were privileged, and so able to preserve their aircraft from desecration at the hands of lesser fry. Dick's *F for Fiasco* was the oldest Beaufort in the squadron, and had received not a few slings and arrows from enemy batteries outraged by Dick's habit of ignoring the niceties of convention in his attacks. An aircraft can be made almost equal to new after quite a severe hammering, but such extensive repairs take time, and my faithful Beaufort of that first flight was not yet repaired, though Maintenance Section were making good progress.

Fanny's aircraft, *D for Donald* (his Christian name), was beautifully maintained by his airmen, carefully supervised by a flight sergeant quite absurdly devoted to Fanny. It had various pieces of armour-plate fitted, no doubt illicitly acquired, and specially arranged to protect the pilot's person! There was also a very well adjusted automatic pilot which received continual attention from one of the flight's instrument repairers. For this to fail when Fanny was at the back of the aircraft conducting one of his turret conversations was unthinkable.

In addition to all this, *D* had several extra guns pointing from unstandard positions where they would be least expected. Fanny left little to chance in the event of an attack by fighters, for his Beaufort could pour forth tracer bullets from every opening, and his personal protection of armour-plate would look after the pilot's safety. I felt that Fanny would never be caught either by fighter attack or in a flying accident, and that the bad luck of a stray shot was his only danger.

Both Dick's and Fanny's aircraft had quite obscene but very amusing crests and mottoes painted on the side of the fuselage. Most pilots invented their own personal insignia, to be painted on their aircraft, often very beautifully, for we had some sign-writers and poster artists among our airmen. I am sorry I never collected photographs of these products of lively imaginations so typical of their owners, but their publication would never have been possible. However, wit was never lacking, and these colourful coats of arms painted in bright colours, not by any means peculiar to our squadron, reflected the spirit in which crews went to war. Humour and lightness of heart camouflaged the grimmer aspects of the struggle. Sometimes hours would be spent in devising a crest for a new pilot, then it would be painstakingly painted on the side of his own Beaufort, for it perhaps to make only one flight, but that would at least be made laughingly, with some Mickey Mouse, Popeye or Donald Duck making light of the enemy.

With my own aircraft *K* in the hangar having autopilot fitted and the wing repaired, I could not resist having some alterations made to my personal taste. I was particularly interested in the question of camouflage, and did not think the under surface of the Beaufort should be painted black, although this was the standard colour. No doubt at night a dull black surface did not reflect searchlight beams, but I thought a battleship-grey colour would be equally effective and infinitely preferable for daylight operations, when it would blend in well with the dirty North Sea, against which black was easily distinguished. Paint sprays were brought into action, and after a day's work no black paint remained visible on Beaufort *K*, whose under surface had become a pleasant-coloured grey. No change was needed on the upper surface, which was painted in the usual camouflage of greens, browns and greys, which merged well enough into a background of either sea or coastline. I was determined not to be seen by the enemy if I could help it.

I also took the opportunity of having the gyro compass changed, since I suspected it of being very erratic and unreliable. When a landfall is repeatedly made far from the point intended, several reasons may account for the error. It may be due to miscalculations of the course or wrong estimation of the wind, both navigational errors made by the observer. If the navigation is not at fault, then inaccurate course steering is the cause, and invariably the pilot will exonerate himself by passing the blame on to his compass. This was exactly what I was doing now. My recent course steering had been under suspicion by my observer, and in self-defence I had cited the gyro compass as the real offender. I intended to have the magnetic compass checked as soon as *K* was ready, and to leave nothing to chance I was having a new gyro compass fitted as well.

It is of the greatest importance for a pilot to steer accurate courses, particularly at night, when map-reading is difficult and navigation almost entirely dependent on calculation. The observer can only produce accurate results if the pilot obeys implicitly his instructions as to the course to be flown and the speed and height at which to fly. An automatic pilot usually does this sort of flying more accurately than a human pilot, for if carefully maintained an automatic pilot flies with robot-like precision. I felt that with my aircraft fitted with one and perfectly adjusted gyro and magnetic compasses my navigator would have no further cause for complaint.

While airmen were busily working on *K for Kitty*, operations by the squadron were continuing as usual. The pilots in my flight, Jimmy and Ian, out together on a daylight Rover, had the incredible luck each to sink a ship in an attack made from extreme range. Jimmy, who had considerable experience, although he was still a Pilot Officer, had been leading, and, meeting with weather that was all that could be desired, had roved eastwards from Texel. After searching outside the Frisian Islands without result, they encountered a convoy in a position very near where Dick had sunk his tanker only a few days before.

The ships were moving very slowly, making not more than five knots, but were not taken by surprise and had put up a curtain of fire from the time the aircraft came in sight and long before they were within torpedo range. Jimmy was by no means lacking in determination, but prudence played an equal part in his operations; he was orthodox in his methods of attack and very sound in judgement—in fact, another H-P in steadiness and reliability.

Confronted with about fifteen ships escorted by several flak ships, all pouring out accurate tracer, Dick would have waded straight into the middle of the convoy to take a preliminary photograph before attending to the real business of the attack. However, Jimmy was much less adventurous, but in the circumstances he played the correct card, and both he and Ian flew in under heavy fire to aim their torpedoes at separate targets from long range. As they made away, two fair-sized ships were seen sinking; one was on fire and the other with its decks already awash.

A pilot only sees the after-effect of his attack and never has a chance to see his torpedo actually hit the target, or the resulting waterspout rising from underneath it, for he is then in the middle of the very critical turn away, when his aircraft is banked steeply and offering an easy target to the ship's defences.

This was an excellent show, at which the Wing Commander danced with joy, for it was both pilots' first success, indeed it was only Ian's third sortie. The exploit was duly recounted in the wireless news that evening, and celebrated in the Mess far into the night. As both pilots were married and living near the station, the Wing Commander gave them the next day off. Two ships in one day was a record for the squadron and by no means a common occurrence. To bomb ports and aerodromes was a pleasant occupation, but sinking ships was the squadron's real work and in a different class of achievement altogether.

The enemy was not blind to our mounting successes or to our methods of attaining them under cover of bad weather, with the result that, gradually, the game was to become less easy. Small ships mounting multiple quick-firing guns, later known as flak ships, were now to be found forming a protective screen to convoys in the same way as destroyers screen a battleship, and placed in the very position in which we wanted to drop our torpedoes. Single ships steaming alone were becoming a rarity, and to find ships in convoy was now the rule when only a few months ago it had been the exception. Also an air escort to these convoys was now being encountered, usually consisting of Heinkel 115 floatplanes. While this was not a type which could actually menace a Beaufort, it was capable of seeing our approach from afar and calling up fighters from nearby aerodromes.

All was changing; slowly the roving pilot was being tracked down and his activities narrowed. He was never to be completely driven from the enemy coastline, but over a period of months he was to become more and more restricted by the steps that the enemy took against him. The game was changing constantly, requiring new rules of conduct and continual overhaul of tactics. To keep abreast of these new developments was essential to continued success. We were not only sinking ships but being a nuisance to the enemy, and against us he was diverting now valuable armaments and great effort; our operations were being justified.

However, not all our shows were these sought after Rover operations, for occasionally a coastal target might require attention which Bomber Command could not give, resulting in a small force of our Beauforts being sent to do the work. To drop bombs on Boulogne harbour was one such mission which had now to be undertaken, and three of our Beauforts were ordered to carry it out. Fanny, Flying Officer 'Dinty' Moore and Jimmy were to operate on this sortie, which appeared similar to our Lorient raids of a few weeks before.

The enemy defends his harbours thoroughly. Lorient, St. Nazaire, Brest, Cherbourg, and Bremerhaven, to mention but a few of our targets, had essentially similar defences, consisting of heavy and light AA guns so aimed as to form a cone of exploding shells and tracer trajectories directly over the harbour. Searchlights were operated in conjunction with the guns, their beams forming a pyramid of light over the target.

The barrage of light and fire thrown up by these defences had to be flown through somehow if the target was to be hit. Some pilots favoured a very low diving attack, by which they claimed to pass under the archway of searchlight and flak meeting harmlessly above them, while others believed that height was the solution to launching an accurate attack in the face of such heavy opposition. Bomber Command practised this method except in special circumstances, but it was not applicable to our squadron, whose Beauforts were not fitted with oxygen equipment. Dizzy heights above 10,000 feet were therefore barred to us, although we sometimes exceeded this limit, as I had done when forced by weather conditions to fly high on my way to Bremerhaven. However, as a rule we adopted as our only choice the tactics of racing through the barrage low down, and found this fairly successful.

Fanny had been impressed by the good results of our early morning attack on Lorient, and now persuaded the Wing Commander to time the Boulogne attack for dusk, when conditions would be similar. Accordingly, the three Beauforts took off at one-minute intervals in the pleasant light of late afternoon, with the intention of reaching the target just after sunset, but before night set in.

Half an hour before their expected time of return, the Wing Commander and I sat in Operations Room in company with the enigmatic position map and blackboard, from which the night's aircraft letters and names of their pilots stared dumbly at us. We talked idly with the Controller and Operations Room staff about recent shows, while waiting for the signals which would tell us that our aircraft were safely on the way home. No wireless messages were ever sent on the outward flight for fear they should be picked up by the enemy, who would then expect a raid and have his defences ready. Only on the return journey could an aircraft start sending wireless messages to its base.

The Wing Commander always sat in Operations Room when his pilots were out, watching over their safety and ready to do all in his power to help an aircraft in trouble. Usually his vigil was uneventful, with the receipt on time of the expected signals revealing that operations were proceeding to plan and aircraft were returning from their mission. But just occasionally there would be complete silence from a solitary aircraft to cause worry. Sometimes this would mean that the wireless had failed, and the aircraft would arrive back in due course, but sometimes it would fail to return, its fate unknown.

Rarely on such occasions was there anything that the Wing Commander could do, except look endlessly into the mirror, which was the map and the blackboard, to see the bare picture of his pilots going out to the target and returning. Inside Operations Room it was a railway running to its timetable, but outside in some Beaufort's cockpit it might be an early explorer's perilous voyage in the grip of an Atlantic storm.

Inside Operations Room all is remote, with fighting an impersonal subject for written report, telephone conversations and idle conjecture. Puppet aircraft are moved at intervals by the plotter across the map, to settle peacefully and absurdly on the target, which is no more than a name, and then to begin a sedate return along the straight drawn tape stretched between target and base. A train running on time, or perhaps inexplicably late. Signals from aircraft in the air are, in the Controller's hands, mere words on paper. Outside, in darkness, real aircraft flown by living people find their way out to the target and home again, often struggling against the elements, cloud, ice and rain, battling with the enemy, and sometimes opposed by misfortune in unexpected guise. The sky in the Control Room is clear, the earth firm beneath the feet; here is a chilly mirror which flashes back no true reflection of a breathless scene, but a bare cold outline of a calculated operation.

Bare names of pilots in puppet aircraft go out over the map and return, while the Wing Commander keeps watch, powerless to fly the aircraft for some young pilot, never able to make a decision of action for him, only able to give advice, and nothing more. The pilot in the air is remote in another world, and is his own master to make momentous decisions. He is responsible for others' safety, for he is master not only of his own fate but of that of his crew. Operations Room staff give every assistance from the ground within their power, but this is limited. They extend all possible help, but are powerless to fly for a pilot; he must help himself.

First a signal came from Fanny, revealing his position, and a plotter moved *D for Donald* over the map some twenty miles on the return journey. Conversation turned to Fanny, and was all admiration for his leadership; he was less rash than Dick but equally successful, was the general opinion, for he tempered his dash with judgement while Dick's impetuous nature was hardly kept in check by his very sound observer, Paddy. Fanny always looked like coming back, hitting hard and flying his Beaufort brilliantly, but although Dick was an equally fine pilot, his recklessness carried him into unnecessary danger. We talked of their fine shows with praise and little censure as Fanny's aircraft moved up the map northwards to his aerodrome, while we waited patiently for signals from the other two Beauforts.

The next signal was one of distress, a stark SOS message from Flying Officer Moore's aircraft, from which we could only surmise that he had been hit over the target and was going down into the sea somewhere on the route. Within a few minutes the Controller had high-speed rescue launches sent out to search the Channel and Thames estuary. Nothing more could be done, we were remote and impotent witnesses of Dinty's plight, reflected by a bare SOS, only able to hope ineffectually that all would be well.

At least the second aircraft was accounted for, but there was still no word from Jimmy, who should by now have been well on his way home. The flare path officer reported that *D for Donald* was circling the aerodrome, so the Wing Commander and I were glad of an excuse to go out and stand in the night air to watch Fanny come in. Approaching smoothly, he made a perfect landing, and within a few minutes he and his crew were with us in Operations Room, recounting their story to the Intelligence Officer.

It appeared that the timing had been at fault, causing an early arrival over the target in little less than broad daylight. Without hesitating, Fanny had dived very fast through the barrage, which was fierce and accurate, dotting the air around his Beaufort with black puffs, some coming near enough for the aircraft to reel under their explosion. His bombs had gone down into the target area, but he had thought it unwise to wait and see the result, and had made away in his usual dive to nought feet. As he turned for home the two other Beauforts had been visible in the middle of even thicker flak than he had flown through, a sight which made him feel glad to have the attack behind him.

This report held little hope for the two missing aircraft. It seemed likely that they had both been hit in the barrage, from which Dinty had just been able to limp away to send an SOS before going down into the sea. Fanny was inclined to blame himself for mistiming the attack, but the Wing Commander would have none of it and stoutly refused to consider the other two aircraft as lost. Single aircraft had been lost before in similar shows, but never more, and precedent seemed as good a reason for optimism as any other.

His confidence was soon justified, for a telephone message was passed to the Controller saying that Dinty had made a forced landing in a field in Norfolk, or rather in several fields, for it appeared that his aircraft had ploughed a furrow through a brick wall, over a stream, and finished up in a young wood, without any of the crew being injured. His Beaufort had been hit by shrapnel over the target, and practically turned over by the explosion which had occurred right underneath it. One engine had failed almost immediately, and Dinty had done well to make dry land before the other also failed. Both engines were later found to be riddled with shrapnel.

This was cheering news of what must have been a great flying effort. To land a Beaufort at night on a well-lit aerodrome often seemed difficult enough, but to land a damaged aircraft on one engine in completely unlit and unknown country, as Dinty had done so skilfully, was beyond praise. Here was an example of Fortune favouring skill and determination, for any real obstacle such as a building or a thick wood might have barred the way, to make a less happy ending. Our second aircraft and crew were now safe, only Jimmy remained unaccounted for.

The hours passed, and with their passing our hopes for Jimmy's safety receded. An aircraft carries sufficient petrol to remain in the air for a limited time, called the "endurance", but it is possible to increase this time by cruising very slowly, and so economizing in petrol. The actual time which the flight to Boulogne and back should have taken was exceeded, first by one hour, then by another. Waiting there in Operations Room, we each silently calculated how much longer remained before the endurance of Jimmy's Beaufort would be spent and he could no longer be flying. An aircraft was never assumed to be lost until its endurance was exceeded by a full hour without any news that it had landed safely at another aerodrome, and as the hours passed it was for such news that we waited.

With a Beaufort's endurance exceeded by nearly two hours, the Wing Commander, Fanny and I left Operations Room; the blank space on the blackboard against Jimmy's "time of landing" had been mocking us too long and we wanted air. As we stepped out into the darkness we suddenly stopped, speechless and listening. From the night sky came the distant sound of aero-engines. The Wing Commander ran, we followed, out over the aerodrome to the floodlight. The flare path was lit, but that alone was not enough; at his order obstruction lights, flares and full floodlight blazed the presence of the aerodrome to the aircraft above, whether friend or foe. The field telephone on the flare path rang in shrill censure; there was an enemy aircraft in the vicinity and we were exceeding the permissible light, it said, to which our reply was to leave the receiver off its hook and so prevent further argument. If the aircraft were Jimmy's the beam of light might attract his attention, while the flare path might be passed unseen. Time was vital, for he would have no petrol to spare to circle or ask permission to land, a procedure Fanny was making unnecessary by flashing green dots and dashes up into the darkness at random.

And a Beaufort came in, approaching steadily to pass us, standing by the floodlight, and touch down a little way up the flare path. A good landing, Jimmy was down, and all three of our aircraft had returned "safely". Where his navigator had taken him Jimmy could never explain; from the time they left the target the wireless had been useless and they had first flown over large stretches of North Sea looking for land, then over most of England searching for the coast. He had realized, immediately he knew he was lost, that a safe return would depend on economizing in petrol consumption, and had cruised very slowly, with an anxious eye continually on his petrol gauges. When at last he had seen the aerodrome, lit up like some peace-time Piccadilly, he had just reached a decision to climb up and order his crew to take to their parachutes, for a deadly nought was reading on every petrol gauge. The Beaufort's endurance was exceeded by two hours and five minutes, a period of flying entirely on borrowed time, but Jimmy had never for one minute lost his head, and, handling his engines carefully, had never given up hope of reaching the aerodrome. To drop our bombs on Boulogne harbour had meant many anxious hours of waiting in Operations Room, but they were now rewarded. To look after his crews is a CO's first duty, and Jimmy never forgot the sight of the forbidden floodlight when all seemed lost.

There were not always such happy stories of narrow escapes to be told at the end of the day's work, and within the next few days we lost Squadron Leader Robinson, on his first operation, the first loss from enemy action since I had been in the squadron. It occurred on a daylight Rover on which he was leading Jimmy, who returned with a full account of what had happened. Apparently Robby had fallen into all the errors of inexperience. He had remained for long periods near one place on the coast, when the very essence of safety on a Rover was to keep moving; he had failed to make detours to avoid suspicious-looking fishing-vessels liable to report his position, and worst of all, had actually circled several likely targets, giving the careful Jimmy agonizing minutes as he obediently followed his leader.

In the end they had come across a mine-laying vessel, which Robby had circled several times just out of range before flying in to attack. Jimmy knew well that these dilatory tactics would be fatal, and rightly kept out of harm's way as Robby flew straight towards the target, without even twisting or turning. The gunners must have long been aware of his presence and were doubtless waiting for this very moment. Accurate fire did its work, and Jimmy saw the Beaufort falter, then dive into the water before a cascade of tracer and bursting shells.

This was a sad and needless loss, for according to Jimmy the target was under 2000 tons and hardly worthwhile attacking with a torpedo. It was never good tactics to fly around in the vicinity of a ship before deciding to attack. To recognize a target quickly and then fly straight into the attack without hesitation were the correct tactics, and the only way to take the defences unawares. Fractions of a second counted, and poor Robby had been playing with minutes.

There was so little time to think on a Rover that a pilot's actions in a certain set of circumstances had to be prepared before the flight. If fighters were met he could either climb into cloud or make a running fight low down near the water. If flak opposition was alert and heavy, it might be wise to sacrifice a few hundred yards of range in order to obtain accurate aim, rather than go in close and take a snap aim under heavy fire.

The rules were clear-cut, decisions had to be made without hesitation, and only when faced with a completely new set of circumstances might a pilot excusably make an error. A lucky shot or good shooting might at any time account for the wisest of pilots, for torpedo range was short and had to be reached whatever the opposition. During the attack the Beaufort was by no means an impossible target to the defences, and it was essential to surprise a ship whenever possible. To lose our Second-in-command in this way was sad, and to me he was an old friend of Gosport days. Yet lessons were to be learnt, and once more it seemed that experience was only to be gained in a hard school.

The next Rover day saw the Wing Commander himself going out, following Dick's inspiring leading, with Jimmy in the formation making a third. He was restricted by the authorities to carrying out only a few operations each month. To hazard an irreplaceable and wise counsellor in action was rightly discouraged, but he would fly just often enough to keep abreast with the ever-changing conditions, and so was able to appreciate the problems of the operations on which he sent us. Despite his night flying accident which had occurred in the summer, the Wing Commander was really an excellent pilot, and to choose to follow Dick rather than to lead, knowing he was a more experienced Rover, was typical of his outlook. He was always ready to listen to suggestions from pilots actually in closer touch with the enemy than himself, and a suggestion made by any of us would always receive consideration and often a thorough trial.

Much to our disappointment, the Wing Commander was very unlucky on Rovers, and this one was no exception. He attacked a target which Dick had ignored, a medium-sized ship steaming close inshore, but his torpedo struck a sandbank before reaching it. The explosion sent up a water-spout a hundred feet high right in front of Jimmy's aircraft, which was also coming in to attack. Jimmy was not a little put out in avoiding what he considered to be an unfair hazard! Nothing else was found to attack and it was a blank day; in fact, the Wing Commander nearly always drew a blank on his sorties, when all the time we hoped so much for a personal success for him.

After nearly a week in the hangar, my Beaufort K was pushed out on the aerodrome, looking resplendent in its new paint, and after the compass had been adjusted I took my crew up to give it a thorough test. The automatic pilot was really a great luxury, and an amusing toy, flying the aircraft unerringly on courses as straight as a line ruled on a map, and it could be made to turn, climb or dive at will. Certainly this was going to be a great aid to night flying, for with the automatic pilot in charge the pilot would be free to take his eyes from the instrument panel and help his observer in searching the darkness for some landmark or light on the ground. My crew were very intrigued with this ghost pilot which flew the aircraft with the pilot's seat unoccupied while I stood nonchalantly beside it, but I never felt Fanny's confidence in it, which allowed him to go aft to the turret and leave it unattended. I was becoming very attached to K, which I had flown on my last four or five operations, and now that it had an automatic pilot K became the only aircraft for me, and very closely guarded.

For our next Rover we were to take a section of Blenheim Fighters with us, not for our own protection against enemy fighters but to divert the target's attention while we made our torpedo attack. This was no new idea, for we had long been asking for some sort of diversion to accompany our attacks and so divide the enemy's ever-increasing defences. Flak ships were being used regularly to protect shipping, and the enemy were no longer taken by surprise with our low attack made in bad weather. These changing conditions demanded a diversion to allow the torpedoes to be carefully aimed, for pilots could not be expected to concentrate on aiming when ringed with flak. It was now intended that Blenheims should spray the decks of the target with their front guns while we came in to attack behind them under cover of their fire. Theoretically this was a sound scheme, but it was never actually carried out until the next summer, when Hurricanes fitted with shell-firing cannons began putting up this sort of diversion and actually sinking flak ships.

But a section of three Blenheims now came up to our aerodrome for this combined operation, and after a preliminary conference we decided how we should operate. I was to take off first, leading Ken and H-P, to form our section of three Beauforts and the Blenheims were to form up and follow some distance above and behind us, diving in front to the attack when the target was sighted.

Accordingly, I got my formation together on the aerodrome circuit and circled, waiting for the escort, until I saw first one Blenheim, then the other two take off, and, expecting them to join formation and follow, I set course for the target. But after a few minutes' flying we were still without our fighter escort, and returning to the aerodrome I saw all the Blenheims on the ground again with their engines switched off. I was just about to break up the formation and land when my wireless operator passed me a message which read: "Proceed without escort".

This was not altogether unwelcome news, for I had some personal doubts about the usefulness of the Blenheims for the work they were to do, and thought that a large force might be detected by the enemy when we alone might pass unnoticed. But nearly an hour had already been wasted in waiting for the escort, and as our time of arrival on the other side had originally been timed for half an hour before sunset, we would have to put on speed to have even ten minutes' roving on the coast. In the end there occurred what had all the time been a foregone conclusion to me; darkness set in before the coast was reached, and as there was no moon it was impossible to find shipping in the total darkness in which we found ourselves flying.

The formation broke up in the dark for each pilot to make his way home independently. I flew back using the automatic pilot, not quite as confident in its instrument flying as I was in my own careful night "driving", and soon I took control myself. On reaching the Lincolnshire coast I experienced my first real night flying trouble, and emulating Jimmy's recent performance I flew hither and thither, quite unable to find the aerodrome. In wartime guiding lights cannot be placed in every field, but there was really little excuse for losing our way, since the wireless set was working and Jim obtained several good positions which told my navigator where we were. We were not really lost, for we kept identifying places on the coast south of the aerodrome, and then north of it, but no flare path could we see in between.

Admittedly this was a really dark night, with the stars completely obscured by cloud, and the first moonless night on which I had flown since my return to night flying. The great difference between the two kinds of flying, visual and instrument, was brought home to me forcibly now. These conditions called for instrument flying pure and simple, for no horizon could be seen nor anything of the ground below. Sometimes, neglecting caution, I would look out to try and distinguish land from sea, only to have to return my attention quickly to the instrument panel to right the aircraft, which in a very short time achieved undesirable attitudes. To fly steadily by instruments was easy enough, but to bring the aircraft back to level flight from a position it should never have been allowed to achieve was quite another matter. I had several unpleasant moments, with the aircraft either very low and diving towards the earth or else climbing steeply and nearing the stall. Not any too soon I gave up trying to supplement my observer's eyes by peering out dangerously into the night and concentrated on the instrument panel.

We flew around in a small area for over an hour, never very far from the aerodrome, before sighting the very welcome lights of the flare path, over which we must have passed several times in our search. After a circuit of the aerodrome and the usual exchange of signals, I received the green light and came in to make an indifferent landing, bouncing up the flare path with brakes screaming, and finally coming to rest just before the boundary.

I now had some idea of what Jimmy must have felt after hours in the air, knowing he was lost and that his petrol was slowly running out, and the night's small experience increased my admiration for his good landing at the end of eight hours' flying at night. If my Intruder operation had been my most successful, then this was certainly the most useless sortie I had ever made.

I was greeted on the tarmac by H-P and Ken, who had been down long before, but I had no time to hear why the Blenheims had not come with us, since I was going out to supper with Dick and his wife Joan and was already late. Fanny, whom I was to take with me, had been stamping impatiently up and down the flare path cursing at my blindness, for hearing a Beaufort passing overhead, not once but many times, he had been flashing the floodlight on and off in an effort to attract my attention. As we drove out to the village where Dick and his wife had a house, he told me that the leading Blenheim's port engine had failed in taking off and the other two pilots had naturally not wanted to go without their leader, with whom all details of the attack had been arranged. However, they were staying the night at North Coates in order to make another attempt if the weather was suitable the next day.

Paddy had arrived at Dick's house long before us and made apologies for our lateness. He had already described my plight as "buzzing round Lincolnshire like a fly trying to settle", and I came in for some leg-pulling from both Dick and Fanny, who never failed to come straight up to the aerodrome. But Joan did not mind our unpunctuality, for it was nothing new to her. A pilot's wife rarely knows when her husband will appear to within an hour, and this was especially true of Dick, whom nobody knew when to expect back from a flight. Joan was a charming and very pretty girl whom I had not met before yet seemed to recognize. This was later explained when she told me she had been a photographic model before her marriage, working for several dress designers. I then realized that I had seen her face smiling from the advertisement pages of fashion magazines only a few years ago. Both she and Dick were very young, yet they had a little boy of eighteen months called Nicholas, who was brought from his cot to grin at us with smiling eyes, an expression that had all of his father's devil in it.

After supper we talked, Joan and Dick, Paddy, Fanny and I, sitting round the fireside, some on chairs, others on the rug, talking shop. Dick was full of the efforts he was making to transfer to fighters. The lure of eight guns at his control and no crew to restrain him was very strong. I think Dick was at heart a true fighter pilot, and his hankering after fighters was not the commonplace desire of almost every pilot but an effort to reach his real vocation. He would have done wonderfully well in single-seaters. I am certain he was feeling that his luck on Beauforts could not last much longer, and he must have felt that there was nothing more he could do to win his DFC. Perhaps he was tiring a little under the strain of operations, but he showed no signs of this and certainly would never have admitted it. Fanny and I were fresh, having hardly started operating, but Dick had months of violent operations behind him.

Luck does not last for ever, nor do pleasant evenings, and in the dark outside their door we said good-night to Dick and Joan, with thanks for an unforgettable evening. Driving home, well past midnight, the struggles and narrow escapes from accident of a few hours earlier were completely forgotten. Both Fanny and I were silent, hiding the same unspoken question: How long could Dick last? But as I went to sleep such momentary pessimism was forgotten, and with happier reflections I felt: This is an evening I shall remember.

If that evening was always to be a pleasant memory, the next is still a nightmare. I crashed. This was not the mild sort of accident which had happened to me at St. Eval, when I had overshot the flare path on landing, but a full-blooded crash in which my Beaufort fell out of the sky to strike the ground far short of the aerodrome, turning cartwheels over and over, in the end coming to rest on its back, a mass of wreckage in a ploughed field. And there were shattered limbs and grievous injury, blood and cries from the crew in the utter blackness of a dark night, suffering and destruction, which I had caused.

I had done what I had always feared to do, I had let the Beaufort fly me instead of keeping an alert and guiding hand upon her. I was tired and neglectful to let her take charge, and she had viciously crashed into that ploughed field, dashing herself to pieces against the furrows as those Atlantic waves pounded on the Cornish sands, breaking into many pieces hurled into the air by the impact, like spray bursting upwards into the sky. My Beaufort, *K for Kitty*, that was new in its spotless grey paint, over which airmen had swarmed, adjusting, polishing, spraying for seven nights and days, lovingly preparing their aircraft which was to go to war and fight, that proud aircraft was now shattered and their work undone beyond repair; I had crashed.

It was Rover weather the day after our party with Dick and Joan, but our fighter escort of Blenheims were recalled to their base for some special work, and the experiment in tactics was left untried. I cannot say we were at all sorry. When a real fighter escort came with us for the first time, in six months' time almost to the day, I was again leading our Beauforts. Then the experiment was completely successful, for the fast and heavily armed single-seater fighters, our escort on that occasion, were very different from the Blenheims which were to have accompanied us now. Hurricanes and Spitfires were a real asset and protection to us, but in all probability the Blenheims would have been a liability and merely attracted attention.

With a favourable Met report, Dick and Pilot Officer Bill Hicks set out in formation about nine o'clock in the morning, making for Dick's usual landfall at Den Helder. They had been out together a few weeks earlier, when both had missed big ships in convoy quite inexplicably, for they had achieved surprise and met little opposition. Dick had engaged a Heinkel 115 floatplane which was protecting the convoy, and for once came out worst in the scrap, returning with a large piece shot out of his starboard wing by a cannon-shell from the heavily armed Heinkel. Now both pilots were anxious to make amends for their last failure. Although Dick was always finding and attacking big ships, he was not very successful with the torpedo, missing in a large proportion of his attacks. I suspect either his aiming or actual torpedo dropping of being faulty, for many of his attacks produced no more result than a close-up photograph and a good story.

Bill returned after an hour with some obscure engine trouble, leaving Dick to continue alone which being an individualist, he no doubt relished. Meanwhile we waited in Operations Room for news that he had attacked a ship or was returning empty-handed. Whenever the squadron had aircraft out on Rovers, some aircraft waited on the aerodrome, loaded and ready to take off, in case a wirelessed report might come in from one of the roving aircraft to say it had sighted a convoy. Consequently there was always excitement while a Rover was in progress, not only for what the roving pilots might have done themselves, but for what they might have seen. I felt a personal interest in Dick's luck, for it was my turn to operate next, and John, who was now completely recovered from his balloon-tilting episode, was to follow me.

At noon, a sighting report came from Dick of a convoy in a position off Texel steaming east. He had attacked, the report said, but without result. My navigator quickly worked out a course to intercept the convoy, based on its speed and position given in Dick's report, and after a few minutes' discussion on the attack we should make, John and I were off to our aircraft; the sooner we could get to the convoy, the less time it would have to disperse or go into harbour.

This was not a Rover operation, but a definite "strike", and so bad weather could only be hoped for and not demanded as our right. But as we neared the enemy coast cloud seemed scarce; there was just an occasional white cloud high out of reach in a clear blue sky, with no sign of a cloud-bank anywhere. This weather was certainly out of character for November, of which this was the last day. However, I pinned my faith in my navigator bringing us straight on to the convoy without having to spend a dangerous time in searching. I then intended to make a quick attack and run unashamedly for home before fighters could answer a call from the convoy and come out to intercept us.

The navigation proved accurate, for before even the outline of the coast was visible, a forest of masts and haze of smoke could be seen projecting above the horizon dead in front of us. As we approached low over the water they became the smoking funnels, and finally the stately hulls, of ships steaming in convoy. Visibility was unlimited, making the coastline beyond the convoy appear ominously near, and the time taken to reach the target infinite, for we must have sighted it first from something approaching twenty miles away. The ideal protective cover of cloudy Rover weather, to which we were accustomed, had spoilt me for the bare conditions I now found. I felt naked in a sky owned and swept clear by the enemy. This was not the coast over which I had flown unconcernedly with Dick under mist and rain, just as if it were our own. This was a strange insidious land, bathed in lethal blue sky and unwanted sunshine.

As we drew nearer I could count eight ships in the convoy, steaming in line ahead and flanked by flak ships positioned as a screen just at torpedo range from the ships they were protecting. As mile succeeded mile I was confidently expecting that they would sight us and open fire; yet strangely, nothing happened. All was peaceful and silent as a summer's day, which, in fact, that last day of November perversely resembled, with its hot sun shining through the perspex into my cockpit and the sea matching the sky in their two colours of blue.

During the long approach I had been manoeuvring to reach a position ahead of the convoy, intending to turn there and fly towards it rather than approach it from the side where I would be seen from every ship. At last I could no longer see the ships as long majestic hulls rising and falling gently in the swell which prevailed, but as narrow top-heavy shapes rolling regularly from side to side, and then I turned towards them. It was my intention to fly along parallel to their course, prepared to turn in to the attack as soon as I came abreast of the largest ship, or when the flak started, whichever happened first.

Thus we passed within a mile of the leading ship, flying so low along its length that we might have been flying-fish temporarily out of our element, yet these tactics were effective for we passed unseen. By this time the open sky above had inured me to danger, for we had been flying under it for some minutes within sight of the enemy and there was still no sign of fighters. I felt that the flak from the ships, which must start at any minute, was a small danger compared with an attack by fighters. Flak was encountered often and its dangers overcome as an everyday occurrence, but fighters were unknown and dreaded. My crew felt the same about the danger as I did, sensing the nakedness of our aircraft trespassing in a foreign sky, and kept a good look-out, particularly towards the blazing sun, from which fighters must dive to the attack. Ships and their flak they had seen before, but fighters they had no wish to meet.

We passed the second ship in the convoy, all the time nearing the fourth and largest ship, on which I had my eye, and still we appeared to be undetected. My feeling was one of suspicion and pleasant disbelief; it was too good to be true. The acute tension which had been present when the target was first sighted had been killed dead by the long flight to the horizon, and was now replaced by an apathetic curiosity. During the whole approach we were thieves of time, for all the while we should have been under heavy fire with fighters on their way to intercept us; instead, we were running down the line of enemy ships under a clear sky, picking and choosing the biggest target. The situation was unreal, the open sky, the steadily steaming ships with the beaches and green fields of Texel behind them, and John and I, within a mile, about to attack.

The mile separating us from our target would become less by painful hundreds of yards, until torpedo range was reached. Seconds would split into agonizing tenths as with the attack the game would start in earnest, we would declare our presence, the torpedo would enter the water with a splash, a glove dropped to challenge the defences, and as we turned away our engines would roar at full throttle as we avoided the fire from a hundred guns.

I rocked my Beaufort's wings just slightly, hardly daring to attract attention, an upraised eyebrow of a signal, but sufficient to send John out of formation and ready to attack. Then I turned in towards the 10,000 ton ship which was my target, steaming slowly and serenely northward unaware of its danger. I ran in towards it, finger on the torpedo release button and an occasional glance at the air-speed indicator to check our speed, but my eyes rarely left the ship which steamed across my line of sight or the flak ship which we had to pass to reach the dropping position.

Where was the flak? I almost prayed for flak to start to relieve the unbearable tension. I was just within dropping range and taking steady aim, when a single stream of tracer crossed in front of me, silver rain against a blue sky, but port-flare to gunpowder. I had dropped my torpedo and was turning away when the convoy became no longer an inoffensive line of ships but a solid fortress. The flak came as never before; it is only "the usual", I said to myself, no worse, no thicker, no more accurate, no more deadly than before. Just the usual tracer and daubs of black smoke hanging absurdly in the air around my Beaufort, just the crackling of flames and tongues of fire from a wall of guns. Light shells can do no harm, I told myself, and remembered those three important shells which had hit my aircraft, it seemed years ago.

Taking violent avoiding action, I never let the Beaufort settle down on a steady course for a split second, always turning first one way and then another, alternately climbing and diving to outwit the defences and see streams of tracer flying wide first on one side then on the other. I thanked providence that I had taken the precaution of flying not in my usual flying suit but in my shirt-sleeves, for this violent flying caused sweat to stream off my forehead; perhaps fear had a little to do with it also. In another moment, a pregnant one, we had reached the safety of extreme range, when the fire was comparatively innocuous and could be ignored, and I had time to relax after the ordeal.

But to me the critical time of the whole day had arrived. During the time when I had been jinking to avoid the AA fire my torpedo should have been running steadily towards the target: was this to be another miss or my first success? I was just turning, almost reluctantly, to see the result of the attack, when my gunner shouted briefly and triumphantly, "She's up", a statement I could hardly wait to prove with my own eyes. Turning quickly, I was just in time to see a column of water falling back like an extinguished fountain around the stern of the ship I had just attacked. The heavy black smoke of explosion still enshrouded the afterpart of the vessel long after the cauldron of foam had died away. As the smoke-cloud in its turn rose to hang like a canopy over the doomed ship, she began to sink slowly by the stern, her bows rising gently from the water. In her last moments she was still stately and unhurried, a torpedoed ship sinking beneath the waves.

My aim had only just met its mark. The extreme stern had been hit, when only a few feet could have separated me from yet another miss. I tried to imagine as I looked at the ship now heeling over drunkenly and giving up her last breath quite how I should have felt if the torpedo had slid harmlessly past the stern, and I blessed those few feet which had meant the difference between success and failure. Fascinated, I wanted to stay and watch the final plunge, but John's Beaufort, once more in formation and hugging mine, reminded me of the open sky and the inevitable call for help which the convoy must have made. It could only be a few minutes before an avenging swarm of fighters would be on the scene. We left with the ship's final sinking unwitnessed: two Beauforts flying close together as one aircraft, hugging the surface of the water, leaving destruction in their wake.

I had not been able to keep an eye on John during the attack, and for all I knew he might have aimed his torpedo at the same ship, but my observer told me he had seen him attacking a ship right at the end of the convoy without any result. However, one big ship for two torpedoes seemed enough for one day, and John himself indicated how pleased he was at our success by grinning broadly and gesticulating as he flew alongside me.

As we flew homeward my crew's exhilaration knew no bounds, and they kept alive a commentary on the state of the sinking ship long after she had vanished under the horizon. My own thoughts were of the story I had to tell, first at the tea-table as I sat down to eggs and bacon, later over cans of beer, until it would be told and retold throughout the evening, gradually becoming unrecognizable with embellishments as midnight chimed. The strange silence from the defences, the clearness of the sky, the unmolested approach, the enormous ship, the waterspout which my gunner claimed to have been three hundred feet high, the slow sinking, and above all these few feet of stern which caught my torpedo as it nearly passed by. Yet my success was empty. I never sat down to tea that day, nor did I hear the wireless news that evening. There were no smiles of congratulations for me. I crashed.

We reached the aerodrome just after three o'clock in the afternoon, to find the Wing Commander and all the other crews lined up on the tarmac waiting for our story, for our signal had already been received giving bare details of the attack. Excitedly we scrambled out of *K for Kitty* almost before she had come to rest, and gabbled our versions of what had happened to the audience which surrounded us. Meanwhile John had landed and his crew came up to join us in the story with picturesque details which had escaped us, of sailors jumping into the sea as our torpedo approached and boats being lowered as the ship settled down. Was the convoy worth another strike? asked the Wing Commander when all had been said, and were the other ships torpedo targets? Certainly there were four or five other ships of between five and eight thousand tons which were well worth attacking, we said, but could they be reached before sunset?

There followed frantic activity. Our aircraft were refuelled and loaded with torpedoes while I rushed to Operations Room to report very briefly on what had happened. Group rang up asking to speak to the pilot who had been out on the "strike", and picking up the receiver I heard the voice of the AOC himself asking, "Is the cloud cover sufficient?" In reply I abandoned caution under the bright light of success and did my best to lie convincingly: "Yes, sir it's quite adequate for a quick attack". And so we were sent off once more. There was to be no leisure time in which to bask in success, but the game

to be played again against the enemy, to outwit the defences, sink his
ships and return unscathed.

This time we were flying alone, for if it were possible to reach the
convoy at all before dark, which was doubtful, it would at least be
dusk by the time we arrived, and to be in formation under these
conditions would be a handicap. The afternoon's attack had been a
daylight operation, but this was going to be equivalent to a night show,
on which we always worked independently and not in formation, for
to carry out a combined attack at night was impossible. I left the
aerodrome before John, whose aircraft was still being refuelled, and
also before Victor, who was to fly a third aircraft which had just
become serviceable. All our aircraft and available pilots were used
that day, for several of our crews were resting from the previous
night's operation and others were on well-earned leave; the target
justified all the effort we could make.

Flying eastwards again over the familiar North Sea, my thoughts
were on further success; another ship, two in one day, then at last I
could rest contented with real work done and enjoy a few pleasant
days of lazy tea-times. I could not know then that the rest I was to
earn was to be an enforced one of many months spent in hospital, and
later convalescent. Now I was concerned only with the failing light,
which was quickly following the sun setting behind it and promised to
shield the convoy from attack.

Eastwards the sky darkened, moonless as on the previous night, and
again it seemed that we had set out on a hopeless pursuit, as we had
last night. In an effort to cheat the decreasing light I increased our
speed into the darkness covering the eastern sky, hoping to reach the
target in the last flickerings of daylight. But the race against time was
lost. Long before our landfall was made, total darkness came to make
sea and sky one in an obscurity in which no ship could have been seen,
much less a torpedo attack have been made. Frustrated, very tired,
with spirits depleted by the aftermath of success and worn out by the
excitement of achievement, I gave up ploughing uselessly through the
darkness and turned for home.

The automatic pilot flew me very accurately and steadily back to
our coast, giving me opportunity to rest, drink tea in comfort and curse
our luck with the crew. In truth, to have reached the convoy in daylight might have been to receive a furious welcome, for it would
probably have been ready for our reception and with fighters overhead
to protect it. Yet the dangers of an attack are usually out of mind until
actually encountered, and we now felt cheated of another ship rather
than relief at the possible dangers we had avoided.

Good navigation and the automatic's accurate flying brought us to a point on the Lincolnshire coast south of the aerodrome, as we had intended, for there were balloons to be avoided northwards and we always made a southern landfall in case of error. I took over from the automatic pilot and followed the coast northwards, flying by instruments and directed by my navigator, for it was a pitch-black night, in which I could see nothing. It was with pleasant surprise that I suddenly saw the aerodrome far ahead, a bright flare path shining distinctly in the night, for I had feared a repetition of last night's wanderings. Grateful at my release from that experience, I made a quick circle of the aerodrome, flashing my letter *K, K, K, for Kitty*, to which the answer was a green light from the flare path, permission for me to land.

With undercarriage lowered, flaps down, and airscrews in fine pitch, I approached the aerodrome, not very steadily, not quite aligned with the flare path, on to which I attempted to turn. Slowly I drew nearer to the first flare, losing height each second, feeling confident of a safe landing and anticipating the sudden glare of the floodlight and then the firm feel of the ground beneath my aircraft's wheels. I had been in the air for eight hours that day, and was unknowingly very tired. Fatigue spelt carelessness, and this, which had already caused me one mild accident, now hurled my Beaufort from the sky to the ground, leaving it a mass of twisted metal in a ploughed field far short of the aerodrome, its crew falling with it.

I was straight in my approach now, and confident of a steady landing, when I made the careless mistake; I took my hand from the twin throttles controlling each engine to make an adjustment to the cockpit light. The throttle levers, momentarily unsupported and loose, closed as if moved by an invisible hand, causing both engines to die away. I saw the flare path, by which I was guided, suddenly reel drunkenly ahead as I appeared to dive beneath it; my hand went instantly to the throttles, the engines roared to life again, but too late.

The aircraft struck the ground with a sickly concussion of metal, only to rebound into the air again, turning slowly over and over until it struck the ground with a final blinding crash of disintegration. My last conscious memory was of the flare path appearing to be moving across the sky above me, but this curious sight brought no realization that we were turning over in the air, I was past such speed of thought and firmly in the grip of the calamity I had caused. Everything had happened so quickly; when I should have been completing an uneventful run up the flare path my Beaufort lay a wreck in the field adjoining the aerodrome, and I and my crew lay stunned and injured among the wreckage that had flown out that day as Beaufort *K*.

Between the field and the aerodrome was a typical Lincolnshire dyke, which prevented the ambulance reaching us immediately, since it had to make a lengthy detour. It was Jimmy who pulled me out of the twisted metal and shattered glass in which I was lying stunned. He had waded, fully clothed, through the intervening dyke, and now worked hurriedly to get us out and away from the aircraft, for petrol was everywhere and fire might break out at any minute. By this time I was quite conscious, and found myself covered in blood from some head wounds, and also by large quantities of Lincolnshire earth into which I had been thrown by the crash. Jimmy afterwards told me that I never ceased to curse fluently as he helped me out of the wreckage, and that I then walked about supporting my right arm with my left hand. All I remember is that my right arm was quite useless and that I was little help to Jimmy in extricating the rest of the crew. However, my wireless operator was quite uninjured, merely a little dazed, and we found him wandering round the field trying to work out what had happened to him. Together the three of us managed to lift the navigator and gunner out of the wreckage and lay them on the ground. Petrol, blood and earth, all surrounded by twisted metal, were illuminated by the light of Jimmy's torch. Blackness of night was all around and the noise of other aircraft could be heard circling the aerodrome; the flare path which I had failed to reach was still alight and mocking me as the ambulance at last came to carry away our useless bodies, not to fly again for many months.

CHAPTER XII

HORIZONTAL

AFTER the crash we were not taken directly to hospital, but first attended at the station sickquarters by our own service doctors. They found, as I expected, that my right arm was broken without any doubt, probably in several places, and so could do nothing except make it fairly comfortable. However, there were two cuts on my head to occupy their attention; these they stitched up neatly after first shaving a lot of my hair away, an action at which I was most unreasonably annoyed. I felt still more annoyed when my flying overalls were cut away to prevent moving my injured arm unnecessarily. Had I been feeling brighter I would have protested loudly at this desecration, for I had flown in these same overalls since Cranwell days, and had become attached to their grimy oil-stained appearance, which had once been a shining white.

As I recovered a little and became more capable of clear thought, I forgot these trivialities of lost hair and torn overalls, and became concerned about the injuries to my crew, but the doctors soon assured me they were not as serious as I feared. For a horrible moment in realization of what had happened, I thought one of them might have been killed. My navigator had broken both his legs, but had no other injury, while my gunner had no broken limbs but was suffering from severe concussion after the impact. The most amazing escape of all was my wireless operator's; Jim had stepped out of the wreckage a little dazed but completely unscratched, and was now standing in the room surveying us as we lay on stretchers, a sorry crew. This was his second miraculous escape, for he had been flying as wireless operator when the Wing Commander had crashed, and had been then the only member of the crew able to walk away from the wreckage.

When the Wing Commander, Dick and Fanny came in to see me I made great efforts to appear cheerful, and succeeded in convincing them that my injuries were so superficial that I would be back with the squadron and flying again within a few weeks' time, an assertion I really believed to be true. Fanny and Dick seemed to think my accident extremely funny, gazing down with cat-like grins at me lying helpless and slightly battered on a stretcher. They talked not so much about the crash, which as good pilots was almost outside their comprehension, as about the day's success, for a sinking ship was much more in their line. The Wing Commander's attitude was more sympathetic, since he himself had crashed in almost identical circumstances, undershooting the flare path when approaching to land at night. Strangely, his aircraft had actually finished up in the same field next to the aerodrome, not very far from the spot where my Beaufort's wreckage now lay.

Friends from Operations Room and other pilots from the squadron came in to see us, both to commiserate and congratulate, but in truth I was by now feeling ill and sick at heart, and not in the least sorry when at last I was carried out on my stretcher to the waiting ambulance. Passing through the doors, I suddenly remembered that the mascot, which I always carried with me in the aircraft, had been forgotten and lost in the crash; I told Fanny of my loss, and he put my mind at rest by saying he would make every effort to find it first thing the next morning.

That night in hospital was followed by successive nights and days in nightmare sequence. I felt wretchedly ill with after-effects of concussion, a splitting headache and sickness. In addition, my whole body was so bruised that it ached as if every bone were broken, making sleep impossible for lack of comfort; every position in which I lay brought new agony, and this discomfort was aggravated by my arm being now encased in plaster of Paris from wrist to shoulder, and my head swathed in bandages. These were days of endless waking hours, in which I had ample time to regret my carelessness, for such was the real cause of the crash, with tiredness after a long day's flying and over-excitement playing their part as well. Although the incident was over, it was not forgotten or forgettable. Day and night I could not help reliving that day's flying in my imagination, and remembering only the night's failure to the exclusion of the day's success, which should have been so sweet. But gradually these memories became part of the past, to which the crash belonged. Its lessons were learnt in the hard familiar school, never to be forgotten. Soon the future became my first concern; how long I should be in hospital? And when I should be able to fly again? These questions were always in my mind, but always remained unanswered.

The Wing Commander had most considerately telephoned my mother on the night of the accident, telling her of the crash and my slight injury, and now she came up to stay near the hospital and visit me daily. Also came friends from the squadron each evening to tell me of the day's work, recount the squadron news and comment politely on the "bad luck" of my crash. On the first evening Dick and Paddy came in with photographs they had taken on a Rover that very morning, showing the masts and top deck of "my" ship projecting above the water, and behind it the coastline so near that the hull must have been aground on a reef.

The Wing Commander also visited me, bringing the good news that Group had agreed to his suggestion that I should remain on the strength of the squadron while in hospital and not be posted to a pool, which was the usual procedure. This was cheering news, which meant that when I returned in, as I thought, a few weeks' time, I would still command C Flight as before. Normally a replacement would have been posted to the squadron to fill the vacancy made by my absence. To crown this good news, Fanny came in holding up my mascot, a soft toy panda, which he had recovered for me.

I am not really superstitious, but to fly on an operation without my panda would be unthinkable. "Ming" always occupied a convenient ledge in the Beaufort, just behind my seat, and sat there looking over my shoulder as if he were taking an active interest in all that was happening; he had now flown with me on each of my twelve operational flights, for after the luck of my first sortie I felt I could never dispense with him. When not flying, he would occupy the "pending" tray on my office desk, often sitting as a paperweight on the files of correspondence seemingly so necessary to the conduct of a war, and sometimes sitting appropriately on my flying log book, as if to guard my flying hours both in the air and on the ground. As I worked at my desk he always faced me, a reminder of the part I knew so well that luck must play in flying operations. This poor panda, when recovered by Fanny that morning, had been floating in the waters of the dyke through which Jimmy had waded to come to our aid, and before long it would have drifted downstream to be lost in the familiar North Sea. It was now little the worse for the experience, although Fanny rudely suggested that it must have been doing the instrument flying for me, since it had developed a slight squint! At all events, Ming was now placed beside my bed, to bring me a quick recovery, a feat which unfortunately proved to be beyond his powers. However, after the narrow escape which we had both experienced, this panda's value to me as a lucky mascot was greater than ever.

The cheerful atmosphere of that first night in hospital was obliterated by the dreaded news which Fanny himself brought me a few evenings later: Dick was missing. They had been out roving together that morning in ideal conditions of cloud and rain, and after covering many miles of coastline Dick had inevitably ended his search at the mouth of the estuary leading to Bremerhaven. The shore batteries there had sighted the two aircraft and sent up a lively barrage of tracer, which combined fiendishly with the real rain falling heavily at the time. It was into this network of fire and water that Fanny saw Dick's Beaufort disappearing for the last time: Dick was never seen again.

Fanny himself had rightly declined to follow such rashness, realizing that to enter this well-defended area by daylight was equivalent to suicide. Nevertheless, for several hours after Fanny's safe home-coming, Dick's aircraft was confidently expected to arrive over the aerodrome until, with the Beaufort's endurance exceeded by many hours, its return became an impossibility and hope forlorn.

Dick was missing – Dick who had sunk ships, bombed ports and engaged any enemy aircraft he encountered. A gallant and fearless fighter, the best we ever had. It was December, and ever since the squadron had started operations in June Dick had been in the thick of the fight, making over fifty sorties of all kinds in those six months, yet he was still undecorated. The lure of the *Bremen* and *Europa* had been too much to resist, in the end overcoming him. I lay in bed remembering the plans which he made to attack those giant liners where they lay, and how I had tried to dissuade him. I recalled his enthusiasm, as, cup of tea in one hand, gesticulating with the other, he would describe how the ships could be reached and a torpedo dropped which would run straight and true. The sinking of one of the liners would have been a crowning achievement, his decoration would have been made certain at last. He and his observer, Paddy, and his crew had done work beyond praise; they were irreplaceable. Many courageous and daring pilots rose and fell in subsequent months, but none comparable with Dick. The evening spent at his house only a few days before came back vividly to me, and I recalled his wish to transfer to fighters, a new start with a clean sheet before his luck should at last give out. "How long can Dick last?" had been my unspoken thought that night; now that question was tragically answered; Dick was missing.

The cuts on my head were superficial and healed quickly, but my right arm was less satisfactory; the break was not clean-cut but splintered, and the bones refused to align themselves to the doctor's satisfaction. Twice during the first few days he tried to set the bones properly, while I was mercifully unaware of what was going on, having been extinguished by some pleasant anaesthetic, but each time I awoke to find that his efforts had been unsuccessful. I was by now feeling less ill and more belligerent, and with every delay I became more impatient, feeling that the three weeks' absence from the squadron, to which I had become resigned, was likely to become four or five. It was just as well that I did not know then that not weeks but months would pass before I made my next sortie. Optimism reigned with ignorance, for I really believed that a broken arm was normally healed in a matter of a few weeks. I never reflected that I was very fortunate to have survived the crash, much less to have escaped with so little injury; in my impatience at enforced inactivity I never gave a thought that my arm might never be strong enough to fly again, otherwise I might have felt gratitude for my escape rather than dissatisfaction with idling in bed.

Everybody at the local hospital was wonderfully kind to me and did everything in their power to make a disgruntled patient comfortable, but at the end of a week I was well enough to move, and was transferred to an RAF hospital near Cranwell. Here I hoped for immediate reassuring news from the doctors that my arm was progressing satisfactorily and would soon be well. Instead, I was given a rude shock by the news that twelve weeks was the shortest time in which a fracture of the humerus could be expected to heal after being properly set, and that my broken arm was not yet correctly set and needed more attention. I had felt elated after my move, thinking that it signified progress, but I felt wretchedly depressed at this delay, for by this time I was feeling quite well again, with the after-effects of the crash completely vanished. Only a broken arm barred my return to the squadron and flying.

Twice more I was wheeled out of the ward, down the passage to the operating theatre, where a delightful anaesthetic called Pentathol was administered to me with a hypodermic needle. Long afterwards I would regain consciousness, to find myself in my bed with a pleasant feeling of intoxication. But the next day an X-ray photograph would reveal that the fracture was not yet set. Impatience prevailed as the days passed without my even making a start on those twelve weeks which the fracture needed to mend after being set.

One morning, my doctor told me that he would have to operate and join the bones together from within, otherwise the arm would never be strong enough to fly again and I might not even have the full use of it. I welcomed this decision, for I thought it would mean immediate action and some progress at last, but actually it caused still further delay, since the operation could not be carried out until some cuts on my arm had healed, for fear of the bone becoming infected. With every delay I was becoming more and more resigned to weeks, perhaps months, of lying idly in hospital; flying seemed far away in the distant future, while my crash equally remote in the past. Christmas, which I had hoped to spend with the squadron, was spent in bed in the company of eight other casualties who shared my ward. Christmas cards from friends in our squadron adorned the mantelpiece and injuries were forgotten in celebration, yet the fate of my arm was still undecided. November 30th was the date of my accident, but it was not until the week after Christmas that I was wheeled out of my ward to the operating theatre for the last time, and was overjoyed, for I knew that with this operation my recovery would start in earnest. I grinned at nurses and orderlies as I made the familiar horizontal journey down the passage to the operating theatre, and beamed at the doctors as I lay on the operating table where I had lain several times before without ill effects, indeed I had rather enjoyed the elevating influence of Pentathol. I little knew what was in store for me.

Afterwards, I felt more ill than I had ever felt before. The after-effects of the crash and concussion dwindled into insignificance in comparison with the aftermath of the operation. Apparently I was becoming inured to Pentathol from my previous doses, and on this occasion, instead of that pleasant anaesthetic given by hypodermic needle, I was given something smelling strongly of gas or ether through a mask. Whatever this concoction was, it certainly was effective, for although I had left the ward, cheerful and optimistic, at nine o'clock in the morning, as I slowly and painfully awoke in my bed I saw with vague surprise that the blinds were drawn and the lights switched on; it was six o'clock in the evening. Waking, I felt so deathly that I wished only to relapse into oblivion. If Pentathol produced a feeling of intoxication, this gas produced effects reminiscent of the worst imaginable hangover, and they were lasting effects. For a whole week I felt the same and would willingly have exchanged my state for death. I considered that a most unfair trick had been played in not forewarning me that I would feel like this. However, the operation had been successful and the work was done at last. The bones were joined internally by a metal band and my arm encased once more in plaster, under which, my nurse told me, was a long line of stitches sealing the incision through which the doctor had worked. As I began to feel better I started counting the weeks in earnest, for I was now well on the road to recovery, which would lead me back to flying again.

Since I had been in hospital I had corresponded with Alec Gammon, also with the Wing Commander and Fanny, writing all my letters left-handed, for my right arm could not be used at all. The Wing Commander, whose knowledge of the time a fractured humerus takes to mend appeared to be as hazy as mine, was amazed to hear that I would not be returning for several months. However, he did not retract his promise of keeping my vacancy, but arranged for my Flight to be taken over temporarily by one of the other pilots until I could return to resume command.

The day after the operation, when I was feeling at my worst, a letter came from Alec with the bare news that Fanny was missing from a sortie on Boxing Day, when he had set out to attack a ship which had been sighted off the Dutch coast. There were no details of how or why in this letter, for Alec, as Adjutant, was little concerned with the flying side of the squadron, but I heard the whole story later from Ian, who had actually been following Fanny at the time. They had found the ship which they had set out to attack, an armed merchant cruiser of about 10,000 tons, protected by E boats; as a target, it was a very tough proposition. Flak had been unusually accurate, and as Fanny turned away from the attack his aircraft was hit and seen to crash into the sea, immediately vanishing from sight beneath the water. That very day Fanny's promotion to Squadron Leader had been announced, since he was filling the position of Second-in-command of the squadron made vacant by the loss of Robby. He had made about twenty-five sorties in the few months he was in the squadron, and it had seemed that he was set for a long successful run of operations. That night his flight sergeant had waited on the tarmac until past midnight, confident that Fanny would return. Yet *D for Donald*, the Beaufort fitted with the extra guns and armour-plate, the aircraft with the immaculately adjusted automatic pilot, never came back; a lucky hit or good shooting must have accounted for it and its crew, for I know that Fanny could not easily have been laid low.

Almost within a month the squadron had lost Robby, the Second-in-command, and two out of the three Flight Commanders, and I, the third, was out of action for an indefinite period. As I read Alec's letter with the bare account of this misfortune, I wondered how the squadron would seem without its best and most energetic leaders, Fanny and Dick, and I wondered, too, how many of my friends would remain when I eventually returned. I realized then, for the first time, that the squadron could never again be quite the same. The Rovers in blinding rain, the gathering round the wireless for the evening news, drinking morning tea in each other's Flight Offices, waiting in the Ops Room for friends to land, dashing out on to the flare path to give someone forbidden light; it was all over. I hoped with all my heart that the Wing Commander would not be posted away from us or meet with disaster before I returned.

As the weeks went by word came of further losses in the squadron, from which I began to feel remote. Thankfully, of those lost none were my old friends, but new pilots recently posted to the squadron, some of whom I did not even know. On one occasion a Beaufort returning from a night sortie had passed straight over the aerodrome, flying out to sea, and had never been heard of again. This was an incident to remind me of my own night wanderings, and of Jimmy's both of which had happier endings, but even the memories of those nights seemed unreal. The life of action in the squadron seemed very distant compared with the slow tempo of hospital existence.

I had started by hating the hospital life of lying idly day after day inactive and bedridden, and longed for the activity to which I was accustomed. However, as time passed, I was surprised to find that my longing for flying receded, eventually to become almost forgotten and hardly missed. Perhaps being out of sight caused flying to be out of mind, and it needed the roar of engines and the rush of air past the cockpit to make the music to which I marched. Now the sight or sound of some remote aircraft overhead touched no chord; flying was out of mind. The feeling of power, the conflict with the elements and the changing cartographic view, failed in their call to me now; I lived without flying.

As I saw more and more cases of serious fractures and severe internal and head injuries, I began at last to realize my comparative good luck in escaping so lightly, a realization which banished all ungrateful discontent from my mind. It was winter, and the hospital the centre of a number of aerodromes from which night bomber squadrons operated. The weather was treacherous with rain and fogs, snow and cold bringing the dreaded ice-forming cloud to menace the bomber pilots, whose aircraft I could hear, as I lay in my comfortable bed, flying out almost nightly to face the elements and attack the enemy.

Often at night, or early in the morning, a crew, injured in some flying accident or hit by flak over their target, would be brought into the hospital. Always doctors and nurses were ready to receive them and fight for their lives, their limbs, or perhaps their looks. Amazing feats of modern surgery were achieved, and limbs recovered when they appeared lost. Bones were grafted or perhaps bolted together to make in time a perfect limb, not only strong enough to use again, but strong enough to use in flying and against the enemy; amputation was extremely rare. Time was the keyword in the hospital. No mending fracture could be hurried on to an early completion, for healing broken bones was time's own work. Nevertheless, time, the healer, was carefully supervised by X-ray photographs of the fracture's progress, and muscles which might waste through idleness were kept active by massage and exercise, so that they would do their work when the bone was ready. So I, with many others, waited on time's pleasure and was satisfied when successive X-rays showed standard progress.

As I lay helpless in bed, with day uneventfully succeeding day, I became an ardent admirer of the fine work the hospital was doing, work whose scope outside my ward I could only imagine from snatches of conversation, the talk of sisters and other patients. Broken limbs were mended and brought once more into use, skin grafted to cover burns, bullets extracted and cuts stitched. Reconstruction went on all around me; all day and every day new cases were being carried in on stretchers while patients walked away cured. It was a fascinating, gripping picture, and I was lost in admiration for the work of doctors and staff.

Particularly did I admire the doctor who attended me; he was responsible for over a hundred cases of fractures, nearly all sustained in flying accidents, and his hasty visit to patients was always eagerly awaited. We all expected some encouraging pronouncement on our recovery, which in fact rarely materialized, yet everyone felt utter confidence in him and thought that even independent Time might become a slave in his hands. After the morning visit he would be operating throughout the day, and often at night also, struggling to save limbs and give some pilot or his crew the chance to fly and fight again. It was fine, inspiring work.

Sisters and nurses also played their part, always cheering us with news of recoveries which they had helped and witnessed. "John Gordon, who was with us for a whole year with a broken back, has just got his DFC", one would announce, and we, to whom flying and the war seemed as remote as past peace-time, would marvel. Some- one would remember the pilot who had been shot down and crash- landed, his aircraft rolling over and over down a hillside, how he had occupied the corner bed, how he had first walked after months in bed, and eventually left with his back straight and strong. Hospital was a little world of its own, and we lived contentedly its little life of horizontal conversations, listening to the wireless, or reading.

The eight officers in my ward were mostly pilots from night bomber squadrons, flying Hampdens, Wellingtons or Whitleys from the neighbouring aerodromes. They, flying always at night, could not understand my preference for daylight operations, while I was quite unable to convince them that cloud could be equal in safety to the cover of night. That I should have difficulty in finding my way in the dark was incomprehensible to them. These were the moths of the service, sleeping part of the day, flying through the night. They usually made not more than one or two sorties each week, for their flights, of ten or twelve hours, perhaps even of longer duration, were tiring and their activities were often restricted by bad weather, either at their base or over the target many hundreds of miles away.

From these night pilots, my companions in these weeks of idleness, I learnt more about the art of night flying and attacking well-defended targets than I could have learnt in a year of night flying in my squadron, for they were experts in this work, which was to us only a sideline. However, their injuries were caused mostly by crashes which were the result of a careless error such as mine, often to be traced to the same reason, tiredness after a long flight. Some had crashed on landing through an error of judgement, others had crashed while returning from a raid in unexpected bad weather; very rarely was the cause engine failure. Whatever the reason for his misfortune, every pilot was ready to fly again as soon as his injuries allowed, keen to get even with the enemy and to profit by the lesson he had learnt. All were cheerful, with a feast of stories about their squadron's shows and narrow escapes combined with humour and tragedy. One thing was common amongst us; we all thought our own squadron the best in the world.

A few weeks after the operation, X-ray photographs showed that my arm was mending "as quickly as could be expected", a medical phrase as tantalizing as the newspaper expression "a near miss", and I was allowed to get up for the first time after eight weeks in bed. With my arm still in plaster and supported in a sling I was now free to walk in the countryside around the hospital, which I knew so well from Cranwell days. I could also for the first time see other parts of the hospital outside my ward, and took the opportunity of visiting my observer. His broken legs had been set correctly at the local hospital in the first instance, and it looked as if he might be using them before my arm mended. All the same, I was the luckier in being able to dress and walk about, although he seemed happy enough propped up in bed in a ward filled with other sergeant-observers and air-gunners in a similar plight. In every ward could be seen rows of broken arms and legs encased in the now familiar plaster of Paris. Some limbs were held to the ceiling by wires and pulleys, others weighted to ensure the fracture setting straight and to the correct length. All the patients became resigned to discomfort, knowing that it was inevitable for their eventual complete recovery. More laughter seemed to echo from these wards than from any school dormitory.

I now met other officers, convalescent like myself, whose broken limbs were well on the way to recovery. Many of these cases were sent, as soon as they could travel, to a famous RAF hospital in the South-West, where their re-formed limbs were exercised back to normal after weeks of idleness, while they recuperated in sunshine. I think my doctor wanted me at hand in case my fracture should even now show an unexpected sign of failing to knit, and while others came and left I remained at the hospital until I was almost the oldest inhabitant. But I was resigned to anything that was ordered, for I could see that all efforts here were directed towards my own good; to be impatient at delay was both useless and ungrateful.

Occasionally some of us would break the day's monotony by walking over to supper at the golf club nearby. It was here that I had played as a cadet, and the professional, who was also the steward, remembered me from those days. He had known successive terms of Cranwell cadets for a decade, for most of us played golf on summer evenings or Sunday afternoons, and so we had mutual friends, about whom we talked often and long. One of my instructors at the college, who had been the idol of the professional's little boy of seven, was now posted as missing from a raid on Kiel. "Nobody flew over the course as low as Dennis" was the child's summoning up of his hero, and I, too, remembered the crazy low flying which Dennis had indulged in while I hung on for dear life in the other cockpit. It was a jolt to meet the memories here, to hear of other cadets who were lost, and realize that all the time the names of friends were appearing in the lengthening casualty lists. The old Air Force was a dying race.

I passed day after day of this uneventful life waiting for time to do its work, knowing that I should soon be able to go on sick leave and eventually return to the squadron. My flying would at first be restricted to short flights, then, if all went well, I should be allowed to resume operations. Reading, playing left-handed darts or writing letters filled the time not occupied by country walks or golf club evenings, until in the first week in February I was granted the expected sick leave, and with my arm still in plaster and still supported in a sling, I left the hospital to join my family in Cornwall. Every summer of my life I had been in Cornwall, either in August or September, but never before at this time of the year. I found it altogether delightful, with wild gales blowing in salt from the Atlantic waves, incomparable seas breaking on to the beaches and the sound of their rollers in my ears at night. These were four carefree weeks of leave spent in the peaceful home atmosphere so rarely gained in wartime. The hospital, flying and danger were equally forgotten. Only occasionally were memories awakened by the sound of an aircraft overhead in the darkness or by the view at night from my bedroom window, which looked out over a curving chain of bays. Twenty miles across the water the beam of the floodlight at St. Eval could be seen guiding in some aircraft to a safe landing, a reminder of the squadron's operations against Lorient, which now seemed long ago.

For the first time I began to long for the use of my right arm again, which had been out of action for nearly four months. Although my left hand through constant use was able to shave and dress me, cut up my meals and do almost anything I wanted, I was tiring of carrying the weight of a useless arm in a sling and of continually being careful lest I bump it. I wanted the freedom of whole limbs with which to play games, which I could use without worry or thought, but this was a luxury I was never to regain. It was the price I had to pay for carelessness.

At the end of four weeks of leave I returned to hospital, with no small regret at leaving the home atmosphere which I was beginning to consider the most desirable thing in all the world, but compensated by the expectation of having the plaster removed from my arm. In this I was disappointed, for when the doctor examined the arm, which, if appearing somewhat shapeless and scarred, felt to me quite strong, he decided that the join was still not strong enough and proceeded to encase it once more in plaster of Paris. By this time I had learnt better than to protest, but I had built up hopes and was disappointed. Admittedly the new cast was smaller and lighter than before, allowing limited movement at the elbow, but it was not what I had hoped for and meant still more delay before I could fly. However, I could now dispense with the sling, and my arm, hidden beneath the sleeve of my tunic, appeared outwardly quite normal. I noticed that the doctor examined my shoulder, to which he had not previously paid much attention, and now that I could move my arm about more freely I found it weak and not very effective. For the first time I began to suspect that arm and shoulder would never be quite the same as before, and hoped that at least they would be strong enough to let me fly.

The doctor now suggested that I should take another four weeks' sick leave, a suggestion I received with mixed feelings. I had been away from the squadron for over four months, but my vacancy was still unfilled. Much as I would have liked to return to Cornwall, I felt that the least I could do in gratitude to the Wing Commander was to try and return to the squadron at once. Although I could not fly, I could run a Flight and make myself useful on the ground.

No promise had yet been made as to when I would be allowed to fly again, but this was not for want of my asking. I had been asking doctors, nursing sisters and even knowledgeable orderlies at intervals since my first day in hospital, but always without result. They were used to this eternal question from their flying patients and could rarely be induced into even a non-committal answer. At the suggestion of more sick leave I took the opportunity to explain the situation to my doctor: I had thought to be absent from the squadron for a few weeks, but had now been away several months and felt I should return as soon as possible. He very reasonably agreed that I would be as well doing a ground job in the squadron as on sick leave, and said I could leave hospital the next day. Made bold by this success, I pressed for an answer to the eternal question, and was promised that if all was found to be well in four weeks' time, when I was to return for an X-ray, I should then be allowed to carry out limited flying. My return to operational flying would follow in due course.

This was the first definite promise I had been given and was as good news as I could possibly hope for. At least I would be back with the squadron and in touch with operations, even if not actually taking part in them. These four weeks before I should fly again seemed negligible compared with the twenty I had already waited. I had not spent all this time in hospital without realizing to the full how very lucky I really was. I saw many young pilots lying there who would never return to their squadrons, nor ever fly again. Others even less fortunate had been carried in during the night only to die before morning, notwithstanding the efforts of doctors and the skill of modern surgery. Some patients had injuries to back or head which might be healed effectively enough to be unnoticed in everyday occupations, but which would never withstand the strain imposed by flying. I knew I was very lucky indeed to have escaped so lightly, and if perhaps my arm might not be as strong as I had hoped, it was an insignificant injury compared with some I had seen, and I was thankful for it.

Before I left, I went to say good-bye to my observer, whose recovery had not outstripped mine after all. He was walking now with the aid of two sticks, and was expecting to be transferred to the convalescent hospital very shortly. Whenever I had visited him in the previous weeks to exchange news of the squadron, which we received from different sources, I was always amazed how both he and my air-gunner regarded the crash as an incident to be taken as part of the day's work. I wondered if I should feel so kindly towards another pilot who let me down. Few of the beds in this ward were occupied by pilots, but mostly by gunners and observers who had been powerless to avoid the crash through which they now suffered. They made me feel lucky to be a pilot, and so to some extent master of my own fate. But my observer, apparently, felt no bitterness at my mistake. Invariably my visits, which were made with the intention of cheering him up, ended with my being immeasurably heartened by his good-humour and the high spirits in the ward. Two broken legs, one with a compound fracture, are far more painful than a mere broken arm.

Saying good-bye to the hospital was almost like the sad parting from a squadron, for I had made many friends there, particularly among the officers in my ward, a slightly changing population with some old inhabitants. The pilot officer who had hit the ground at over two hundred miles an hour when night flying in a Blenheim, and had been thrown out, landing unbelievably in a thick snowdrift which saved his life; I remembered the morning he had been carried into the ward with a fractured thigh and cuts on his head, looking as pale as the snow which saved him and the sheets in which he was laid; now he was recovering well. The Hampden pilot, returning from a long flight to Kiel on one engine, who had lost control as he came in to land, just when he must have felt he was safe at last. His aircraft had spun into the ground from seven hundred feet, yet, amazingly, he had escaped with a broken ankle and minor head injuries. Another Hampden pilot, who had stalled his aircraft after taking off, being thrown out as it crashed, the only survivor of his crew, with a broken arm and ribs. These were my friends to whom I said goodbye, and to the sisters and orderlies who looked after our ward. I was returning to my squadron, and they thought me very lucky.

CHAPTER XIII

NEARLY, BUT NOT QUITE

AS I had feared, the squadron was not quite the same; it was good to be back and among friends, but there were many strangers in the Mess and old friends were missed. Fanny and Dick had left a gap which was unfilled; they had been leaders not only in the air at the head of formations, first into the attack and making decisions of moment to those who followed them in complete confidence, but also leaders on the ground, in their flights, in the Mess and even further afield. While I missed them personally as my friends, the squadron, too, was missing their unquenchable high spirits and infectious energy, which had influenced all around them to think only of success, never of risk or failure. Yet, on the credit side, Wing Commander Braithwaite was still with us, a wise counsellor as CO, and Alec was still the squadron's servant as Adjutant, both holding the squadron together through its losses and contributing in the background in no small measure towards every success.

The vacancy caused by the loss of Fanny had been filled soon afterwards by the posting to the squadron of Jackie Fishwick, who will be remembered as one of the original six who had met that November morning at Leuchars years ago, complaining bitterly about their Fleet Air Arm postings. He had since served in the *Glorious* until the Navy took full control of the Air Arm, when he had become a flying instructor. However, I never saw him as a member of the squadron, for his tenure of command of the flight was short-lived; he arrived in February while I was in hospital and was missing from his first operation, a mine-laying sortie at night. Joe, too was lost a few weeks later, shot down, it was believed, by Messerschmitt 110's before he could reach cloud. He had been an Oxford double blue, playing rugger in the pack and also boxing; he was both a former pupil of mine in Training Unit and a member of my flight. I missed him dearly, and so did his white bull-terrier named "Dockitt", which used to lie curled up in a corner of the Flight Office while his master was flying; when Joe was overdue, the dog was bewildered, unable to understand that he would never return. Ken probably missed Joe more than anybody else, for they had been together since their entry into the service, and were inseparable friends. The squadron's face had changed in four months, but there still remained Ian, Jimmy, now very experienced and with a ship to his credit, and also Ken, who had been showing dash on his operations reminiscent of Dick's. Others too remained, less conspicuous, but nevertheless playing their part; the squadron was not the same, but it was still good to be back.

H-P had been posted away from the squadron just after Christmas, having completed over fifty operations; bravery had been recognized by a DFM and now steadiness was rewarded with a rest. A new scheme had just been introduced, setting a limit on the number of operational flights a pilot should undertake before being rested from the strain in some less hazardous work. H-P was the first in the squadron to reach the limit, and left us to instruct at a flying training school. This scheme was welcomed by all, for it gave some objective for a crew to aim at, a rest in sight at the end of good work in a squadron. I reflected that Dick would have been saved by this scheme, had it come into force earlier, but I knew that it was only now made possible by the increasing number of crews being trained both in England and by the Empire training scheme. Victor also had left, being posted to command the Training Unit from which I had struggled to escape. Somebody had to do the inconspicuous but valuable work of instructing the air-crews who would eventually fight in torpedo squadrons such as ours, and at least Victor had tested, while in the squadron, a little of the reality of operations on which to base instruction. In truth he was not reluctant to leave, since he was newly married; the luck of war was no respecter of sentiment, and, sadly, several of our pilots who were married, with wives living near the station, became casualties.

The squadron had also undergone some internal reorganization in my absence; the number of Flights was reduced from three to two, but the squadron was no smaller, for the size of the Flights was increased and they were no longer commanded by Flight Lieutenants but by Squadron Leaders. The post of Second-in-command of the squadron was abolished, so if the Wing Commander was away, the senior Flight Commander took charge. In this way our organization was brought into line with the Bomber Command squadrons, all of which were commanded by a Wing Commander, with two Squadron Leaders as Flight Commanders. The fact that a Squadron Leader does not command the squadron is confusing to outsiders, but is explained when one realizes that a flight today is often larger than a whole squadron in time past, and the squadron itself several times its former size.

My return to the squadron was timely, for on the very next day after my arrival my promotion to Squadron Leader was announced. This was an "automatic" promotion, based on time of service, for I had been a Flight Lieutenant exactly a year, and reading the promotion list I saw that what remained of my term at Cranwell had gone up in rank simultaneously. Promotion, which had been accelerated by the expansion, was now very rapid; in peace-time it might have taken twelve years to reach this rank, yet I was a Squadron Leader five years after leaving Cranwell. This was a pleasant surprise to find myself promoted so soon, although I would in any case have been granted acting rank for filling the Flight Commander's vacancy. A few weeks later came more good news, with the posting to the squadron of Eddie Culverwell, not only one of the original six who had joined the Fleet Air Arm at the same time, but a cadet at Cranwell with me and a fellow instructor at Gosport. He, too, was a newly promoted Squadron Leader, and came to command the other flight.

In these months we were often short of pilots; losses seemed to be exceeding the replacement rate, for the training of Beaufort pilots had only just started in earnest. In the same way as he had helped me to join the squadron, the Wing Commander would try and have others posted to us who were torpedo pilots and longing to escape from some dull job which might be done by another less valuable pilot. In this way Tony Gadd, an old friend from Torpedo Development Unit, came to my flight. He was a Flight Lieutenant, and in five years had dropped over a thousand experimental torpedoes; now he was anxious to see for himself what one would really do when dropped in anger.

In hospital I had learnt many good lessons from conversations with other pilots, and now I learnt even more during these weeks in which I ran my flight and watched the squadron operating without being able to take any part in the flying. There was ample time to read the Intelligence reports, talk to pilots after their operations, and form a picture of the changes which had occurred in my months of absence. It appeared that the game was becoming more difficult than ever, for Blenheim squadrons of Bomber Command had started extensive daylight operations in what we considered to be "our" area off the Dutch coast and Frisian Islands, and had stirred the enemy into taking considerable defensive measures.

Intelligence revealed that aerodromes near the seaboard all held fighter squadrons, Messerschmitt 109's or 110's, whose readiness had already been proved by Joe's loss and the near escapes of several others. John (of the balloon cable incident), to whom something untoward happened whenever he took to the air, if only for a circuit and landing on the aerodrome, had been chased by two Me 109's until they had exhausted their ammunition. On landing, his Beaufort had resembled a sieve, being riddled with countless holes, both from machine-gun bullets and cannon-shells; the navigator afterwards found no less than eight bullet holes in his clothing, yet was unscratched. It appeared that John had been trespassing near the coast without cloud cover, and he was lucky to return to tell his story. Nor was this interception an isolated case; fighters were being encountered more frequently, and several of our pilots returned from Rovers with their aircraft holed. There was evidence that the enemy was receiving very accurate warning of our approach to his coast, and it was suspected that he was using a system of radiolocation similar to our own. It seemed to me to be now of greater importance than ever to fly low, tactics which reduced the risk of detection by the new system no less than with the old method of sound location.

There was more enemy shipping at sea now, no doubt due to the disorganization of interior communications, canals, railways and roads, by the heavy raids of Bomber Command on such places as Cologne, Antwerp and Hamburg. By these the enemy were forced to make more use of coastal shipping, which with increased importance became better defended than ever; ships were now being found in strong convoys, invariably protected by large numbers of flak ships. The solitary large ship, which had formerly been our easy prey, was now never encountered in daylight. The squadron's successes were being achieved more and more by night, and recently both Jimmy and Ken, out on moonlight Rovers, had sunk good targets.

But the weather conditions required for these night operations were too limiting for them to become our sole occupation, for only on about ten nights in each month was the moonlight bright enough to make ships visible from the air, and of these ten moonlight nights several would be made useless by cloud or rain. However, we took every advantage which a moon period offered, and, with the increasing success of enemy fighters, moonlight Rovers began to supplant daylight attacks in our pilots' estimation. I was sorry to see this fall from favour of the daylight Rover, and wondered if it were not in fact due to the lack of leaders that our former success by day was not being achieved.

The very week of my return saw two more losses, both occurring on daylight Rovers, and it seemed that they came as a warning to me, as if to illustrate the changing scene of operations as I imagined it. One pilot was shot down by fighters, due, I think, to his ignoring the rules of cloud cover and wandering near the coast under a clear sky. The other, a newly arrived Squadron Leader who came to replace Fishy, was lost, like his predecessor, on his very first operation; the German news told us that he had been shot down by a mine-laying vessel. This was an incident to remind me of my own first sortie and a similar attack on a mine-layer from which I was lucky to return; they were always well-defended vessels and not really big enough to be a torpedo target. This loss seemed to me yet another case of a pilot new to operations failing to realize danger when it was near, for there were several points about it in common with Robby's fate. Fanny and Dick had held the fort for half a year, but their replacements were continuously unlucky, and successive Flight Commanders failed to last more than a few weeks, while all the time some of the squadron's younger pilots were making sortie after sortie unscathed. It was not until the summer that the Flight Commanders again came into some luck, and Tony and I, commanding the two flights, were able to see our number of operations pass the thirty mark without being separated.

More heartening were our successes, for in March, while I looked on from my Flight Office, unable to take part, the squadron sank nearly 17,000 tons of shipping. Ken sank two ships, one by day and another by night, and Jimmy also had two to his credit, both sunk on night sorties. On another occasion Ken had a field day; he dropped a torpedo at a ship in daylight, but missed; this did not seem to him to be a good reason for returning, so he roved on until he found another. This time he had nothing with which to attack the target except his guns, which he used to such advantage that the crew decided to take to the boats. Ken's observer took a magnificent photograph showing a boatload of frightened sailors pulling away from the ship which they had so lightly abandoned. Ken had then left the scene and soon found a gun emplacement on one of the islands, which he proceeded to spray with his front guns. He was so busy diving and zooming around the gun post that he quite failed to notice the arrival on the scene of two Messerschmitt 110's, who signified their presence by some accurate bursts into Ken's Beaufort, their bullets passing through the aircraft and breaking the pilot's windscreen! Ken just made cloud in time with the 110's hot on his tail, and thought it wise now to call the day's work complete. On reaching the aerodrome, he found that his hydraulic system had been shot away, and was forced to land ingloriously with his undercarriage retracted. Shades of Dick were in the Mess that night.

The night bombing operations, with which the squadron used to reinforce Bomber Command in attacks on coastal targets, were now becoming a thing of the past, for many new bomber squadrons had been formed, to make this diversion from our own work unnecessary, and we were left for the most part to our specialized anti-shipping operations. However, we did occasionally carry bombs on our shipping sorties, and although not so effective as a torpedo, they were popular with some pilots, for while a torpedo had to be brought back if no ships were found, bombs could be dropped on harbours or coastal aerodromes. But we were a torpedo squadron, and while "hit and run" bombing raids were a welcome change, most of us would willingly take a torpedo out on several sorties and bring it back without finding a target; the result of a hit after several barren operations always seemed worthwhile. To strike a ship below the waterline was for it to sink without a doubt, but to score a hit with a bomb was not always so effective.

Single aircraft or pairs now gave way to formations of three for our daylight sorties. This change was made partly to combat the fighter menace, for the fire power from the turrets of three Beauforts together offered each aircraft mutual protection against fighter attack. Also for three aircraft to attack a target simultaneously served to spread the defenders' fire and prevent it concentrating on a single aircraft, thus giving each pilot a better chance to aim his torpedo with the least possible distraction from flak. If the enemy was taking steps against us, so were we alive to the situation and still keeping a pace ahead of him. In fact, we were never driven from the daylight sky on his coastline, nor did a month pass without his ships being sunk. Our success could not be judged alone on the tonnage which we sank, for part of our role was to be a nuisance to the enemy, who, not knowing when or where we might strike next, had to keep immobilized many fighter squadrons on coastline and spare many guns for his ships, both of which he must have wished to employ actively elsewhere. Bomber Command, with its crushing raids on the interior of Germany, was making the enemy turn more and more to his ships for transporting the essentials of war, and we were making it both difficult and costly in effort for him to use his shipping routes.

It is only fair to mention that Blenheims of one of the Bomber Groups had been since the new year operating very extensively by daylight against shipping. They had been particularly active off the

Dutch coast, and, always using bombs, had great success in their attacks on shipping, indeed their work probably surpassed ours; we were only one squadron, while they were many. However, the presence of other aircraft operating in the area in daytime was in one way advantageous to us, for it resulted in many more sighting reports of shipping being received. Such sighting reports enabled us to send a force to attack a target in a specified position, which was far preferable to having to search for ships ourselves, for time spent within the enemy's sight and hearing was becoming increasingly perilous. Operating conditions were much changed since I left in November, and now I listened and learnt, knowing that I would soon be operating again, and then both my safety and success would depend on my ability to recognize the signposts on that uneasy road.

In the first week in April I returned to hospital, and the plaster of Paris was taken off my arm for good. The X-ray photographs showed that the fracture was firmly joined, and my doctor was at last satisfied. He told me that I could now start flying again, but not carry out flights of longer than two hours' duration; I was to return in six months' time, when, if the arm had made normal progress, I would be allowed to carry out operational flying again. My right arm would not be normal for another year, and the shoulder would always be weak, but apparently both would stand up to the strain of flying. I hardly thought of the real meaning of his words in my relief at feeling my arm completely free after being restricted for so long; the mention of flying obliterated any misgivings. After visiting my old ward, in which one or two of my contemporaries still remained, I hurried back to the squadron with the news that I could fly again.

But I returned to find an empty Mess with no one to hear my good news, for while I had been away these few days at hospital all the Squadron's serviceable aircraft and crews together with some maintenance personnel had been moved to St. Eval to carry out some special work. They were expected to be away only a few weeks, and I imagined that the operations would be similar to our raids on Lorient from the same aerodrome in the previous November. Meanwhile Alec and I were left in charge of what remained of the squadron, a few hundreds of airmen and the usual large number of aircraft under repair. Our work was to prepare aircraft to replace losses and crashes at St. Eval and generally to take all possible administration work off the Wing Commander's hands, for his energies would be taken up in directing operations and actually flying himself.

For five weeks the squadron was detached thus, using St. Eval as an advanced base for mine-laying operations by night and torpedo attacks by day in the Brest area. News of the squadron's work reached us through Operations Room, where reports were received of all operations carried out by our aircraft, and as usual this news reflected both success and failure. We heard that Tony had led an attack against destroyers, gaining a probable hit, but from this sortie one of the formation was missing, shot down by fighters. Tony himself had only just escaped when attacked by two Me 109s; his aircraft had been holed in several places and on his return to the aircraft he was compelled to land with his undercarriage up. A story of his nonchalance during the attack is still being told: "Yellow-nosed Messerschmitts coming up astern," his gunner shouted excitedly, to which Tony replied, "What colour did you say?" at the same time diving and turning towards the water. Tony was a beautiful handler of an aircraft, very steady and completely without imagination; in short, he had the qualities of an ideal wartime pilot, and in fact lasted out his time in the squadron. Eddie had led a second attack against the same target a few hours later, not a pleasant task, for he must have known fighters would be in the area and the destroyers ready for him. However, he manoeuvred his formation cleverly, and after launching his attack unmolested was able to lead the force of three Beauforts home intact.

The work at St. Eval was exacting and dangerous, with operations every night if the weather allowed and daylight attacks whenever a target was sighted. This was an unlucky period for the squadron, which lost four crews in these five weeks, among them Ian and Ken, both from my flight. Ian was missing from a mine-laying mission to a particularly well-defended harbour, and it was assumed he had been shot down. Ken had failed to return from a dawn torpedo attack on the *Scharnhorst* and *Gneisenau*, the two German battle-cruisers lying in Brest harbour. This appeared to me a suicidal operation, for Brest is notoriously well defended, and to enter its harbour in daylight was no less dangerous than flying into Bremerhaven, as Dick had done fatally. However, this was not a case of rashness but of courage, for the operation had been ordered; it was not a Rover but a definite "strike". Ken had been seen to go in to attack, and it was rumoured that before being shot down he had hit one of the targets. This was a fine show of determination and bravery, and one which we long hoped would be recognized by a posthumous decoration, for Ken had already done good work and completed some twenty operations; however, the months passed and nothing resulted from our hopes. Dick's successor in dash and fighting spirit had followed closely in his fate, remembered but undecorated.

While the squadron was away I was flying again regularly, and found that my long absence had not affected my judgement at all. My right arm was not as strong as I would have liked, nor had I yet full movement in it, but this did not restrict my flying in any way. I flew nearly every day, testing the aircraft which had been repaired in Maintenance Section, and sometimes delivering one to St. Eval, to bring back in its place another Beaufort requiring overhaul.

All our crews there were beginning to weary of the long absence from their own station and were longing to complete the work and return. The Wing Commander felt strongly the loss of his crews, and was carrying out many sorties himself, taking turns equally with other pilots. He was a pillar of strength to the squadron, which was now composed largely of young and inexperienced crews, and his personal influence was far reaching. Everyone trusted his judgement, which on all operational questions was unerring; his leadership was above all else sound yet unspectacular, and inspired confidence in us all. Alec's devotion to the squadron was equally effective in another sphere in gaining the confidence of the airmen, from whom he had a great following. These latter, whose work was no less essential to the squadron than the more attractive role of flying, are apt normally to be neglected, but Alec made every airman, from barrack room orderly to wireless mechanic, feel that a ship sunk by one of our pilots was partially his own success, which indeed it was. It was a very happy squadron despite the heavy losses and hazardous operations, and this contentment went hand in hand with the efforts of the Wing Commander and Alec in their different ways.

Before the squadron returned, a quite unexpected event occurred: Dick and Fanny were posthumously mentioned in despatches! It was good to know that, after all, our two Flight Commanders, who had done such sterling work, were not quite forgotten. Here was belatedly at least some of the praise which we felt to be their due now bestowed officially by the authorities. Their real worth would be revealed by a glance through the squadron's album of action photographs, which would show that the most excellent photographs obtained since the squadron started operating were taken on sorties carried out by these two pilots; indeed the album is something of a memorial to both of them. "Who on earth took that?" asks a new pilot in astonishment, not entirely unjustified, for the particular photograph shows a close-up view of the bow of some ship from which the name can easily be read. This was a memory of Paddy, and in that album are reminders of all three, Dick, Fanny and Paddy.

I contemplated night flying again not entirely without misgiving; it was never my first love in flying, but I knew that I would have to put in some practice before I could fly on night operations, and reluctantly decided to make a start. To go back to the beginning and learn all over again with dual instruction seemed unnecessary, for it was only practice that I needed, and so I started flying at dusk, making circuits and landings until it became quite dark. Not surprisingly I was super-careful, not intending to trust again to my good fortune to escape serious injury in a crash. After several nights of uneventful take-offs and steady landings I felt quite confident to operate again at night, although I still liked night flying no better than before: my preference was for day operations, for I was prepared to risk being seen by the enemy if I myself could see the sky around me and the earth beneath. After months in hospital from a night flying crash, the darkness of night appeared to me a fickle two-edged sword, shielding an aircraft from the enemy but luring it into other dangers.

At the end of April the squadron returned from St. Eval to its base, after five weeks of continuous and hazardous operations; four crews had been lost and several Beauforts wrecked in crashes while landing at night, fortunately without injuring the crews. Night landings were always to claim an occasional casualty in aircraft, but such crashes rarely amounted to more than a Beaufort running through the aero-drome boundary or breaking its undercarriage after a giant bounce; serious errors such as mine or the Wing Commander's were rare. At morning tea for several days after their return pilots talked of their experiences, narrow escapes and good luck, the differences of operating in a strange area, the flak and searchlights at Brest, the bad luck of the missing crews and their own gladness to be back in the squadron's own hangars and offices which were its home; the five weeks at St. Eval had been a hard time, which was now over. Hearing these stories, I felt I had missed a chapter of the squadron's history and longed more than ever to rid myself of the role of spectator.

However, the time was drawing near when I should be allowed to operate once more, to have me counting first the weeks, then, as May progressed, the days before I should return to hospital and hear the long-waited decision that my arm was strong enough to stand up to long flights and operations. With the last week of May the great day came, and in excited anticipation, stimulated by the idle flying of the last few weeks, I set out for the hospital, returning happy that evening with the news that my arm was completely mended and that I could start fighting at last.

My first operation after the crash very nearly took the form of an attack on a battleship! When the German battleship *Bismarck* was sighted one day at the end of May lying in a Norwegian fjord, there were indications that she was going to make for open sea; the presence of tankers and supply ships, which were seen alongside her, pointed to preparations for a long voyage. It was assumed she would make for the Atlantic to prey upon our shipping there and generally create a diversion to our forces, but there was only one channel of escape open to her, through the Denmark straits between the North of Scotland and Iceland.

To combat this menace to our Atlantic convoys, two air forces were needed—a reconnaissance force to find and shadow her, and a striking force to cripple her, reduce her speed and allow her to be caught and finished off by our heavy naval forces. Naturally, our squadron was chosen as the spearhead of the striking force; operations against warships were the real reason for its existence, and only the complete absence of German naval craft within our range had caused us to specialize in attacks on merchant shipping. The torpedo was the ideal weapon with which to strike at a battleship, which was assumed at this time to be unsinkable by bombs and only capable of being severely damaged by hits beneath the waterline. We were always waiting to attack such a target, so when it was known that the *Bismarck* might be at sea, enthusiasm in the squadron rose high.

We went north at short notice, to Wick, an aerodrome almost within sight of John o' Groat's, twelve Beauforts strong, led by the Wing Commander with Eddie, Tony and I leading sections of three; spare aircraft were to follow later as reserves. In Operations Room at Wick I saw the original reconnaissance photograph, a bird's-eye view, taken from many thousands of feet, which showed the *Bismarck* in its hiding-place, attended by several smaller vessels. This photograph was taken from one of the long-range Spitfires belonging to a unit specializing in such work. This was a "PRU" (Photographic Reconnaissance Unit), whose pilots do amazing work, flying at great heights to the interior of Germany and Italy, or covering many miles of every occupied territory. Nothing is hidden from the eyes of PRUs; the cameras on their aircraft record indelibly vital information. Watching the movements of shipping, the building of aerodromes or fortifications, or the results of bombing raids, are but a few of their varied activities. The pilots usually fly at great heights in special single-seater aircraft, bringing back from their sorties not stories of enemy aircraft shot down or targets destroyed, but clear invaluable photographs of enemy territory and reconnaissance reports of inestimable importance. This photograph of the *Bismarck* had been obtained casually on the return from a flight with quite a different objective; a strange ship had been seen below, a mere speck on the sheltered Norwegian waters, but it had appeared suspicious to the pilot, so he photographed it as a matter of course. It was this photograph which, when printed and expertly analysed, revealed the presence of the *Bismarck* and started the train of preparations which led to its eventual destruction after a wild dash for the freedom of the Atlantic.

On arrival at Wick, half our force was ordered to move again, this time further north still, to Iceland, so the Wing Commander and Eddie took their two sections over the long stretch of sea to the RAF Aerodrome at Kaldarharnes, leaving Tony and me with our six Beauforts at Wick. In this way our force was ideally disposed to guard the straits, with six Beauforts on either side, each half forming the jaws of a nut-cracker ready to close on the target which must pass between them. Excitement among the crews was high, for it seemed certain that the long-awaited chance for the squadron to attack a battleship would now be presented. Operations Room was visited hourly, and the question on every pilot's lips was: "Has she moved yet?"

However, we had reckoned without the weather. Just as cloud was our cover from fighters, so was bad weather the *Bismarck's* protection from aerial reconnaissance and attack. Three days of low cloud, mist and rain followed upon our arrival, making it impossible for the battle-ship to be watched from the air; aircraft could not take off from their aerodromes nor could they have flown in the weather prevailing in the North Sea and on the Norwegian coast; naval forces were also similarly restricted by the appalling weather. The situation, which had appeared to be well in hand, with the ship being watched from the air day and night as she lay in hiding, now became critical. As day succeeded day with no break in the weather, it seemed certain that the *Bismarck* would take advantage of the conditions to escape from our grasp and soon become lost in the vastness of an open sea. When the three days of unsummer weather had passed, the fjord was at once found to be empty, and the chase began. Three days' steaming was a good start, and would take the *Bismarck* almost out of range of most shore-based reconnaissance aircraft, certainly out of range of our Beauforts. Reconnaissance aircraft of Coastal Command searched like telescopic eyes over hundreds of miles of ocean, until the crew of a Catalina flying boat picked up the quarry when it had almost escaped from aircraft range into comparative safety.

Although many hundreds of miles out of range of our waiting Beauforts, she was yet to meet her fate at the hands of torpedo-dropping aircraft. The Navy had its aircraft carriers in waiting, and flew off squadrons of Swordfish to attack the *Bismarck*. These aircraft, which I knew so well, were flown by some pilots who were contemporaries of mine in the Fleet Air Arm and others who had been our pupils in Training Unit. Their attacks, in the face of very accurate gunfire, were beyond praise, and a hit was made on the stern, reducing the battleship's speed sufficiently to allow our naval craft to finish off the task with more torpedoes and gunfire. So ended an epic hunt, starting in Norway and ending in the Atlantic some hundreds of miles west of Lands End. The nails in the *Bismarck's* coffin were the all-seeing eyes of the Photographic aircraft, the wide network of Coastal Command's reconnaissance, and finally the sure aim of a single Fleet Air Arm torpedo.

So our force returned to its base, feeling somewhat cheated of its prey but having enjoyed a change of scenery and air. I myself was sorry to have missed the few days in Iceland and also disappointed at the escape of the target which had at first seemed so certain to come within striking distance. The Iceland party brought back vivid stories of the grandeur of the scenery and the strangeness of flying over great wastes of glacial country; there is always a view from the air, and it is often an inspiring one, but I felt no sight could be more impressive than the great battleship ploughing its way through rain and heavy seas beneath low clouds, a sight which had been denied us. Later I met one of the Swordfish pilots who had taken part in the successful attack. The ship, he said, had opened fire when the attackers were several miles away, and they had flown in under continuous fire to drop their torpedoes against what appeared a giant firework of blazing gunfire. His leader's aircraft had been hit at four miles' range, losing a wing tip, yet continued as if nothing had happened. I knew well how slow the faithful Swordfish were, and could imagine the suspense of their pilots as the target was approached, when time must have seemed to be standing still. Theirs was a great achievement, and their success may become a portent of the growing ascendancy of the air over the sea, aircraft over ships.

CHAPTER XIV

NORTH SEA AND CHANNEL

MY return to operations was signalized by a week of engaging and diverse operations which were among the most successful I ever undertook, and certainly no flying week before or since had been so full of incident. All were my favourite daylight "strikes", and on each occasion I was leading formations of three or more Beauforts, a circumstance which never failed to instil in me the confidence of strength in numbers, the feeling of being in the company of friends when amongst enemies. Not always were weather conditions ideal, nor were any of these sorties straightforward and lacking in danger, but luck, personified by my watching panda, back in the air after its long retirement, was again with me. This June week saw a lightning start to my new lease of fighting life; all the energies stored up in six months of enforced absence from operations were unleashed equally on the destruction of the enemy and the solution of the problems it involved. I was aching with a desire for activity after weeks spent in watching pilots set out and listening to their stories on their return, stories inflaming my desire no longer to be a spectator, but a participator in the fight that was raging all around me. In the last weeks I had been unable to do more than run my flight, test an occasional Beaufort or help in organizing the sorties on which other pilots set out. Now at last I was to set out myself, not the ignorant beginner of my first operation, to be caught unawares by a simple enemy trap, but armed with hard-earned and somewhat bitter experience and forewarned by a knowledge of fighting conditions drawn from all I had heard and read during these weeks of inactivity. I was straining to escape from my cage and hunt.

My observer, Steve, who had been wounded while flying with me over Lorient, was now completely recovered and in my crew once more. He had escaped my crash through himself being in hospital at the time, recovering from his shrapnel wound; now he was again my navigator, to remain with me until I left the squadron at the end of the year. Also flying with me again was Jim, the lucky wireless operator with the habit of walking away unscathed from crashes; I would not have liked to do without his excellent operating of the wireless or lose the only member of my original crew. Surprisingly, he still appeared to have confidence in my flying, and neither he nor Steve wanted a change of pilot, although they would have been quite justified in seeking a more reliable "driver", since my past performances had hardly been inspiring. My air-gunner, Flight Sergeant Bill Pierce, was a newcomer, a cheerful and good marksman, a quality that was to prove his worth in some later combats with fighters.

These three remained with me as my crew until the end, flying with me on every operation except one, never failing me; it is to them, who supported me in the air, and the ground staff who prepared my aircraft on the ground, that I owe very much. They were great companions in the air, Steve busy with chart, pencil and dividers, Jim tapping out messages, and Bill scanning the sky for sign of an enemy fighter; all conspired to help me fly out to the target and return safely: I just flew the aircraft, always completely dependent on them, and always my confidence was justified. How lucky I was to have them with me. In my first twelve operations I had lost three observers and two air-gunners, either wounded in action or injured in the crash; now through double that number of operations and in more exacting circumstances I did not lose another member of my crew. Wisdom had been learnt in those intervening six months of discomfort and impatience; perhaps it was not attainable in any other way. Certainly after my return I was more successful, steadier, with less rashness and greater reliability than before. If I admired Dick and Fanny, personifications of dash and bravery, no less in my estimation were H-P and Jimmy, who still lived on as examples of steadiness rewarded. Perhaps the squadron benefited equally from both types, for we always had at least one daring pilot and one eminently steady operator among other less outstanding but nevertheless invaluable pilots, the rank and file of the squadron.

This first sortie was a straightforward daylight Rover, on which I was the leader of a formation of three, the other two pilots being Dougie Attewell, who was a newcomer to the squadron and on his first operation, and a sergeant pilot, a wild Irishman always longing to come to closer grips with the enemy in spite of the twenty operations behind him. Since our load was bombs, I fully intended to attack a coastal target if no shipping was found, and had several of the smaller Dutch harbours in mind as our secondary objective. Flying out over the familiar North Sea with a Beaufort on either side, it seemed as if I had never ceased operations and that my six months of absence were but the few days between sorties. My experience of that very first operation was still with me, unforgotten, and my last view of the enemy coast, the forest of masts that was a convoy, and the sinking ship, all were still bright in my memory.

Ample cloud cover had been promised by the Met Officer, but perversely, as we neared the enemy coast, there was no sign of cloud in an open sky, conditions in which I might well have turned back there and then. I was unwilling to risk my formation by continuing to the coast under a clear sky, yet at the same time reluctant to throw away the opportunity which I had awaited so long of striking my first blow at the enemy. I decided to compromise, and, turning, flew parallel to the coastline at a safe distance of twenty miles out, running low over the water on a westerly course, just out of sight of the low land which lay beyond the horizon. I was searching now not for ships but for cloud, and flew thus from the Frisian Islands right into the English Channel before a layer of stratus cloud appeared ahead to justify my decision to remain roving.

Then I forsook our usual tactics and left the surface of the water, climbing through the thin layer of cloud to fly along above its feathery ceiling, southwards, towards the French coast. The cloud-base was some 2000 feet high, too far from the surface to be reached in the event of fighter attack, but in order to continue I was prepared to risk detection by radar, which flying high involved. However, I was now intent on attacking not shipping but one of the Belgian or Dutch harbours on which bombs could be dropped from just beneath the safety of the cloud-layer. I knew these tactics were unorthodox, but I based them on reasoning, and from every angle the project seemed fairly sound. Cloud passed beneath our propellers like grass under the blades of a mower; our three Beauforts hugged the level cloud-ceiling as if it had been the customary sea over which they flew; to be near cloud was to be quite safe, and the cloud persisted.

Through a tiny gap my observer caught a glimpse of the French coast near Dunkirk, at which we turned, running parallel to the coastline on a north-easterly course. Seeing the Kursaal and bathing-beaches of Ostend through another convenient break in the cloud, I was half inclined to dive through and attack the harbour there, but before I could see any shipping the gap closed, making the decision for me to continue further up the coast.

For some time afterwards nothing was visible below but fleecy white cloud over which we skimmed, until I caught sight through parting cloud of the harbour and famous mole of Zeebrugge, where several ships could be seen moored alongside. This was the opportunity I had hoped for, a lucky gap in the cloud with a target beneath, and rocking my Beaufort wings in the familiar signal for the formation to attack, I turned without further ado and dived straight through the closing gap towards the harbour. Although we had been flying high, the defences did not seem ready for the attack, and as, one after the other, we broke cloud diving steeply at the mole, few guns barked to greet us. Opening my bomb doors during the dive, I turned slightly to bring the aircraft on aim at a fair-sized ship, which appeared to be unloading; then, with 1000 feet indicated on the altimeter, I pressed the bomb release, letting fly a stick of six bombs, afterwards turning quickly to climb away towards the cloud with the speed I had gained in the dive. It was all done in a flash; the sight of the target, the dive, with 200 then 300 knots reading on the airspeed indicator, the release of the bombs, followed by a steep climb away, it was all over in, perhaps, twenty seconds. The guns, rudely awakened by bombs bursting around them, fired wildly as we climbed away from the attack, one after another, for the following aircraft had been close behind me in the dive, releasing their bombs within a few seconds of mine, an excellent piece of flying on the part of their two pilots. Just as we were gaining cloud, Bill, from the turret, told me that he could see fighters approaching from a distance, so, taking no risks, I used cloud cover for the first time, flying hidden in its safety for ten minutes, until I knew the menace from fighters must have passed.

After the attack, the formation had become separated in the cloud, but, by a previous arrangement for this happening, each pilot returned independently, and we found ourselves together again on the aerodrome circuit of our base. As I taxied up to the hangar, the Wing Commander was on the tarmac to welcome me back after my first operation since my return, and was delighted with the news of our attack. The other crews also seemed enthusiastic over this unusual but effective operation, talking excitedly as they all crowded into the Intelligence Office to piece together the full story. Bombs had been seen to burst all around the target, but no one had waited behind to see the actual damage on account of the danger from fighters and the flak coming up from the well-defended mole and harbour. The presence of fighters, suggested by my airgunner, was confirmed by the other gunners, one of whom claimed he had seen an enemy fighter shot down by their own AA fire. An unlikely but not impossible happening. It appeared that, after all, we had not taken the enemy unawares and a force of fighters was in the air and ready for us in case we should come out into open sky. Considering how unpromising the weather had been, the day was a success, with three loads of bombs deposited on a worthwhile target at some annoyance to the enemy and great pleasure to ourselves. I felt good to have my first operation behind me, to have seen flak again and to know that I was no longer a passenger in the squadron but once more a leader, taking my place in a direct line of leaders.

In the midst of the celebrations that evening a message was received for six of our aircraft to move to Scotland for some special work, and at first light next morning six Beauforts were forming up over the aerodrome to fly northwards, while I lay peacefully in bed. This formation was led by Eddie, who commanded the other flight, for we took it in turns between the flights to go on these detachments. It transpired later in the day that the pocket battleship *Lützow* was believed to be at sea off Norway and our force was to search that night in an effort to intercept her. It seemed to me essential for this to be a night operation, for the *Lützow* could proceed down the Norwegian coast by day under a strong escort of its own fighters while safely out of reach of ours, and the only chance to attack her was under cover of night.

Word came the next morning that she had been hit by a torpedo during the night, but the successful pilot belonged not to us but to another Beaufort squadron, based on an aerodrome in Scotland and also taking part in the search. A big force had been out that night, for the target was a rare and important one. The ship had last been sighted off the south coast of Norway limping slowly for harbour, which was thought most likely to be Kristiansand, and although hit and crippled she was known to be still afloat. As I sat at breakfast wondering how our pilots had fared during the night, an order came for three of our Beauforts to take off immediately to try and attack the *Lützow* with torpedoes before she reached harbour. This mission appeared extremely hazardous, since the damaged pocket battleship would inevitably have a fighter "umbrella" and be otherwise well protected by surface craft, destroyers or E boats; also, after the night attack, she would certainly expect further attention. However, if the mission was dangerous it was no less attractive, for the *Lützow* was a target of importance which could not be allowed to pass out of our range unmolested.

Again I found myself crossing the North Sea, this time not eastwards towards the familiar Frisian Islands, but on a more northerly course to the Skaggerak, the stretch of sea between Norway and Denmark. On one side of me was Jimmy, who had recently been awarded the DFC and was now the most experienced pilot in the squadron, with fifty operations to his credit; on the other side flew another Ian, on his first operation. New crews were continually joining the squadron to take the place of those we lost, and on almost every sortie some new pilot would set out on his first operation and the long journey through operations to the promised period of rest. All our newcomers were full of fighting spirit and aggressive to strike their first blow after long months spent in training and waiting for the day when they should first set out. Above all, new crews were always optimistic of their chances of success, despite the knowledge that they might be replacing a crew of some experience, lost perhaps after many operations, lost perhaps inexplicably after months of success and good luck. Not one took off on a mission with a faint thought flickering in his mind that he would not come back; confidence in their own ability banished any such thought from the minds of these fresh new crews. That luck might play a part and turn against them, that the hazards of warfare might be too great to overcome, that the enemy might outwit and outgun them was unthinkable; yet few crews reached that prescribed limit of operations to retire to their well-earned rest, somehow they were always claimed, often dearly missed, yet always replaced. Always there came replacement crews, ready to take up the sword. And now on one side of me was Jimmy, about to leave the squadron after a run through a year of operations, and on the other Ian, just starting his time, and sadly not destined to last as Jimmy had; few did.

To the Skaggerak was a long flight; one hour passed and yet another, with lonely sea stretching all around to the horizons without sight of land. At intervals Steve would hand me a message slip with a small change of course to steer, due to some change of wind which he had calculated; on such a long flight it was essential for navigation to be accurate. After two hours' flying we were four hundred miles from the English coast with still another half-hour before us to reach our destination; only the cold North Sea intervened between us and home, making me thankful for the monotonous beat of the engines and steady readings of their gauges on the instrument panel, a message which told me all was well, as engine failure here would mean a watery end for pilot and crew.

Towards the end of this last half-hour my observer told me to expect the Norwegian coast to appear ahead and on the port side, a warning which had me looking questioningly at the sky, in which there was all too little cloud amidst wide stretches of clear blue; it was a lovely June day whose sky offered us little cover. I flew, as usual, low over the water, wanting to remain unseen and undetected by radar, while gradually the line on the horizon became visible as the grey of Norwegian cliffs, backed by lighter coloured mountains and ringed by the white of surf. We searched eastwards, flying at some ten miles out from this hostile coast, feeling very vulnerable and far from home, and trying to bury ourselves from sight in the slight swell which prevailed in an otherwise flat sea.

Finding no sign of the target on this part of the Norwegian coast, we made further south and eastwards to the Danish coast, where the cliffs towered out of the water in great headlands, and green hills rolled into the interior. Thus we crossed and recrossed the stretch of water between the two countries, each time progressing further and further within the straits, each time becoming more enmeshed in the net of enemy defences. Ahead I could see the town of Kristiansand quite plainly, with snow capped mountains rising in the background, while the Danish cliffs and headlands were still visible behind me, and yet there was no trace of the *Lützow* within our sight, which was unlimited to the straight horizon of sea or boundaries of coastline. We flew thus for a whole hour searching the Skaggerak, right within the very jaws of the enemy—the most uncomfortable hour's flying I have ever spent. There was no cloud above, over four hundred miles separating us from friends, and enemy fighter aerodromes on either side of us with squadrons at readiness to pounce on hapless intruders: yet strangely we went unopposed. Just as I was about to make a decision to turn for home, a decision which would shortly have been forced on me by our diminishing petrol, we ran into a fleet of mine-sweepers, sweeping across the straits in line abreast. Sighting us before I could make a detour to avoid them, they immediately started flashing morse to the shore, a message which I knew reported our presence and a warning to me that it was time to run for home.

Some more accurate navigation by Steve brought the formation straight over the aerodrome which we had left six hours before, and my longest operational flight was at an end. Not one of us was sorry it was over, for we knew that we had been playing with fire and had been lucky to escape the penalty. Jimmy's demeanour I particularly admired, for with his experience he knew the risks we ran even better than I did, and to make the flight more agonizing, he knew beforehand that it was to be his last before reaching the limit. We joked together about little incidents of the flight afterwards, as he told me how often his gunner had warned him of the approach of mythical fighters and how he himself had sighted the target several times, only to find it was in his imagination. The flight must have been torture to him, yet he had followed unhesitatingly and several times I had caught his encouraging smile from his Beaufort's cockpit: Jimmy was a real trouper, whose help on the night of my crash I never forgot. Very soon afterwards he left the squadron to take his deserved rest from operations as an instructor, one of the very few to run the gauntlet. It was a victory of good generalship, assisted by the essential of good luck.

I myself realized that this mission was the most dangerous I had yet undertaken, and the hour spent searching the Skaggerak within sight of two hostile coastlines had been one of great tension. My crew and I were continually searching the sky above us for fighters and the horizon all around for sign of our target, incredulous at our continued safety and expecting it to be rudely shattered at any minute. Although no flak was fired at us, no fighters seen, no target was found nor an attack made, yet of all my operations, before and afterwards, this was the most arduous; the difficulty of interpreting my elastic instructions, which were to try and find the target without taking undue risk, had added to my responsibility for the other two aircraft which followed me. As I stood on the tarmac stretching cramped arms and legs and watching Jimmy and Ian landing, I felt that if Luck never flew with me again, it had that day been with me, and indispensable.

The evening, however, was crowned not by celebration of our escape and tales of new lands, but with some bad news; if I had that day been under the eye of good fortune, bad luck had dogged Eddie the previous night. He had taken off in darkness at the same time as our other aircraft on a search of the Norwegian coast for the *Lützow*, only to find after a few minutes in the air that the turret of his aircraft was jammed and useless. Returning to the aerodrome he landed, changed to a reserve aircraft, and taking off an hour later was never seen or heard of again. Our other pilots, returning to North Coates the next day, told me that the weather had been good on the enemy coast that night, with a bright moon, but night fighters had been seen near the target. No one could tell what befell Eddie, who was experienced in operations and a very careful pilot, yet, whatever the cause of the loss, it was to me another friend missing, an old friend who had occupied a room next to mine at Cranwell, joined the Fleet Air Arm at the same time, bewailing with me our mutual bad luck. Together we had instructed in Training Unit in peace-time and struggled to escape to a squadron when war came; like Dick, Ian and so many others who became casualties, he was married only a few months before. This loss was just another case of "bad luck"; what else would you call it?

Our visit to the Skaggerak took place on a Sunday, the date I now read in my log book as June 13th, a figure that escaped my notice at the time. At any rate it was the date on which the Wing Commander was due to go on leave, but with typical concern for his crews he had waited in Operations Room until a wireless message told him we were safely on our way home, and then left on the week's leave which he had long been looking forward to. He believed in leave as a tonic for himself no less than for us, and indeed he needed rest after nights in Operations Room spent waiting, nearly always worriedly, for the return of his aircraft, and full days spent in organizing operations and administering his squadron of five hundred men and twenty complex aircraft. I myself had not taken leave since returning to flying, as I felt I had a long rest behind me and should now do all I could to make up for lost time, but my crew could not be expected to forgo their leave, and now went away for three days. If I wanted to fly in their absence I proposed to borrow a crew, but since I was temporarily CO I expected to find my time fully occupied in the office.

But when Tuesday came promising good cloud cover, I could not resist leading a Rover myself, and obtaining Group's permission to send three aircraft, I set out once more over the North Sea, eastwards, a Beaufort on either side of me and a crew borrowed from another pilot at their posts in my aircraft. With the enemy coast due to come in sight within a few minutes, cloud was again noticeably absent; scanning the sky and remembering that perseverance had found cloud on my last Rover, I set off southwards, flying again a safe distance from the coast. Sure enough cloud was found, and in abundance, a great grey sky under which we flew in to make a landfall near Amsterdam, where we turned and commenced a run northwards. Cover continued along the flat Dutch coast as we passed within sight of Ymuiden and then Den Helder, which I had explored intimately with Dick. Now I gave it a wide berth and passed some ten miles out to sea, for although the cloud appeared adequate I did not feel free to stir up trouble in waters too shallow for the torpedoes we carried.

We flew thus along over a hundred miles of coastline well within sight of towns and beaches, yet were not intercepted, a fact which illustrates that three Beauforts flying low over the water are invisible and inaudible to a casual watcher only a few miles away. Passing the island of Borkum, I was reminded suddenly of that last day in November by Jim, who pointed excitedly to a wreck far away near the shore; it was "my" ship! There it still lay, with masts and funnel projecting above the waterline, and waves lapping over the hatches, looking exactly as in the photographs which Paddy had shown me in hospital. Now I would have liked to go closer and examine my trophy, but to do so was hardly justifiable; from where we were flying, any shipping between us and the coast could be seen easily and it was pointless to stir up trouble for sentiment's sake. I was doing my best to stifle any rashness and substitute careful calculation, and that now told me to keep clear of the coast and concentrate on the shipping route.

However, my calculations did not allow for the presence of a convoy on our seaward side; ships were expected to be steaming between our formation and the coast, for they rarely came into open sea, and it was this small ribbon of water that my observer and I had been scanning throughout the flight, hardly giving any attention to the wide stretch of sea on our other side. Happening to take my eyes off the Texel coast and glance seawards, I was amazed to find we were nearly abreast of a small convoy which was proceeding placidly on its way, apparently equally ignorant of our presence. If surprise was to be achieved, there was no time to lose, and quickly signalling to my followers to spread for an attack, I turned in towards a ship of about 6000 tons steaming at the head of the convoy. It was for the other pilots to decide whether to share a target with me or select their own, and favouring the latter choice they made for their own ships somewhere in the middle of the convoy.

This attack from the landward side probably came as a complete surprise to the line of ships, whose look-out would be directed seawards and whose guns would also be pointing in the same direction, the one from which an attack would normally be expected; coming from the land we may have been thought friendly or not noticed until too late, and these tactics of approach, which I had found by accident, I remembered for another day. Not until I was within torpedo range of my target did tracer from a single flak ship flanking the convoy start halfheartedly to draw lines across the sky, and I was able to aim my torpedo from much closer range than was usually possible, turning away from the attack without the characteristic barrage of fire which I expected. Only when I was nearing the safety of extreme range did the flak commence in earnest; we had achieved the sort of surprise a torpedo pilot dreams about.

This was my borrowed crew's first operation, and a memorable one for all of us, for while I was dodging the black puffs of flak which pursued us rather inaccurately, my gunner shouted inarticulately something about an explosion. Now well out of range of gunfire, I manoeuvred the aircraft to give myself a view of the leading ship completely stationary, with a column of black smoke issuing from its deck, the result of a hit amidships. This was an exciting result of an attack which had taken only a few seconds from sighting the target to dropping the torpedo; the hit confirmed beyond doubt what I had always known, that short range of drop is the key to success in a torpedo attack, and only by taking the target by surprise could that desirable short range be achieved. Often we dropped torpedoes, but rarely in the ideal conditions I had experienced in the attack, more usually in a blaze of fire from all sides, from which the pilot felt enmeshed in a network of shells, a position hardly conducive to careful deliberate aiming at the correct low height and slow speed.

As I had a camera in the aircraft, I decided to climb up beneath the cloud-layer, where, out of range of gunfire and safe from fighters, my observer could take some photographs of the burning ship, now almost obscured by smoke. This climb was a revelation to me; the cloud-base, which from the surface of the water had appeared to be 1000 feet high, was not reached until more than 3000 feet was showing on the altimeter. Had fighters appeared, we could never have gained the shelter of such remote cover before falling victims to their greater speed and heavy armament. After this experience I always remembered that the precise height of cloud is difficult to judge from an aircraft flying at sea-level; henceforward when out roving I was continually appraising the cloud above me for its value as cover, and when on a later operation I actually met Me 109s for the first time, I did not find my cloud cover lacking.

Unfortunately my observer could not get the camera to work, and after hovering under the cloud-layer for several minutes I had to turn unwillingly for home without the coveted photograph of a sinking ship. Yet in my memory I carry a clear picture, a view from an unwonted height of the little convoy below, with all its ships stationary around one stricken ship, from which a smoke-trail ascended into the grey sky, and in the background extended the seemingly innocuous green of the Dutch Islands so rarely seen thus so far below, yet so close. I might have gazed longer on the scene had I known I should not see success again that year.

From such operations pilots usually returned independently of their leader, since, once broken up for the attack, aircraft became separated and seldom rejoined, so on reaching our base I was not at all disturbed to find the other two aircraft had not yet returned. I had seen no results of their attacks, nor indeed any sign of them afterwards as I circled trying to take photographs, and I assumed that they had rightly made straight for home without remaining longer than necessary near the scene of the attack.

While telling my story to the Intelligence Officer news came to Operations Room that one of the aircraft had landed safely on the aerodrome, and a few minutes later the pilot came in with his report. He had taken a target in the middle of the line, which he had just missed, for the torpedo's track had been easily visible on the surface, passing only a few feet ahead of its objective. He had seen me attacking at the front of the convoy, and thought that the other pilot had made for the rearmost ship. I still felt no anxiety for the aircraft which had yet to return, for frequently when formations were split up in an attack, half an hour or more separated aircraft on their return; that it had not been seen was no cause for alarm, for during an attack each crew concentrates on its own affairs and contact with other aircraft is usually lost.

Yet time passed without news of the third aircraft, inexplicably overdue, and with the slow passing of hours the Beaufort's endurance was exceeded, for it to be posted on the board as missing. What had caused this loss was beyond the realm of conjecture; fighters had not been seen and the flak had been the lightest imaginable. The only solution was that an unlucky hit had done its work, for the pilot was experienced and very reliable. Sitting in Operations Room waiting, at first confidently, then anxiously, for news, thinking each time the telephone rang that we should hear the aircraft was safe, talking for hour after hour about trivialities with the Controller, I realized for the first time the Wing Commander's responsibility; he did this every day of the week, so small wonder that he needed leave. This was the first and only aircraft lost from among those which followed me on all my operations, and the only one lost during the several periods when I was deputizing for the Wing Commander in his absence; it was a loss which I had been powerless to avoid. Nevertheless, the fact remained that a crew had been lost while I was leading, and although a ship had been hit, the day's success was turned into something of a failure.

I was given little time to ponder on this strange loss and hazard explanations, for we were on the move again that very evening. Just as I was sitting down to tea, which was very welcome since I had again missed lunch, I was called to the telephone; six Beauforts were to move immediately to Thorney Island, an aerodrome in Hampshire, with the possibility of being ordered to St. Eval the next day. With only a few hours to prepare the aircraft, pack a few clothes and reach our destination before dark, the squadron was stirred into a turmoil of activity, with the result that the six Beauforts reached Thorney Island just before eleven o'clock that evening, when the last rays of daylight were fading and the aerodrome surface just distinguishable without the use of a flare path or floodlight. Each aircraft was packed tight with all the paraphernalia of a move, its crew of four, airmen and their tools, suitcases, our parachutes, and not least important, mascot. We were ready for unknown work and an indefinite stay.

Always we were moving north to operate from Scottish aerodromes on the Norwegian coast, south to attack shipping creeping down the Channel, or west to the familiar Cornwall and Brest peninsula. We never knew when we might move or how long we should be away; there was no permanency at our base, for no sooner were we settled than a move would be ordered, usually unexpectedly and at short notice, to have crews tumbling clothes into suitcases, baggage into their aircraft, and flying away northwards or westwards. We complained loudly and bitterly, but at heart we loved it. Other Beaufort squadrons were in existence and more were forming, but we were the original squadron and proud of our record. At this time we were the experts in torpedo attacks on shipping, the squadron to be called upon for every and any special anti-shipping operation wherever it might be, off Iceland or in the Bay of Biscay; an enemy battleship stirring in some harbour, expected to run for open sea; some destroyers sighted or perhaps some special mining operation in well-defended waters; very often a false alarm, but whatever the reason, we moved. Sometimes a small force, three Beauforts to look for shipping, sometimes larger, twelve to intercept a battleship; very often the threat which we had moved to forestall failed eventually to materialize, and our aircraft would return to their base without having operated. Normally, however, we sought action, and wherever we went, if the original target failed to appear, we tried to find other work; "Can we search?" we asked when the weather was suitable, and three of us would take off to fly along strange coastlines on a quest for shipping. The squadron owns wrecks off Norway, wrecks in the Channel and wrecks off the west coast of France; how the enemy must have hated the three Beauforts which might appear anywhere on his coastline, flying always in bad weather; we must have been the menace to his ships on cloudy days that his fighters were to us in a clear sky.

At this time there was always some activity in the squadron to keep hands busy and minds occupied, always something new to prevent pondering over losses, risks or ill luck. The inflexible leave scheme kept up a stream of continual comings and goings; always some crew was going on leave or returning fresh from the change of atmosphere which brought with it forgetfulness and strength. The squadron was never static in these days, always in a healthy state of flux. Torpedoes were loaded and operations minutely prepared; pilots went out on sorties, attacked targets and returned with their reports; ships were sunk, others missed. Crews were lost, new crews came in their place, aircraft crashed and new aircraft were delivered to replace them. The only brake on our wheel of activity was the supply of serviceable aircraft, and when all else was still there remained always the endless struggle in workshops through day and night, the struggle to supply us with faultless aircraft to maintain the inspired offensive and keep our forces strong in numbers, ready to answer any call.

Reporting at Operations Room I was told we were not required to operate that night, news which I received thankfully, for it had been a full day in which a Rover had been organized, a ship hit and probably sunk, an aircraft and crew lost, and finally six aircraft had moved and were now ready to operate. I had decided to lead the detachment myself, partly because six Beauforts were the greater part of our serviceable aircraft and I did not want to remain behind commanding the static part of the squadron, partly because I was unwilling to be left out of the fast current of operations in which I had just begun to swim. I had no hesitation in leaving the squadron, for it would be safe in Alec's hands, and I felt that flying was the first consideration, with office work well able to wait until quieter times. But I was tired after nearly six hours' flying that day and the business of organizing the move; the detailing of crews to aircraft, the preparation of the route to be flown, and a hundred lesser details had all to be attended to. That night I slept soundly; the excitement of a success was forgotten equally with the sad unavoidable loss of a crew; such thoughts always dispersed before the bustle and commotion of eternal moving and fighting. There was little enough time for preparation against the future, much less for idle reflection on things past.

The next morning we received the expected order to move on to St. Eval from which we assumed that the battle-cruisers *Scharnhorst* and *Gneisenau* were showing signs of restlessness in their lair at Brest and our force was being moved to anticipate any attempt on their part to run for open sea. These ships were old enemies of ours, and were known throughout the service as "Salmon and Gluckstein", a nickname originated, I think, by our Wing Commander. A pleasant flight over two cathedral towns, Winchester and Salisbury, thence to Taunton, brought us to Cornwall, the sea and St. Eval. A visit to Operations Room there revealed that we were not, after all, required, since the two warships now showed no sign of leaving their berths, but our orders were to remain at St. Eval for a few days. That afternoon was spent lazily on one of those incomparable Cornish beaches, the murmur of the sea a delightful relief to our ears after the roar of aero-engines, and our idleness in the sun a rest from the rush and excite-ment of the previous day. The love for Cornwall which I had felt in childhood came back now in all its old strength, the sea, salt air and firm beach seemed so far above the exhausting jar of machinery; between them, I thought, lay the gap between peace and war. How desirable peacefulness seemed, how equally desirable was the security and leisure for which we fought. Reluctantly we left the beach as the sun was setting, and looking back on the peaceful scene of dying colours, greens and blues and greys all tinged with red, I knew instinctively that the future of a past childhood was worth fighting for.

The next morning brought an urgent signal for us to return without delay, not to our base at Thorney Island, but once again to North Coates, for an immediate but unspecified operation. Within an hour of receiving the order we were packed and in the air again, six Beauforts, in two formations of three, carrying their crews back to war again after a day's rest, with the prospect of real work ahead. This time we took a sea route, flying past Plymouth, Torquay and Wey-mouth, all jewelled in the sapphire sea of a summer's day. The sun beating down on its chalk cliffs made the Isle of Wight visible from afar, and skirting its headlands and beaches we turned in towards the Hampshire coast. Three and three the two formations circled the aerodrome, then, separating into single aircraft, came in to land one by one; six Beauforts taxied over the grass one after another to be lined up at intervals at the aerodrome boundary while transport came out to take the crews to Operations Room.

We reached Thorney Island at three o'clock in the afternoon, and were in the air again at four-fifteen, not a move this time but an operation. There was excitement and anticipation in the air of Operations Room as we entered, and looking at the map I saw the reason in a flash why we had been moved so hurriedly from St. Eval, why the Controller was so pleased at our arrival, why there was an air of expectancy in the airmen who had begun to refuel our aircraft almost before their engines had stopped and in the driver of the truck which collected us. Two enemy destroyers were steaming down the Channel, a rare and important happening in a piece of water we claimed as our own.

They had been first sighted earlier in the day, steaming westward just off Calais, by one of the fighter reconnaissance aircraft which daily patrolled the Channel from dawn until dusk, always flying at a great height from which any movement of shipping could be seen in the narrow neck of the Channel. These pilots were nicknamed "Jim Crows", on account of their watching continuously from the roof of the sky. The destroyers' progress had been carefully noted by a succession of these, and when we arrived at three o'clock a reconnaissance pilot out over the Channel was expected at any minute to land on the aerodrome with the latest news of our targets; everyone waited in suppressed excitement, and when at last a Spitfire was reported circling the aerodrome, we could hardly wait for its news.

At half-past three the reconnaissance pilot himself in the person of a Polish pilot walked into Operations Room with the position and speed of the two destroyers when he had last seen them at three o'clock. They were, it appeared, still steaming fast in a westerly direction, making about twenty-five knots and all the time hugging the coastline; their formation was line ahead, with only a few lengths separating the two vessels. Now I was glad of the presence of my observer, Steve, who had finished his leave and rejoined us at St. Eval with the rest of my crew, for navigation was going to play no small part in intercepting this fast-moving target. While Group were being told the latest information by telephone, Steve plotted the destroyers' position on a chart at half-hour intervals along the track we expected them to take; but we could not work out our course, for we had not yet been given our time of take-off. As minutes passed I became impatient at the delay, for while we waited our target was moving, and might conceivably make harbour before we reached it.

But a message from Group explained the delay and brought news which was joyously received and well worth waiting for: we were to have a fighter escort. I was called to the telephone myself and with paper and pencil took down the hurried instructions; several single-seater fighter squadrons were coming with us, and we were to make a rendezvous at 16.45 at 2000 feet over their aerodrome in Dorset. I was warned on no account to be late at the meeting-place, not to fly at less than 180 miles an hour, which was the cruising speed of the fighters, and above all to find the target without searching for more than a few minutes, since the endurance of the fighters was very limited and if I wasted time they would run out of petrol. Group wished us luck; looking at the scribbled instructions in my hand, I wished only for time, time in which to think and prepare.

The whole operation promised to be completely novel. The squadron had never before flown with a fighter escort, nor had it attacked a fast-moving naval target; we had never previously operated more than three Beauforts at one time, and now we were to use six.

Yet there was little enough time to digest my instructions or make plans; by the time I had finished talking to Group it was nearly four o'clock and we were still a hundred miles from our rendezvous. More frantic consultation with Steve and rapid calculation on his part revealed that we must take off not later than four-fifteen to reach the meeting-place in time, and if we left there punctually we should intercept the target off the Cherbourg peninsula. Fast moves we had made before, but none like this one from Operations Room to our waiting aircraft; it was fortunate that everybody knew in advance what to expect of the opposition and how I proposed to attack, for I had filled in a few waiting minutes by running through our plan of action.

At one minute before a quarter to five we were circling the fighters' Dorset aerodrome at 2000 feet, two formations of Beauforts, one behind the other, led by Tony and me. We were dead on time, and my first responsibility was met. As we circled there were signs of activity on the aerodrome below, paths, of grass blown flat in the slipstreams of racing propellers, toy figures which were pilots running out towards their toy aircraft shining in the sun. Within a few minutes these aircraft, which I recognized as Spitfires and Hurricanes, came to life and one by one taxied out over the grass surface like so many buzzing insects, ready for the take-off. Squadron after squadron, forming up on the ground in V formation, took off together as one aircraft, filling the sky with noise as they climbed up to join us. We, who were accustomed to work alone and fend for ourselves, found this a fascinating, almost unbelievable sight, as flights of fighters formed up on either side of our formation, above and behind us, to make the sky around seem full of their little single-seaters. It was a dream, a flat contradiction of everything we had known; we were flying high in an open sky, and there were six of us surrounded by countless fighters, on our way to attack destroyers, yet I did not think the operation strange, I was only concerned with its success and burdened with responsibility.

The seemingly endless stream of fighters continued to come up from the aerodrome below, and as I set course for the target, feeling I should not delay longer, aircraft were still racing across the surface while others were still running their engines on the ground, leaving paths of flattened grass and little clouds of dust behind them. I knew that with their superior speed they could easily catch us up, and to delay longer might be to allow the destroyers to escape by entering Cherbourg harbour, which Steve estimated they would reach at five-thirty. Reluctantly I left this hornets' nest, turning southwards on to our course with the throng that was our escort wheeling into line behind us.

Very different was this short Channel crossing, which would only take some twenty minutes, from the long wearying journey over the wide North Sea to the Skaggerak of a few days before. Although blue sky surrounded us, relieved only by a summer heat haze near the water, these clear conditions caused no misgivings; the countless fighters on either side of us inspired confidence, and in such a company I could have flown into the middle of Germany without fear for our safety. As Portland Bill dissolved in the haze behind us, I began a shallow dive to gain our usual position near the surface, while at the same time our escort began to climb away to the great height at which they liked to fly, watchful above us and ready to swoop to our protection if we were molested.

We seemed hardly to have left our coast before Steve began to glance frequently at his watch and gaze expectantly into the haze ahead; he was not unnaturally a little nervous, for his was an important part in the operation, since an error in his calculations would result in the target escaping us, an unthinkable end to such an auspicious setting out. I, too, felt uncomfortable, with the responsibility of leading so large a force against such an important target weighing very heavily; I was anxious for the mission to be a success and to add to the squadron's reputation.

We had just completed the shallow dive and reached the water when the French coast became visible as a dark line on the haze horizon, with Cherbourg itself discernible in a long bay between two promontories. Steve had estimated that the destroyers would be steaming across the bay as we arrived, and this proved an excellent piece of timing, for just ahead could be seen two white wakes, one behind the other, lashed up by two fast-moving ships. This first sight of our targets produced in me not the usual feeling of tension before an attack, but one of relief that we would not return in disgrace without finding our quarry. As we closed rapidly on their tell-tale lines of foam, the grey-painted hulls of two destroyers began to stand out from the darker cliffs behind, until the lettering on their sides, their guns and the crew on deck could clearly be seen. Signalling to Tony, whose formation was behind me, that I was about to attack, I spread my own formation and turned in towards the leading destroyer, casting a quick glance upwards at the dots in the sky that were our escort, a glance which confirmed my feeling of confidence. Although near the coast, we had the unwonted luxury of being able to ignore completely the danger of enemy fighters and concentrate only on the attack.

Perhaps I was not alone in looking skywards, for the destroyers appeared to be taken unawares and it seems possible that the attention of their crews was distracted from our little force, approaching low and unheard, by the horde of fighters droning and pirouetting high above them. At all events, my three Beauforts were surprisingly able to go in, drop their torpedoes and start to turn away before fire started, at first hesitatingly, then in earnest. Tony's formation, coming in just behind mine, were less lucky, for they were left to face the trouble which we had stirred to life. But only a second or two separated the two waves, the attack was launched and over almost before it had begun, and all the aircraft escaped unhit.

Two enemy destroyers, looking new and clean with the sun shining on their light grey paint, speed westwards in line ahead, leaving twin white furrows behind them in a calm blue sea; their barking guns fill the air with smoke and silver traces to break the peace of the summer evening. Such was my impression of the target as I approached to aim the torpedo, a picture on which I had to turn my back as I manoeuvred away to avoid the increasing fire. Escaping from reach of the guns, I turned back towards the target, expecting to find that at least one of the six torpedoes we had launched would find its mark, but on neither ship was there sign of the awaited explosion: we had all missed. There was no great waterspout, only the churning of the wakes, no cloud of black smoke but just an occasional wisp of grey from the guns, no explosion but the tiny flashes of fire. It was a disappointing, unbelievable end.

The destroyers were no longer in line ahead steaming westwards, but had turned into line abreast in the direction from which the attack was launched. They had taken excellent avoiding action, turning towards the threatening torpedoes just after we had dropped them, thus combing their tracks, which were visible as straight lines of bubbles on the surface passing innocuously down either side of the leading destroyer. Bitterly disappointed I turned for home, with my two other aircraft forming up on either side of me and Tony's formation also taking up position behind, while the fighters wheeled in the sky above us to return to their base. Reluctantly I left the scene, wishing uselessly that we all carried a second torpedo to enable us to make a second attack; yet another prized target had escaped, and this time we had failed before the eyes of critical fighter pilots. Our home-coming was as dejected as the outward flight had been expectant; six Beauforts, three and three, now returned disconsolately to explain a failure.

On our return Tony and I discussed the attack long and exhaustively in an effort to find our mistake; superficially the whole operation, including the actual attack, had gone according to plan, yet something had miscarried, for no hit had resulted. In the end I blamed myself for the attack's failure, reaching the conclusion that I had made an error in range and failed to press in close enough; it seemed the only possible solution. Judging distance, never an easy task with a calm sea, had been made no easier by the haze hanging over the water; on reflection it did seem likely that we had in fact dropped at very long range, giving the destroyers ample time to avoid our torpedoes. It was my responsibility, a leader's error, and now all I could do was to remember this lesson for the next occasion we attacked destroyers, a chance which never occurred again.

To console myself I reflected that there were great differences between attacking merchantmen and naval vessels, and the day's task had been a difficult one. The merchant ships, which the squadron encountered every week, rarely steamed at more than six or seven knots and could never turn quickly enough to avoid a torpedo. On the other hand, destroyers could turn almost within their own length and might make thirty-five or even forty knots. Such ships were to us like slippery eels, and not only were they a fleeting, twisting target but also a very small one less than two hundred feet long. Nevertheless the fact remained, one of six torpedoes should have hit, and whether speed was misjudged, aim was in error, or the range too long, the attack was a failure.

However, as the evening wore on, the novelty of the day's operation made us forget its lack of success. Over cans of beer we discussed the flight from beginning to end, speculating on the actual strength of our escort, whether six squadrons or more, and wondering what they had seen from their lofty viewpoint. All agreed that Steve's navigation was the achievement of the day, that to have a fighter escort was a great luxury and to be a fighter pilot must be the top of all flying. Not one of us then realized what I learned later, that while we were attacking the target there had been a wild dog-fight going on far above us, in which fighters from both sides had been shot down. It certainly was good to have an escort.

My memory of that June day is still clear, but if I wish I can revive it by a glance at a photograph taken from Tony's aircraft after the attack. There are the two destroyers, puffs of smoke emitting from their guns, the wakes behind them semicircular after their turn, arcs etched on the surface of the water, and in the background rise the cliffs of the French coast. The photograph reproduces exactly the calmness of the sea, the heat of the haze, the vastness of an open sky, and above all the peacefulness of that June evening; two ships enjoying a peace which we failed to shatter.

So ended my first week of operations since the previous November; an attack on Zeebrugge with bombs on a Friday, on Sunday a mission to the Skaggerak in search of a battleship, a hit on a ship off Texel on Tuesday, and finally Thursday saw this unsuccessful attack on the two destroyers. All were daylight sorties on which I led formations, and none was completely devoid of success, for there can be minor successes within failures. These four are my favourites among all my operations, carried out in a June week when I was fresh from a long rest and anxious to atone for an error of judgement made on a November night not yet forgotten. It was a wonderful week of action, yet more memorable than its fears and hopes, achievements and failures, tension and relief, was the peace of a beach in Cornwall. Unforgettable was that lazy afternoon stolen from bustle and activity, when we lay free from the clanging of war on Cornish sand and listened to the sweeter sound of incoming waves.

CHAPTER XV

DEAD MEN'S SHOES

THE end of May had seen the commencement of fighter sweeps over the Channel and Northern France, by which our fighter squadrons gained the mastery of the daylight sky over their German opponents, allowing bombers to be escorted on their missions of destruction to factories and aerodromes in the interior. For the first time since the withdrawal from France we were taking the offensive on a large scale by daylight, tactics which were only made possible by our growing fighter strength. This supremacy in the air was exactly what the enemy had attempted to achieve over the South coast during the Battle of Britain less than a year earlier, when his squadrons were checked and driven off by our greater hearted but numerically inferior little band. Now the tables were turned, with hordes of our aircraft crossing the Channel almost daily in the fine second summer of war, always challenging their opponents to come up and give fight, often compelling them to do so by taking with them squadrons of bombers which the enemy could not afford to ignore. Both sides suffered losses in the conflicts which resulted, but the initiative was with our fighter wings, and the bombers reached their targets and returned unmolested as an almost invariable rule, thanks to efficient fighter protection.

With these conditions of air superiority reigning anywhere within our fighters' rather limited range, it was a logical step to try and close the Channel completely to the enemy shipping which was known to be using these waters, creeping from port to port and hugging closely the intervening coastline. Ships would steal from Ostend, past Boulogne and Calais to Le Havre and Cherbourg, perhaps continuing to St. Malo or even to Brest. Interior communications, railways and roads were being regularly disrupted by the fighter sweeps, and to make the discomfort of the enemy complete, the sea-route had also to be effectively disorganized.

When the two destroyers which we attacked unsuccessfully that June evening off Cherbourg passed unscathed down the whole length of the Channel from Ostend, where they were first sighted, to be last seen steaming peacefully westward, the authorities woke to the fact that the Channel was still open to the enemy and not yet properly policed. A torpedo squadron had not been at hand when required, and the very fact that we had to be called from St. Eval accounted partly for the destroyers' escape. Had we been available immediately the target was first sighted, not one but repeated attacks could have been made until a hit was scored, but owing to the delay caused by our move, when we actually reached the scene only one attack was possible before the target steamed out of fighter range.

There seems no doubt that the authorities were disturbed at the way these ships had run unharmed and almost unchallenged down the Channel, not even under cover of bad weather but openly under the clear sky which we could now so easily rule. The incident stirred them to action, and to the decision that the Channel should be closed to enemy shipping of all kinds, a course now made possible for the first time by our increasing fighter supremacy; within a Spitfire's range we could dictate. The squadrons associated at this time with daylight attacks on shipping were Blenheim squadrons of Bomber Command, of which there were many, and of course the very few Beaufort squadrons of Coastal, the one using bombs, the other torpedoes. Some of the Blenheim squadrons had already been taking part in the sweeps, making bombing attacks on inland targets, and were based conveniently for operating in the Channel area; there was, however, not a single Beaufort squadron on the South coast. Normally if a torpedo striking force was needed anywhere, either north or south, a section of our squadron was moved to a convenient base for that particular operation, for movements of shipping were usually anticipated and the time taken by the move was of no account. It now appeared that a permanent torpedo force was needed on the South coast, with its aircraft ready at short notice to act on any sighting report from the vigilant reconnaissance high over the Channel. Ours was to be that squadron.

Hardly had our six Beauforts returned to North Coates after their few days on the South coast when an order was received for the squadron to move. This was not the customary move of a few aircraft, crews and airmen for a few weeks' stay at another aerodrome, but a complete uprooting of the whole squadron from hangars, workshops, offices and Mess to settle on a new station as our permanent base, and that station was to be the pleasant Thorney Island which we had just left. North Coates was an excellent base for operating around the Frisian Islands, but we were by no means indispensable there, for the more numerous Blenheim squadrons would continue to harass shipping in that area we knew so well and had once called our own. But in any case Beauforts were not to be absent long from the scene of many of their successes, for we were to be replaced shortly by a newly formed Beaufort squadron which was almost ready to take up our role. The Channel operations were going to be important and require the experience which our squadron possessed, while the Frisian Islands were an excellent beginners' hunting-ground for the new squadron, which would start operating mostly at night.

The squadron was not unduly sorry to be leaving its Lincolnshire base for the South coast, or to forsake the North Sea for the Channel, for if North Coates and the Dutch Islands had been the scene of many successes, they had witnessed equally many losses. I personally had felt for some time that the daylight game was temporarily played out off the Dutch coastline, particularly since summer would give few days with the requisite cloud cover, and I welcomed the move to the Channel with the new operations which it promised. Flights would be shorter, for distances were not so great; there would be more specific targets to attack and less dangerous searching to be done in an effort to find our own prey, for reconnaissance would be our look-out. Above all, there would be the comfort of a fighter escort for most of our sorties, which would no longer be limited to bad weather conditions, and being thus unrestricted it seemed that our daylight operations might increase in frequency and success.

Everything promised well for the squadron's future at Thorney Island, not least the pleasant situation of the aerodrome right on the Hampshire coast, with the Officers' Mess on the water's edge itself, looking southwards over the Channel we hoped to sweep clear of the enemy. Our visit of a few days before had shown the countryside radiant under the June sun, a contrast to the unfriendly bleakness of the Lincolnshire coast to which we had returned. Summer months, pleasant surroundings and completely new operations on an unfamiliar coastline held out an attractive future.

And I myself was glad to be leaving an atmosphere so heavily weighted with memories of lost friends; we had been at North Coates for over a year and had lost more crews than I liked to remember. As I packed flying clothing and a few personal belongings in my Flight Office, I came across pair after pair of black shoes, worn and dusty, hidden away in a dark corner. The realization came as a shock that these were dead men's shoes, the shoes of missing pilots of my Flight who had changed them in this very office for flying boots before taking off on the sortie from which they never returned. Here, standing in pair after pair, far too numerous, were the ghosts of pilots who had passed through that door as I sat at my desk, or perhaps lay in hospital, always a cheerful word on their lips and a promise to return with something achieved; but they had not. There stood ghosts in forgotten shoes: of Joe, Ken, Fanny, Dick, Eddie and Ian, and so many others less remembered but not forgotten, all lined up in my memory. Small wonder that I was leaving without regret, for the office had suddenly by this chance upturning become a graveyard. It had been a good time while it lasted, the winter months of the past year when success had been easy and the game new, but since then it had slowly become a fight against odds; I welcomed the new lease of life the move promised for the squadron and its operations, a promise that was not to be fulfilled.

Within a few days the squadron had moved its aircraft, several hundreds of airmen and equipment, and was settled in its new home. A hangar buzzed with the eternal maintenance of aircraft. Tony and I were installed in our Flight Offices, for he had replaced Eddie as the other Flight Commander, and the Wing Commander and Alec were established close at hand. New crews came, aircraft waited and the weather was fine; only one thing was lacking—operations.

Group, like us, anticipated that daylight sorties would take place almost every day, so to meet their requirements we arranged for a section of three Beauforts to be always at immediate readiness from dawn until dusk. Torpedoes were ready loaded, aircraft warmed up at intervals, and pilots waited at hand, prepared to take off at a moment's notice, meet their fighter escort and cross the Channel to attack some target sighted by reconnaissance; but alas he rarely gave us a call. There was the squadron, straining at the leash to attack, just like some fighter squadron waiting to repel an enemy who never came, for hardly a target presented itself. The rosy possibilities for a torpedo force, which we had imagined the area contained, faded before inactivity. Not only was the presence of shipping on the opposite coast rare, but we were often prevented from attacking those few ships which did actually appear by two considerations; either the ship was too small a target for us or she would be steaming in waters too shallow to launch a torpedo. Only the small ships seemed to pass down the Channel, and they hugged the coast so closely that they were often found in waters far too shallow for a torpedo attack. During our first few weeks at Thorney Island we were continually on our toes, waiting for the order to jump into our aircraft and away. Once or twice small ships were sighted and Blenheims would be sent against them with bombs, an occurrence which only increased our restlessness and impatience. Always we were waiting during these weeks for a call which never came.

We were essentially an active squadron, used to finding our own targets and generally in the habit of looking for trouble, and thus to be kept idle appealed not at all to our pilots and crews, who grew restive waiting for operations. As the weeks passed for July to become August with only an occasional daylight sortie, the squadron gradually reverted almost to its former role. As first moonlight Rovers on the French coast recommenced, since they did not interfere with the daylight readiness for which a force had still to be reserved. Then minelaying was ordered almost nightly, and we would send three or sometimes six Beauforts to lay mines outside the Channel ports. Eventually Group must have realized that we were not, after all, to be fully occupied in daylight sorties, and our readiness throughout the day was relaxed, thus enabling us on the few suitable days to carry out Rovers in the Channel and off the Dutch coast. Before a few months had passed the squadron's operations became almost what they had formerly been at North Coates; the promised change to exhilarating daylight raids under fighter protection never materialized. Although several such operations did take place, they were exceptional, and night sorties remained our mainstay.

Nor was the squadron successful in operations from its new base, for, of the few ships found and attacked that summer, only one or two were hit, but with the decrease in activity losses of aircraft were reduced; it seemed as if success had to be dearly paid for. Before many weeks had passed we were longing for our former base and the Frisian Islands again, where, if operations were fraught with danger, they were at least rewarded with success. We missed the former bustle of activity, for with our move the fast tempo of operations, the comings and goings of crews, the losses and successes, had slackened to a funeral pace. Life at Thorney Island was easier, safer, more comfortable, but most of us pined for incident even if accompanied by danger.

But this unaccustomed slow tempo did at least have one good effect on the squadron, it allowed the replacement of crews to catch up with losses, which during the winter months had exceeded the rate of training. Now crews were flowing steadily out to Beaufort squadrons from Training Unit, and for the first time for many months the squadron had its full complement of crews, enabling our generous allowance of leave to be still further increased and causing a crew's turn to operate to come round less frequently. There arose a new stability in the squadron; if operations were less spectacular they were more regular, for previously dependence on weather had made the incidence of operations sporadic, with occasional days of intense activity separating weeks of idle waiting. Now, after the first disappointing weeks of waiting continually at readiness to no purpose, night operations went on regularly, mining on dark nights. Rovers when the moon was up, their regularity interrupted only by occasional bad weather. Daylight sorties were restricted to a rare strike with an escort at some target reconnaissance had espied, or a Rover along the opposite coastline on the few days when the summer weather offered cloud cover. Distances were short, and flights averaged two or three hours compared with the five and six hour flights over the North Sea. Hardly ever either in daylight or in darkness did Rovers prove productive; there really was very little enemy shipping in the Channel, and the objective of sweeping clear its waters was gained almost without a blow being struck.

The change in operating conditions, with the diminishing number of attacks, could not do otherwise than influence the squadron's character, and there became apparent in our pilots much less dash than in former days, when so much had depended on the individual and his initiative. Now steadiness predominated, a quality demanded by the uneventful operations of almost reconnaissance character, for we were often hunting where we knew no prey lurked and when there was only a remote chance of a kill. Perhaps the squadron was growing up from its early days, when it was young, rash and adventurous, to become now of a sober age, reliable and circumspect. The very presence of a torpedo squadron on the South coast must have been a deterrent to the enemy to send his ships into the Channel, and perhaps our most productive work was the few daylight strikes we undertook unsuccessfully, for if we did not hit these infrequent targets, we did at least show that no ship would pass unopposed. I personally regretted in many ways the passing of the old order in the squadron, while recognizing that the new conditions were in some ways beneficial; the squadron was given time to recuperate after a hard winter.

While changes were being wrought within the squadron, new influences were also beginning to be felt without. Since the new year, when Blenheims had started their attacks on shipping the authorities had been showing an increasing preference for using bombs rather than torpedoes. The latter are expensive, taking long to produce and actually costing over a thousand pounds, while a bomb costs a fraction of that amount and is quickly manufactured. With the Blenheims' mounting success it seemed that the bomb was preferable to a torpedo, which had to be well aimed and carefully dropped to be effective, while the low-level bombing which the Blenheims favoured required no such precision. Certainly the bomber squadrons were wonderfully successful, their pilots flying at the target at mast height to release their sticks of bombs as they flashed overhead, but their losses, like ours, were high, the inevitable toll of daylight anti-shipping operations.

Not only were Blenheims with bombs challenging the Beaufort and the torpedo, for as the year progressed more and more ships were sunk by Coastal Command Hudsons, using bombs and operating mainly at night. These aircraft searched for ships on moonlight nights just as we had done on Rovers, but they operated not only off the Frisian Islands, but on the Norwegian and Danish coasts, in the Channel and the Bay of Biscay. Theirs was a mounting list of ships hit, with a low casualty rate, their safety derived largely from the cover of night. The Hudson was the standard reconnaissance aircraft in Coastal Command, and so there were many of these squadrons based all round our coast. Gradually Blenheims operating by daylight and Hudsons at night, both types carrying bombs, began to take the ascendancy in shipping attacks away from the Beaufort squadrons, which were numerically very inferior. In truth, although attached personally to the combination of torpedo and Beaufort by long association, I felt that bombs were the correct weapon against all but the largest merchant vessels, and that torpedoes should be reserved for heavily armoured warships. Nevertheless I watched with interest and somewhat sadly the gradual eclipse of the torpedo throughout the summer at Thorney Island. The squadron began to feel neglected as it became diverted to odd mining and reconnaissance work, and it was evident to all that its proud days were over; a change had occurred which I hated to see.

Metaphorically we had missed the *Bismarck* by perhaps a few hours; only too literally our torpedoes had missed the two destroyers, and no other naval target appeared that summer to give us a chance to make amends. Although several mighty ships stirred in their lairs, at Brest and Kiel, Wilhelmshaven or Oslo, and their movements were quickly reported by the photographic Spitfires, to have us packing hurriedly and moving north and west, we never made the hoped-for-attack. Each time we had a vision before us of the whole squadron attacking in many waves of three Beauforts, filling the water with torpedoes to hit some battleship in its most vulnerable spot, a vision which was never realized. Often we moved that summer, but never did we strike.

Attacks on shipping, by day or by night, with torpedoes or bombs, against phantom battleships or real tankers, the squadron was always associated with these operations, the first squadron of all to take the field against shipping, the first Beaufort squadron in the service. Gradually more Beaufort squadrons were forming at various bases up and down the country, making our moves less frequent and giving greater permanency at our base. June and July, August and September were fine summer months spent in pleasant surroundings. The lapping of the sea on the stony beach could be heard from my bedroom window, hay was made from the aerodrome grass, and trees surrounding the Mess were thick with leaves. Yet we would all have sacrificed this easy living for the bare existence which had been the squadron's life at North Coates and for the dashing successes of its former days.

As if to sound the knell to the squadron's past and blot out for ever memories of its great and volatile days of the last winter, my flying log book was destroyed in a crash. Dougie, who had followed me in the Zeebrugge raid and at Cherbourg, was killed in an accident at the time of the squadron's move to the south. He was following me in formation when we encountered bad weather about which I had received no warning; fair weather had been forecast and we met instead very low cloud. I was at first incredulous at these unexpected conditions, and, thinking they might be only local, tried to fly in the narrow gap between ground and cloud, only to find this impossible. In the circumstances all I could do was to climb up through the cloud-layer and turn for home. In such a situation we always broke formation to rejoin above the clouds, and on this occasion, reaching the blue sky above, I found my right-hand aircraft, but no sign of Dougie on my left, and I was forced to return without him. It later appeared that he had made an error, and instead of climbing up had tried to continue in sight of the ground in spite of the low cloud, almost equivalent to fog. Unseeing, he crashed into rising ground, his aircraft split into a thousand pieces around him, and he was killed instantly.

In retrospect I blamed myself for this accident, for not only as leader of the formation but as Dougie's Flight Commander I was responsible for his safety. Many times we had discussed the subject of cloud flying in the Flight Office, the eternal question of what decision to make when meeting bad weather, and always I had emphasized that a pilot must climb up and instrument-fly at a safe height until a gap appears in the cloud or a wireless message tells him all is clear beneath. Dougie had made an error and had not escaped. It was sad that he should be killed in this way after safely negotiating his first few operations, to which he had looked forward after a year of training, but luckily we had few such accidents in the squadron. Just very rarely an error of judgement resulted fatally, more often an accident would be the result of some haphazard landing, injuring no one but ending with a Beaufort being towed lamely into the hangar for repair.

Now my log book was lost, which had been in Dougie's aircraft as he crashed, and was shattered into many torn and bruised pages. Its loss to me was almost that of an old friend, for a flying log book to a pilot is something more than a personal diary chronicling events; it is a prized possession, a structure which he has built, his flying pedigree, and I felt this loss almost as a writer would view the destruction by fire of a long-worked-on manuscript; it was irreplaceable. Thankfully, I recovered the most valuable pages intact, those containing the laconic entries recording my wartime flights, and I was able to find details of my total flying times, but, alas, many pages of "Hind" flying in 98 Squadron, floatplane days at Calshot and earlier Cranwell flying were irrevocably missing. It was my happy past completely blotted out.

Now I had to start a brand new log book, whose ruled unfilled pages recalled to me Cranwell days, and my first flight there, when I had sat down at the flight desk and written proudly on the first bare page. "Avro Tutor, Air experience, 10 minutes' passenger flying" had been that first entry, to which my new log book now answered, "Total flying, all types, 1192 hours and 15 minutes," a total of flying experience which gazed tolerantly back upon the years between, while the ominous blank pages cried a challenge to the years ahead. But my old log book had gone with old friends, the pages bringing to life flights with Eddie and Fishy at Cranwell, with Fanny and Robby at Gosport, all had vanished. They only stood now as ghosts in unclaimed shoes, with Dougie sadly joining the dead to increase their young number, and the squadron still going on. Beauforts circle noisily while pilots change into flying boots in my Flight Office; somebody sits at the desk making entries in his log book; I talk to my flight sergeant about the aircraft; the noise of repair echoes from within the hangar. It is a new office, and there are no unclaimed shoes, nor yet some dog puzzled at the over-long absence of his master. The squadron has moved, is expectant of new operations, rejuvenated in its new surroundings at Thorney Island, June 1941.

CHAPTER XVI

RED, WITH YELLOW NOSES

Of the sorties I undertook from the squadron's new base in the summer months, not a single one was rewarded, although few were completely devoid of incident. Such disappointment was not peculiar to me, but was shared by our other pilots, to whom success did not mean a safe return from a routine patrol, but a torpedo attack leaving destruction in its wake. Too often, indeed with the utmost regularity, our pilots returned from moonlight Rovers with a wide area of sea painstakingly searched, but no target found, and as torpedoes were nearly always carried, alternative land targets could not be attacked.

I had still to make my first night sortie after my return to flying, and was lucky enough to carry out a Rover on a perfect night of the July full moon. Not a cloud was in the sky as we took off towards the sea, and once my eyes were accustomed not to abject darkness but to bright moonlight, flying became as easy as by daylight. Only a short half-hour after take-off we reached the opposite coast near Le Havre, flying over a speckled silver sea in smooth night air, under a dark blue canopy that was the moonlit sky. Outside Le Havre was a likely anchorage for shipping, but we found none there. Lights flashed from the cliffs and piers to guide ships, but stillness reigned in the town itself; neither searchlights nor flak challenged us as we flew low, undetected and unheard. I felt a confidence I had never before experienced at night, skimming the water as if it were in daylight, seeing clearly all around me, flying comfortably in the warmth of a July night.

Flying eastwards, we searched coastwise to Cherbourg, where searchlight cones and intermittent flashes from guns revealed from afar that the port was receiving a visit from Bomber Command. I approached close enough to see into the entrance of the harbour and the town itself towering in the background, a sight to remind me that the squadron had once sent six aircraft to drop torpedoes there. From all accounts it had been a memorable attack in the face of fierce opposition, with all aircraft being hit, but only one failing to return; at most places on the enemy coast the squadron had a grave, but nearly always a hulk of a sunken ship was a nearby flag flying to avenge the loss.

Passing on our way, we skirted the Channel Islands, where no life seemed to stir; thence on to St. Malo, where every coastal rock silhouetted in a moonbeam appeared to be a ship, only to be recognised on closer inspection and left disappointedly behind. A hundred, two hundred miles of coastline were covered without a single enemy ship found sailing the Channel waters. Luckily our load that night was bombs, and we had previously selected an alternative target to attack in case our search for ships was fruitless. So, with my search at an end, I climbed to 5000 feet, a safe enough height to attack the little port of St. Brieuc, which we had chosen as both easy to find and of some importance, for it is on an estuary, with the main Paris-Brest railway passing through it. My navigator's directions were hardly needed, for I could see the town lying at the end of a silver finger which was the estuary. As we approached, there returned something of the excitement of old times, reminiscent of the raids on Bremerhaven and Lorient, for searchlights were darting their beams to and fro in opposition to the steady moon and flame spurted intermittently from batteries around the little town. But the defences were not really formidable, allowing us to sail leisurely through and drop our bombs with steady aim at a railway yard, whose metals glinted clearly in the moonlight. As we left the scene, a flare path lit up west of the town, only to be extinguished a few minutes later, an indication that the enemy's night fighters were in the air. Already I had seen strange coloured lights and an occasional flare in the sky around us, signs of enemy fighter activity, and under the full moon it seemed that to find an aircraft would be as simple a task as in daylight; yet we were allowed to leave for home unmolested.

Returning homeward, I felt disappointed in this sortie, which seemed so uneventful when compared with past operations; a mere protective reconnaissance was no substitute for the vigorous strikes the squadron once undertook, and the cover of night seemed a slight to the Beaufort's speed and defence. But the trip was not yet over; I was flying with the automatic pilot in action, and, as if to give the lie to the lack of incident of the flight, I found myself suddenly jerked out of my seat up to the roof of the aircraft: the automatic pilot, "George" had gone mad and stood the aircraft on its nose in a vertical dive. We had been flying along at a seemingly safe 2000 feet when this happened, yet it was all too little height to deal with the situation. I must somehow have managed to regain my seat and switch the automatic out of action just in time, for no height at all was registered on the altimeter by the time I had righted the aircraft, and the sea appeared so close beneath us that I could see drops of spray from little waves, and imagine waiting fishes.

The incident had been so sudden and my actions so automatic that, when it was all over, I was not so much frightened as pained with surprise and out of breath from sudden movement. "It's all right," I said to the crew through my microphone, "we're quite all right." This was greeted with replies from the three shaken voices asking for explanations. My gunner had been shot against the top of the turret, Steve had sailed to the roof accompanied by his pencils, charts and all the paraphernalia of navigation, while my wireless operator had smashed most of the valves in his set. It was a lucky escape; had we been a few hundred feet lower, another Beaufort would inexplicably have failed to return. My crew would never let me use the automatic pilot again at night, saying that even my doubtful instrument flying was preferable.

All was calm again in my aircraft when the white cliffs of the Isle of Wight came into sight, standing out clearly in the moonlight, and we altered course a few degrees to reach the Hampshire coast. The welcome aerodrome lights, the red of obstruction lights on the top of hangars and wireless masts, and the white dots of flare path were visible from a long way off, and I wondered, as I approached, how I could have flown so often over the aerodrome at North Coates one night last winter without seeing it; night flying had suddenly become easy under the moon. I flew round on the circuit to receive the flashing green light from the flare path, then came in to land, approaching very carefully to make a safe landing right in the floodlight beam. Other aircraft of the squadron returned soon afterwards from the same patrol, having searched for shipping without success, and, like me, bombed an alternative target. Nearly always our night Rovers were like this, a fruitless search of the French coast, where no ships appeared to sail.

Later in the month came an operation much more after my own heart, a daylight torpedo strike against quite a large ship off the French coast. It had been sighted and attacked by a Blenheim

squadron off Le Touquet in the early morning, but later reconnaissance brought news that the ship was crippled but still moving
slowly down the coast. She was reported to be a 5000-ton tanker, well
worth the expending of a few torpedoes, and we were overjoyed when
an order was received for six of our Beauforts to meet a fighter wing
at Beachy Head and cross to attack her. The last sighting report
showed her to be moving eastwards from Le Touquet screened by
several flak ships and circled by Messerschmitt 109's overhead. With
this information before us, Steve and I got busy with the navigation,
and arranged to fly to a point on the French coast well ahead of the
tanker's anticipated position, then turn and run up the coastline to
attack from the landward side. I hoped such an attack might take the
defences by surprise, as it had done once before.

Off we flew to Beachy, two formations of three Beauforts, with
Johnny Lander, a young but very able Pilot Officer, leading the second
flight. We passed Bognor and then Brighton, two seaside towns
bathed in summer weather, and reached the headland five minutes
before the time of rendezvous, marking time there in great wide
circles. Round and round we went, my eyes glancing anxiously at the
clock and searching the sky for our escort, for the time of meeting was
reached and passed, first by five minutes, then by ten. At last I could
bear waiting no longer; so rarely did we have a chance to attack such
a target, and with every minute passing its chances of escaping us and
making port increased. Almost in despair I told Jim to send a message
back to our base asking if we could proceed without escort. We were
a strong force, and I was willing to risk opposition for the prize which
was offered, but just as I was becoming impatient for a reply to my
message, we found ourselves surrounded by Spitfires; our escort had
arrived, and, completing a last circle, we set off.

We crossed the Channel low down, with squadrons of fighters on
either side and others high up behind us, and made a landfall just
north of Le Havre, where we turned eastwards to fly up the coastal
shipping route, close inshore. As we passed beneath the cliffs an
occasional shore battery would fire ineffectively at us, but we took no
notice; it seemed that nothing could harm a force of six Beauforts and
seven Spitfire squadrons all droning their way through the sky,
relentlessly towards their target. Just as on the last occasion, when we
had been escorted to the destroyer attack off Cherbourg, there was a
clear blue sky above with a thick heat haze on the water, characteristic
of a July day and limiting visibility on the surface to only a few miles.

As we ran along the coast I thought every little fishing-vessel which
loomed up ahead through the haze was our target; as mile after mile

was covered, I began to wonder if we had made an error in navigation and allowed the target to escape us. Leading a big force was always a heavy responsibility, with many points to be considered, and not least of these was the limited endurance of the Spitfires; it was essential to find the target quickly or the escort would run out of petrol before it reached home. Just when Steve and I were giving up hope and preparing to turn for home, the tanker was sighted, not on the seaward side as we anticipated, but very close inshore, opposite the little town of Fécamp; it was quite stationary and surrounded by six flak ships.

If I had time for any feelings at all, they were of relief at finding our objective in time, but the target had loomed up so quickly and was so unexpectedly close inshore, that all feelings gave way to action. I made a signal to Johnny that I was going to attack, and at the same time spread my own formation, turning towards the target. There appeared little doubt that the enemy had been forewarned of our coming by coastal observers, under whose positions on the cliffs we had passed in our search from the west, for fire opened simultaneously and without hesitation from the cluster of ships as soon as we came within range. Tracer crossed the sky horizontally, staccato cracking of explosions could be heard above the roar of engines, daubs of black smoke filled the air, and the water around us seethed with waterspouts thrown up by exploding shells. Here was a scene of formidable opposition, to put even old times to shame, a trellis-work fence of fire, a fine mesh into which we flew.

It seemed an endless time under fire before torpedo-dropping range was reached, but at last I found myself on a steady aim at the sitting target, and hanging on for just another half-second to make sure, I pressed the release button, hesitated a moment, then turned and ran out of the hottest spot I ever wish to enter. Taking their time from me, all three aircraft of the first wave dropped their torpedoes together, and turned away as Johnny's flight came in behind. Once more six torpedoes were in the water and running towards the target, this time neither moving at twenty-five knots, nor turning, but quite stationary.

Afterwards I climbed up a few hundred feet for Jim to take some photographs, all the time watching the target intently, not wishing to miss the expected explosion. Suddenly, a great waterspout rose into the air, and I thought we had hit, but it was not at the target, but just short of it; the torpedo had hit a sandbank or a submerged wreck and exploded prematurely. I waited still in expectation of success, but the scene remained almost unchanged since our arrival. Smoke hung in the breathless summer air like a grey canopy above the tanker, gun muzzles smoked and spat tongues of flame, the sky around us was still daubed with vanishing smudges of black smoke, but nothing happened; we had missed again. Sick with disappointment, I turned away; these were not days of second chances, we rarely had the opportunity to attack with torpedoes, and now that a target had appeared at last, we had thrown away our chance; we had failed.

Before the white cliffs of Beachy Head were reached I had caught up the others and regained the lead, while our escort, who had waited in the background during the attack, were buzzing around us once more, bringing a nice sense of comfort and security. We had survived the flak and could wink at enemy fighters, thanks to our company of Spitfires. Reaching the English coast, we turned westwards towards our aerodrome, while the fighter escort left us, the Spitfires saying goodbye by diving past our formation and rolling over and over in their exuberance. Perhaps they thought we had made a good attack, perhaps they had watched us flying through the wall of flak, perhaps they had seen the torpedoes dropped and running; they too may have been disappointed, as we were, and they may have wished to cheer us by a friendly gesture; Spitfires rolling over on their backs, saying goodbye.

At our base we carried out the usual post-mortem in an effort to find out quite what had gone wrong with the attack. Last time I had taken the blame on myself for dropping at long range, but this time I had made certain of a "good shot" by ignoring the opposition and going right in to short range before dropping. On the first occasion an error was perhaps permissible, but on a second there had to be no room for doubt. Johnny, who had been right behind my flight when we dropped, saw all three torpedoes enter the water perfectly, with lines of bubbles to show they were starting their run towards the target. His flight had dropped their "fish" in the splash marks of ours; six torpedoes had been aimed, not one had hit. It was both baffling and bitterly disappointing. Torpedoes were in little favour enough at this time without this expensive failure occurring to aggravate the situation. In the end, after endless discussion and much reference to the chart of the Northern French coastline, on which depth of water was indicated, we decided that there must have been insufficient depth for torpedoes where the tanker had been lying. She had been much closer inshore than reconnaissance had reported, and the premature explosion which I had seen from one torpedo did point to the conclusion we reached.

Perhaps, after all, a bombing force would have done better than we had done, perhaps the error was Group's in sending us to attack in shallow water, or perhaps they could be excused by the inaccuracy of the sighting's report, but at all events we had done our best. Two of our Beauforts had been hit by shrapnel, but not in any vital part, and all the pilots had enjoyed the change of taking part in a real live operation, just as schoolboys enjoy a field-day. Before the operation my heart had leapt at the mention of a tanker to attack, remembering the photograph taken by Paddy of the great oil fire which Dick had started last winter. Now I returned with a good enough photograph taken by Kim which showed the tanker lying stationary within its protective circle of flak ships, and even details, such as the lines of shell explosions in the water and wisps of smoke from the guns, were quite clear; the photograph itself was excellent, it was the subject which had failed to play its part, that of a burning, sinking ship.

These two contrasting operations, an uninspiring search at night along the enemy coastline, and the eventful daylight attack under a fighter escort, illustrate so well the change which actually resulted from the squadron's move from the east coast to the Channel, and the conditions for which we had hoped. It seemed as if, with our decision to close the Channel by vigorous attacks on enemy ships found at sea, the enemy itself had made a simultaneous decision to withdraw his shipping for use on other, more tenable routes. Our growing fighter supremacy must have pointed to the mastery of the Channel as a natural sequence, and the enemy was not choosing to challenge us. We may, as a squadron, have contributed to the achievement of this objective by our very presence on the South coast, but our role, threatening but passive, did not suit a squadron used to aggression and activity.

But excitement was not always wanting, and no small stir was caused some weeks later, by the alleged sighting of an enemy battleship in the Channel, said to be off Cherbourg and steaming eastwards. This was one of the very rare occasions when the squadron put its whole strength of available aircraft into the air, and luckily we had more aircraft serviceable than usual to make a good show. The order to sweep the Channel with our full force came just as we were sitting down to supper on a hot evening after a fine day; we could not have been more surprised or more excited, for the order was most unexpected, a "flap" at the end of an inactive day. Always it seemed to be cloudless weather on the South coast throughout the summer, and this fine evening was no exception, to make us grateful for the promised fighter escort, which was now usual for these operations. One by one we took off, twelve Beauforts climbing into the air to form up on the aerodrome circuit in four flights of three, one behind the other like a ladder in the evening sky. The Wing Commander himself was leading the first flight, with the second flight following him, while I was leading the third flight with the last three Beauforts behind me, this arrangement on account of our intention to attack in two waves of six. The squadron together in the air was an inspiring and rare sight, and we longed for a target important enough to justify the launching of the twelve torpedoes which we carried.

We circled the rendezvous and picked up our escort in the usual way, but we set out over the Channel flying much higher than usual in order to see further afield; detection of our force by the enemy mattered not at all with fighters all around us only too willing to engage any opponents who care to come up and fight. The Wing Commander led the force across to Le Havre, swept down the Channel westwards to Cherbourg without any sign of the rumoured target, and was then forced to turn reluctantly for home by the fighter's limited range. In truth we had doubted the report immediately it was received, for the presence of a battleship in what we now thought of as "our" Channel seemed ridiculously unthinkable. Nevertheless, Group had been right in taking immediate action on the report, since there had been no time to confirm it with another reconnaissance before dark, and in any case we were glad enough of any glimpse of the enemy coast, even at the expense of an interrupted supper.

We reached the Hampshire coast just as the sun was setting, and parted there from the escort to return to our separate aerodromes. I often wondered who these Spitfire pilots were and what they thought; these rare sorties which we made in daylight were one of many to them, perhaps their third sortie in a busy day of sweeps. I think I envied them their attractive aircraft and active role. Arriving at the aerodrome, we flew low over the Mess in close formation to let other squadrons know we were back, to let everybody know we were a power to be reckoned with. Then the formation broke up from twelve into threes, and these circled, broke up in turn and landed singly on the aerodrome, over which hung long shadows. It had been an unforgettable evening flight, on account of its unusualness; hardly ever did we put a larger force than six into the air, and generally three Beauforts was an adequate number for the targets we were given. The sight of twelve Beauforts surrounded by a horde of smaller fighters was a heartening one, to make us wish more than ever for a worthwhile target to fall to our hand. To be unchallenged by the enemy, who had allowed us to look down into Le Havre and Cherbourg harbours unmolested, was proof indeed of our fighters' ownership of the Channel. I felt more than a momentary stab of envy for their attractive, interesting work, almost wholly confined to aggressive daylight sweeps. I was, like Dick before me, beginning to feel strongly the lure of the single-seater fighter, its eight guns and attractive role.

The squadron put a force of twelve aircraft into the line again not long afterwards, when the battle-cruiser *Scharnhorst* was found to have left Brest and sailed into the Bay of Biscay during the night. She had slipped away out of the virtual blockade of Brest much as the *Bismarck* had slipped from our sight in its Norwegian fjord, under cover of darkness and bad weather, and when found the next day she was alongside the mole at La Pallice, a little harbour not far from Lorient. As it was known she might move at any minute, the squadron was inevitably and at short notice moved to St. Eval; twelve Beauforts were available again, and soon all were lined up on the Cornish aerodrome, all loaded with torpedoes and waiting for action. Still fortune did not favour us, and our quest for a worthy prey seemed destined always to be a fruitless one; our target eluded us. The *Scharnhorst* moved back to Brest under cover of a moonless night on which it was impossible to launch a torpedo attack, and twelve Beauforts started up, taxied out and returned to their base, once more cheated of their quarry.

Just as I had seen the reconnaissance photograph of the *Bismarck* hiding on the Norwegian coast while I waited with my flight at Wick in the hope of intercepting her, so I now saw at St. Eval a similar photograph of the *Scharnhorst* at La Pallice. Although taken from a great height, the ship appeared right in the centre of the photograph and vital details could be clearly seen. A wisp of smoke wound upwards from the funnel, hands were on deck, and in the water around the ship were the thin shadows of torpedo nets. I always had the greatest admiration for the pilots of these photographic reconnaissance aircraft, who were restricted only by weather conditions in carrying out their invaluable work. Their aircraft were fast and of great range, and no opposition either from flak or from fighters ever prevented them flying where their work might take them. I was beginning to be envious of any unit which was continuously active by daylight, and compared the desultory night operations of our squadron unfavourably with these critical high speed, long range photographic flights into the heart of enemy country.

As if to remind me of time past and more exciting sorties, there occurred in August a most unexpected happening; Dick, six months after he had been missing and presumed to be killed, was awarded a DFC. What story lay behind the delay in making the award, nobody knew; it was completely unexpected; we had not forgotten Dick, but had thought that the matter of his decoration was a sad story of the past. Now the squadron picked up the morning paper at breakfast to find that he had been awarded a DFC for continuous offensive operations against shipping in which he displayed great skill and gallantry. Although few remained in the squadron who remembered him personally, all knew him by reputation, and so the news was received with great acclaim, for the squadron at this time had not a single decorated pilot. When we had been carrying out operations deserving recognition, those who should have received decorations always became missing, and now the squadron was doing nothing worthy of notice. Dick's DFC earned about ten times over, reminded me of happy North Coates days, his longing for single-seater fighters, his flying a Beaufort as if it were as easy as a Tutor, his pretty wife and little boy. I could not help feeling that the great days of the squadron, which he personified, had passed for ever with the passing of winter and the squadron's move to the South coast.

Just as I was feeling that incident and excitement were things of the past in the operations, I went on two Rovers which could hardly have been more eventful, for on each occasion my formation was attacked by fighters. While the threat of fighter attack was always a real one and of considerable influence on our operations, and although I knew that several of our pilots had been chased by fighters and not a few shot down, I myself had never even seen one. Consequently I was beginning to feel that the threat was being overestimated.

The first Saturday in August brought weather typical of so many peace-time Bank holidays; it was a miserable day with low grey clouds from which rain poured intermittently on to the parched aerodrome grass. But while this was no weather for holiday-makers, to us it was a paradise of cover for which we had hoped through many weeks of clear blue sky and sunny days; we could rove on the French coast. While reconnaissance had rarely during the previous weeks spied any ships at sea, Intelligence reports showed that there were in harbour at Le Havre and Cherbourg one or two good-sized ships. It was most probable that these vessels moved under cover of dark nights on which there was no moon to reveal their presence, but it was just possible that they might sneak up the coast in daytime in bad weather when a reconnaissance pilot's vision, normally spread over the whole Channel from Calais to Cherbourg, would be restricted to a few miles. Whatever the chances of success, we were most anxious to have an outing to try our luck, particularly as the night operation would almost certainly be cancelled in such bad weather, and at our request Group gave per mission for three Beauforts to do the first Rover on the South coast.

Steve and I worked out a route which took us down the French coast from Le Touquet westwards, and we intended to rove as far as the Channel Islands if cloud cover allowed. But as the Met Office could only promise good cloud as far as Le Havre, I left the decision open as to whether we should continue further or return home.

I flew off down the coast to the familiar Beachy Head, which was chosen as a convenient starting-point, leading once more three Beauforts on a freelance operation, with great hopes of stemming with a success the mounting list of failures, both the squadron's and my own. Certainly the weather seemed in our favour, for as we turned seawards I could see the top of Beachy Head, only a few hundred feet high, vanishing in the cloud. The crossing seemed so short that the white cliffs had hardly been swallowed up in the mist before the bathing beaches and villas of Le Touquet appeared in front of us. Here we turned westwards, running down the Normandy coast under high cliffs and past little harbours and fishing villages, sometimes flying at less than a mile from the shore, for we were in safety under the unbroken sheet of low cloud. But not a ship was seen; the nearest approach to a target was an occasional tiny red-sailed fishing-boat dragging nets close inshore, or even a solitary rowing-boat in which a man sat, rod in hand, pipe in mouth, philosophically fishing, ignoring completely the aircraft which disturbed his peace.

We passed Fécamp, the scene of the failure against the tanker of the previous month, but it now looked peaceful as any Cornish fishing-village, a little cluster of buildings in a hollow around a few quays which were its harbour. Now and then I would be told by my gunner that a shore battery was firing down on us from the height of the cliffs, and I would turn out to sea, only to return to the coast after a few minutes. I hoped in this way to bluff the enemy's observation posts into thinking we had left their shores to return to our base, a ruse which was to prove unsuccessful. As we neared the area where the chance of finding shipping was best, just off Le Havre, the cloud-base began to rise and the cover appeared less complete. I had been keeping a watchful eye on the cloud during the run down the coast, since Met had warned me that it would become less dependable as we flew westward. I knew equally well that our presence on the coast could not be hidden any longer, and if the enemy thought it possible to catch us in open sky he would not hesitate to send out a fighter force, for there was no shortage of convenient fighter aerodromes in this area. In fact, I had reluctantly reached a decision to turn for home, considering the cover insufficient, when a small ship appeared straight ahead, and, thinking to photograph it or investigate, I carried on.

Almost immediately Bill sang down the intercom that there were fighters coming out from the land; they were a pair of Me 109s, he said, coming up behind and closing rapidly. A pilot is completely dependent on his rear-gunner for information during fighter attack, for he is the only member of the crew who is facing backwards and can see exactly what is happening, so a pilot will normally manoeuvre his aircraft according to the gunner's instructions. Bill now kept up an admirable running commentary from his turret, letting me know where the fighters were and when they were turning in to attack; he even had time to describe our opponents as being painted red with yellow noses! The climb to cover seemed endless; I twisted and turned, but not violently, as there was a Beaufort trying to keep formation on either side, while all the time Bill's voice in my ear told me that two unseen fighters were spraying first the right-hand aircraft, then my own, and across to the left of the formation. His steady voice continued over the roar of engines at full throttle and the din of guns firing, poetry to the accompaniment of a brass band. Normally we only tested our guns by firing a short burst into the sea at the start of every flight, but now this was firing in earnest. As the interior of the Beaufort filled with burnt gunpowder smoke I could hear the clatter of spent cartridge cases above the bark of machine guns, and all the time Bill's unvarying commentary, calm as ever but becoming more pointed as the fight went on. With tracer pouring over my port wing, I looked backwards for an instant to see one of these enemy fighters for myself, just turning away from the attack, while tracer from the other streamed between me and the right-hand Beaufort, whose gunner was sending a steady flow of lead back at his assailant. The pair must have made five attacks before we made cloud at just over 1000 feet above the water; not a moment too soon, I thought, with some relief.

Once we were safely enveloped in the friendly grey cloak of cloud, a buzz of conversation broke out among the crew, as everyone tried to find out exactly what had been going on; only Bill knew. He came up to my cockpit to show me his hands and face, black with oil and smoke from his guns, and pointed down the corridor, where I could see Jim wading ankle-deep in spent bullet cases. We rocked with laughter when we heard that he had been holding the camera out of the hatch as the attack started, intending to photograph the little ship we were investigating; he had been so amazed to see a fighter within a few hundred yards that he had not known whether to photograph or shoot it. He had just gazed at the spectacle open-mouthed with astonishment until he saw bullets streaming past; that had made him throw away the camera and dive for the side guns. At all events, we were pleased with the fight, Bill even thinking that the formation had given back more than it had taken, but I was more than a little anxious for my two followers, who appeared to have borne the brunt of the battle.

On reaching the aerodrome, I was relieved to find both the other Beauforts on the circuit with mine, and on landing we all gathered round the aircraft, examining each other's damage with animated and gestulating descriptions of what had happened to whom. My Beaufort had only two or three significant bullet holes in it, and the left-hand aircraft was undamaged, but the right-hand Beaufort had received one accurate burst of bullets and cannon-shells, making some twenty holes in fuselage and wings, luckily without touching any of the crew or hitting any vital part.

Pilots and observers decided that had the cloud been only a hundred feet higher, one of the formation must have been shot down, but the air-gunners, who had regarded the fight as a rare field-day, maintained that they had kept the attackers from coming in dangerously close by their turret fire. My personal opinion was that we had been lucky in our opponents, whom I thought rather poor performers, not pressing home their attacks but content to spray us inaccurately from the safety of long range. All the same, I saw no reason to revise previous views on the menace of fighter attack or the necessity of cloud cover, which I considered proved by the incident. Amusement was considerable when I recounted the story in Operations Room, and later, with subtle embellishment, in the Mess; in fact, the escape of the formation that day was quite a minor success. Nothing spectacular was achieved on that Rover, but a length of coastline had been swept and the enemy stirred to reply; it seemed worthwhile. After nearly a year in the squadron I had seen enemy fighters, I knew now how Me 109s behaved and what they looked like in the flesh; they were bright red, with yellow noses.

The very next Saturday I was out on a Rover again, only to meet opposition once more, a pair of Me 109s like the last time, only much better flown and more determined. I was roving in the west of the Channel, leading, as usual, with Ian on my right and one of our sergeant-pilots on the left, both experienced and very reliable. The weather had promised to be cloudy, and I intended making a landfall at Cherbourg and roving round the Channel Islands to St. Malo, and perhaps further west if conditions allowed. But on sighting the Cherbourg peninsula I looked up to find the cloud-base not lower than

3000 feet, no sort of conditions in which to continue. However, I knew from previous study of the weather chart that bad weather was approaching from the west, so altered course to fly down the middle of the Channel until low cloud materialized, then turned southwards towards the Brittany coast. We had just reached land and started to run parallel to the shore in our usual manner, when I sighted six mine-sweepers, sweeping in line abreast off Les Sept Isles, and made a detour seawards to avoid them, knowing they would report our presence if we were sighted.

I asked Jim to photograph them from a distance, as they might be of interest to Intelligence section, which in fact was interested in almost any photograph of enemy activity. As I was manoeuvring to give Jim a clear view I myself saw two fighters approaching low and extremely fast from ahead, looking aggressive in bright red paint. This was an unexpected interception, for, unlike last time, when we had been flying within sight of the enemy coast for half an hour, we had now only just sighted land a few minutes before. I quickly turned away from the coast and made for cloud, for it was always a good plan to draw fighters out to sea and away from their bases, since their small range may cause them to break off engagement with their work uncompleted; also it cannot be the easiest task in all the world to attack turret-defended formations far out at sea in a single-engined fighter, whose liquid-cooled engine is vulnerable to single bullets. The two other Beauforts came closer in formation in order to concentrate our fire, and soon Bill's commentary was in full swing, with clouds of smoke and the smell of burnt gunpowder drifting up to my cockpit to add colour to the ear-splitting chatter of machine guns, ours and the enemy's.

This time the pair were extremely determined, closing to within fifty yards before breaking away—in fact, at one time I thought they had joined the formation. Bill held his fire admirably, and I would see not only streams of tracer bullets but the broad ribbon of tracer shells streaming past my cockpit's perspex to fall away in a gentle curve downwards, when I would hear the noise of short intermittent bursts from the turret to tell me that the enemy was within range and Bill was giving all he could. His commentary was lucid, but somewhat highly coloured, and this made me realize that we were dealing with quite a different pair of fighters from our last opponents. These were 109 Fs, the latest and fastest German fighter, and very aggressive. Also they had the effrontery to concentrate on my aircraft as the formation leader, and I was not always quite happy, particularly as I could see a great deal of what was going on, and what I saw, I did not like at all.

Luckily cloud was only at a few hundred feet, and we were soon in cover, but our opponents persisted in following us into the cloud, making me feel very hapless and not a little annoyed to be flying by instruments yet hearing the turret still firing and Bill's commentary continuing. However, they lost us eventually or gave up, and I made anxiously for home, knowing my aircraft was riddled with holes and hoping nothing vital in the engines had been hit, which might make me take a dinghy voyage. Also I was worried about the other two aircraft, for which I was responsible, but I reflected that they had entered cloud at the same time as I, and were probably on the way home too. If my crew had been uproarious after last week's episode, this time they were not quite so pleased, for in reality it had been a narrow shave, and Bill's good firing had done much to avert disaster. I was firmly requested by Steve not to go out on the following Saturday, lest a third fight might not be so lucky.

Again, three crews met safely at the aerodrome, fortified now by safety and greatly amused by their escape. My aircraft had innumerable holes in petrol tank, wings and fuselage, but none in vital places, though several were unpleasantly near Bill's turret, and made me realize that to face attacking fighters, as he did, was not the most pleasant task imaginable. Of the other two aircraft, only Ian's had been hit by two bullets, one of which had punctured his tail wheel and given him a bumpy landing.

This was another sortie on which little was achieved, but it had made the enemy put his defences into action; although we had met only one pair of fighters, others may have been in the air, and many more at readiness on their aerodromes. I did not feel that the flight was wasted, certainly not by the experience it brought me. If our escape from the previous encounter had inclined me to belittle a fighter's powers, that misconception was now rectified, for I considered the formation very lucky to have escaped without loss. Our own fighter pilots spoke highly of their German counterparts and their aircraft, and now I could see the reason for the respect, born of everyday knowledge; for a pilot to underestimate the enemy was for him not to last long. I had seen Beauforts return from sorties riddled with many more holes than mine, not merely bullet holes but jagged rents from explosive cannon-shells; all the same, such an escape was a rarity, the exception to prove the rule, for of all those who encountered fighters in open sky, few returned to tell the tale of the combat. This pair of Messerschmitts were formidable aircraft, handled by determined pilots, and only cloud saved us.

August, which had been a happy, eventful month, with Dick's

award, attacks by fighters and one or two daylight torpedo attacks, came to an end with a sad event; our Wing Commander was posted. He had been with the squadron for fifteen months, a term of command longer than the usual year of office, and now left to command a station. His going left Flight Lieutenant Alec Gammon and me as the oldest members of the squadron, the only two who could remember the winter months of last year in the squadron's history; both of us looked back regretfully to the past and forward with some doubt at the future. The past was never allowed to die for Alec, who carried on interminable correspondence with the squadron's very few prisoners of war and the many relatives of missing crews, some of whom would never abandon hope of good news even after many months had passed, while others would like to hear news of the squadron, to which they felt attached by their loss.

While Alec, who was devoted to the squadron, hoped to remain indefinitely as its Adjutant, seeking no promotion or advancement, I knew that my time in the squadron was drawing to a close. For I was nearing the limit of operations and would soon be posted away. I was dreading the thought of leaving the squadron, and looked forward with aversion to the dull routine work of instructing or staff appointment which would take the place of the occasional exciting operation. At the same time I felt that the sands of my luck were running low, and that I had already used my fair share of good fortune to the full; luck couldn't last. Every pilot nearing completion of his tour felt the same; not one ever wanted to leave, yet all knew in their inner hearts that within their next few sorties bad luck might claim them. The last few operations were as critical as the first; with many narrow escapes and fine successes behind a crew, it seemed that all would be worthless if they were lost with their ultimate goal within sight, yet sadly not a few were. If the first six sorties were a wide fat river which a crew must cross, the last six were a tantalizing, dangerous path which led to rest.

Losses in operations from our new base had been reduced by the less exacting nature of the work, but there still remained the occasional flying accident or inexplicable failure to return, inevitable sacrifices to war. A new pilot stalled after a night take-off, another descending through cloud crashed into a hillside; such accidents were due to human errors of judgement and inseparable from operational flying.

Yet I continued flying, dull routine operations, for September to come and remind me that with the end of the month I would have completed a year in the squadron, since my name had remained on the strength all the time I was in hospital. The squadron appeared static under a newly found permanency, with a new Wing Commander as CO, Alec an invaluable pillar of continuity as Adjutant, and Tony and myself still holding the fort as Flight Commanders. Johnny was the most outstanding among the younger pilots, the only survivor of four crews who had arrived together from Training Unit in June, of which Ian and Dougie had been others. He was both a determined and able pilot, just a little inclined to rashness, but with an excellent crew to guide his judgement; the squadron had never lacked a daring offensive fighter, and here was one in the direct succession of Fanny, Dick and Ken. Nor was steadiness lacking, for Jimmy and H-P, who had both been decorated and were now instructing, had their followers also. There were always two or three eminently reliable crews in the squadron, whose operational flights seemed always to run to schedule, no fireworks about them but complete steadiness. Between these two extremes were others no less useful but not outstanding, the rank and file of the squadron's pilots who might at any time blossom out, and were perhaps merely awaiting their opportunity.

Just occasionally there would be a rare and very sad failure, the pilot who could not face the enemy. Such a case appeared to me above all else to be a sad and understandable happening, someone to be lacking in the mental or physical equipment to face danger. After the initial desire to strike their blow at the enemy had been satisfied, most crews steadied themselves to a task which they realized from first experience was far from pleasant, looking forward to a rest after completing their tour, a rest which they would have earned. The pilot who failed completely was extremely rare; most people who found the task beyond them would try to overcome their inadequacy, with the result that their efforts were rewarded by a rest from operations long before it was really due. It was inspiring to see such efforts being made, to see the rather nervous, not very skilful pilot going out in his turn; this surpassed mere bravery, it was a triumph, and rightly recognized as such.

My last few sorties were carried out on the Norwegian coast, operating from a Scottish aerodrome to which we had been ordered to move at the usual short notice; some battleship had stirred and steps were being taken against the remote chance of her putting to sea. But by the time we had arrived the alarm was found to be false and the squadron was cheated, as always, of a naval target. However, we remained in the North to do other work, some tricky mine-laying in Norwegian fjords by night and some Rovers on the coast in daytime. The sea-crossing from Scotland to Norway was a long one, three hundred miles compared with our usual Channel crossing of thirty, but these flights were a change from our recent barren operations, something new which the squadron always welcomed.

On our first show I led a section of three, Johnny and another pilot of my flight, Pilot Officer Roy Orrock, on a Rover off Stavanger, on which Johnny sank a large ship. Weather on the distant coast was not easily predictable; what we had expected to be ideal turned out to be incredibly bad, not the usual blue sky and lack of cover, but the opposite, rain and fog, which gave the worst imaginable flying conditions. In these circumstances the formation became separated, each pilot continuing to search for a target by himself. Time on the coast was limited by our aircraft's endurance and I had no luck, spending most of the time flying by instruments in cloud or driving through sheets of rain low over the water, seeing nothing except a new coastline on which appeared no ship. Johnny, however, had roved in the other direction and returned with quite a different story. He had come suddenly upon some shipping lying at anchor in a bay, and attacked the largest ship, which burst into flames as he made away in the rain. This was Johnny's first personal success, indeed the squadron's first success for many weeks, and was duly celebrated as such that evening in a tavern called "The Cross Keys".

A few days later I walked into Operations Room first thing in the morning and saw indicated on the map a merchant-vessel steaming down from the north past the harbour of Kristiansand. On inquiry I found it had been sighted by a Blenheim at dawn, but nothing had been sent out against it. From our present aerodrome it was well out of range, but I saw that we could reach it easily from Wick, so I put the proposition to Group, suggesting we should send a striking force of three. Within half an hour the formation was in the air, Johnny and Roy again flying on either side of me, a neat arrowhead of three grey Beauforts against green Scottish hills. This was to be my last operation, and I was wishing intensely for a success.

We flew the two hundred miles north to Wick in the worst weather through which I have ever flown, for we ran into rain and low cloud down to the surface of the water, and the formation only managed to get through intact due to the excellent formation flying of Johnny and Roy. At Wick the aircraft were refuelled while we visited Operations Room to obtain the latest information about our target. There was little new to be learnt, except that the Blenheim had flown very low over the ship in order to photograph it, and the Controller thought it might have turned into harbour, knowing it had been sighted. Nevertheless I set out on the longest sea-crossing which a Beaufort's range allowed in high hopes of finding some ship or other to attack, since these waters had not been swept clear like the Channel.

The Norwegian coast has no shallows such as restricted our activities in the Channel, but is interlaced with fjords, narrow inland waters, through which passes the shipping route. Hardly ever is it necessary for ships to come out into the open sea, for they can sail down these sheltered waters, concealed behind steep cliffs and virtually immune from air attack on account of the narrowness of the waters and height of the surrounding mountains. It is a coast a pilot needs to know well, and one which I knew not at all. However, Intelligence told me that ships must come into open sea off Stetlandet, a headland midway between Kristiansand in the south and Bergen in the north. In view of recent experience I also showed not a little interest in the position of fighter aerodromes, but Intelligence revealed that there were few fighter aerodromes in the area, and none where we intended inter-cepting the target. At Stetlandet our force would be virtually safe, since it was at extreme range from the nearest fighter bases to the north and south; an extremely satisfactory state of affairs,

Steve's navigation was characteristically accurate, bringing us in according to plan some hundred and fifty miles north of Stetlandet after a two-and-a-half-hour flight. The coastline was new to me and very beautiful, with mountains rising steeply out of the sea, islands dotted close inshore and narrow cavernous-looking estuaries, whose waters vanished from sight between precipitous cliffs. There was still snow on the mountain-tops of the interior, and their white, combining with the green of woods and grey of the cliffs, made a more peaceful picture than any I had seen while flying. Perhaps this impression was accentuated by contrast with the view of endless barren sea which had been our horizon for several hours, but I remember equally now both sea, grey and unfriendly, and the land, so very attractive.

We had passed fishing-vessels, little hamlets and lighthouses with our peace undisturbed, when Bill, whose look-out was always excel-lent, told me there were six aircraft approaching, and Steve at the same time joined in to say there was a single aircraft creeping up the coast towards us. I was not slow in making a wide detour out to sea, to be passed by six Junkers 88's flying north in formation, followed closely by a Junkers 52 troop carrier. I was half inclined to wade in to attack, but caution prevailed; they were a strong force and we were handicapped by the weight of the torpedoes; to start a fight would be a diversion from our objective. It was unreal to see these enemy aircraft pass so near us, the drone of their engines audible and the crosses painted on the side of their fuselage quite clear; their paint was not this time an aggressive red or yellow, but a sinister dark grey. I could not help wondering where they were going, and if they had seen and ignored us; perhaps they too had work to do and would not be diverted from it.

Cloud above us was variable, but I was not really concerned with cover, knowing that geographically we were fairly safe from fighters. Certainly our presence on the coast must have been known, for we covered two hundred miles without seeing a larger vessel than a fishing-boat. Nothing was achieved but an unforgettable view of the coastline of rugged grandeur, an unchallenged sweep down the coast to no effect. Compelled by time to turn for home, I left the scene reluctantly behind, switching in the automatic pilot to allow me to drink tea with the crew, munch chocolate and talk of old times, good times of flak and fighters, ships and searchlights, flare paths and accidents. The flight home was a long tiring one, and my last in the squadron, a disappointing end to a story.

We refuelled the aircraft again at Wick and were soon in the air, flying south in an effort to reach our base before darkness. Three Beauforts circle the aerodrome in V formation, with first one and then the other aircraft peeling off on the circuit to allow the leader to land first. He approaches steadily, rather carefully, in the half-light of evening; the propellers, reflecting the glint of the dying sun, shine like spinning bronze discs hanging in the sky; the Beaufort touches down firmly at the end of the concrete runway and runs up the strip to a standstill. A momentary pause, as if to feel the solid earth beneath him, and the pilot taxies away to disperse his aircraft on the aerodrome boundary, where airmen wait to receive their charge. One by one the crew climb down the ladder, stiff and tired after nine hours in the air; the pilot in dirty overalls, which have once been white, rubs an injured arm, not yet quite healed; the navigator carries rulers, charts and a log of the flight, while gunner and wireless operator between them carry the camera. There they stand, talking, grinning and watching critically the other Beauforts coming in to land. It is a crew who have flown together on many sorties, and inevitably are friends. With their pilot they walk together over the aerodrome, not only with a day's work completed, but with a years' operations behind them. They have completed their operational tour in a squadron, run the gauntlet and won the promised rest, and are sad at the thought of parting. The pilot carries under his arm a panda.

On the aerodrome, long after the crew have gone, airmen refuel the aircraft; petrol surges into its tanks, oil is replenished, plugs are changed and tyres checked. Even the dull grey paint shines a little in the last light of day as the aircraft is covered, picketed down to the ground and left for the night; the airmen cross the aerodrome, their day also finished. As the moon rises out of the North Sea a guard patrols the dispersed aircraft, Beauforts lined up at intervals around the aerodrome boundary, ghostly shapes silhouetted against the dark blue sky of night. He looks up casually at the nose of an aircraft and notices a crest painted there: two hands gripping an old-time broadsword, holding it aloft as if to strike. Underneath is the pilot's name.

CHAPTER XVII

A STAR SHINES AHEAD

AND so it all ended, with the usual, unacceptable signal condemning me to an unwelcome future: "Post S/Ldr P. Gibbs..." it said, and I was once more an impersonal parcel to be packed, labelled and posted according to instructions. Perversely I was bitter at this news; it suddenly seemed as if I had done nothing at all, that there had been no success, and all had been failure. This was the signal which I had hoped for, and also dreaded; it was, in fact, no death-sentence, but a timely reprieve for which I should have been grateful. Yet as I set at my desk in the Flight Office reading and re-reading the message before me, I felt discontented once more; the old conflicts and confusions returned to add their doubts; where had I been, and where was I going?

Staring at me from the wall opposite my desk is the aircraft service-ability board, made up to date each morning by the Flight Sergeant. Beaufort *A for Apple* is having a routine inspection; during the morning I shall go into the hangar and see how the work is getting on. *G for George* is so badly smashed that it is awaiting return to the makers for rebuilding. I wonder if Hank Sharman will ever make a pilot? *C, D* and *E* are serviceable, loaded with torpedoes and ready to operate; but there is nothing in the air, and no longer anything for me. I am finished, swept up from the floor like ashes to be thrown on some bleak pile, ignominiously to rot with my feet upon the earth.

Outside, an aircraft's engines are running up; it is *F for Freddy*, which is going up on test. The noise is slowly getting on my nerves. I am sick of the sight of these familiar aircraft letters, which have remained coldly unchanged while a dozen different Beauforts have borne them this year. I am tired of the everlasting waiting for orders, of the call from my bed in the middle of a dark, wet night, weary of the roar of engines and the eternal staring at instruments. Why has their note continued unfaltering, why have the pointers remained steady on their dials? I am tired of the clash of war, sick of the fiendish colour of its flames; I have been burnt by its fire and frozen by its ice. I am weary of the endless discordant clanging in that forge of destruction.

My panda sits respectfully in my "pending" tray; an aircraft-hand brings in three outsize cups of tea. Johnny is reading, or rather laughing, about the doings of a certain Pilot Officer Prune, who is not altogether unknown to the world at large; Roy is sitting at the other side of the desk, making up his flying log book. The dirtiest white flying overalls imaginable hang from a hook on the door and a flying helmet dangles in its RT wires; muddy flying boots keep a parachute company in the corner. Outside, somebody has started to run up those ruddy engines again, while from the hangar can be heard the machine-gun-like rattle of mechanical riveters.

Suddenly something in me snaps; the roar of engines reaches a crescendo, making the windows rattle in their frames. The tea is finished, Johnny and Roy are arguing, a cup falls off the desk and breaks into fragments on the floor. Noises of repair in the hangar make it sound like Vulcan's forge. The hand which holds the signal shakes uncontrollably. Yes, I don't care who knows that I am tired of it all, tired of the everlasting struggle to keep aircraft serviceable, tired of the wearisome flying at night and in bad weather, tired of being the target at which all guns point, and above all tired of being a mere name to be moved impersonally about the map. So something snaps; the signal is torn up into little fragments, a chair is hurled on to the floor, and the door is slammed behind me. As I walk out into the open air Roy turns to Johnny and says, "I think Pat's had it", and of course he's right; I have.

To leave a squadron in peace-time had been a difficult parting, but to leave the squadron which I had served in wartime was an unforgettable experience; nerves which had played no part in operations suddenly declared their presence. I found I was attached to the squadron by ties stronger than could be severed by the few words covering a handshake. By falling out of the team I felt almost that I was letting it down. But I had to go; the posting signal was an inflexible order to which there was no reply. Air-crews reaching the limit of operations were posted as a matter of course to a training appointment for some months; my posting was to the Beaufort Training Unit, where I was to instruct the crews who would eventually fly in squadrons such as this. I recalled the struggle of the previous year to escape from the boredom of instructing, and looked forward not at all to its dull routine. Yet there was no alternative, this was a posting which I had known must come, and on black days of losses and failure a posting for which I had secretly longed. But now that this safety was mine it seemed unattractive, a dull future of uneventful circuits and landings.

So it was good-bye again: to the corporal-clerk who had typed my numerous letters to Group, requesting more guns for our aircraft, a more suitable camouflage scheme, or suggesting we operated in stronger forces; to the aircraft-hand who ran the Flight tea swindle, to the airmen who had kept my aircraft shining and faultless, and to countless others who had made up the team, I said good-bye. If my outstretched hand shook a little, it was because I was not as fresh as I had once been; if my voice was not quite steady, it was because it could find no words to say what my heart felt; and if my eyes looked as if they might at any minute disgrace me, it was because I was the survivor who remembered others who had left without saying good-bye. Small wonder that I wanted it over quickly; I said good-bye, I packed my car, and I ran for it.

This was almost like a peace-time move, the back of my car filled with suitcases, parachute bags, flying clothing, odds and ends accumulated in a year of travelling, with my panda astride the lot. I had a week's leave before taking up my new appointment, and was off to London to spend it. Once away from the aerodrome, out of sight of the familiar aircraft scattered around its boundary and away from the sound of friends' voices, I was suddenly glad of the change, grateful at my release and looking forward to the week of freedom before me. You're lucky, lucky, lucky, sang the wheels on the wet road, and for the first time I felt lucky, felt good to be alive, and then I realized that for the past weeks I had been dead in all but fact. Yes, Johnny was right; I'd had it.

But that week passed all too quickly. As I pored over my paper at breakfast on Thursday I realized with regret that only one more day remained before my leave was over, and that then I was to return not to the squadron but to Training Unit. The previous day I had been walking along Oxford Street when an enormous photograph, filling the window of the RAF recruiting office, attracted my attention. There was Dick and his crew, standing larger than life on the wing of a Beaufort. Ready to start out on one of their incredible operations. Strangely, that very evening I was turning over the pages of *Vogue* when I found Joan's face smiling at me from a fashion-plate. Her smile and Dick's diabolical grin brought back to life a winter's evening of a year ago, and with that memory the germ of an idea.

For now that it was Thursday, with my leave nearly spent, I was beginning again to feel unhappy about my new appointment; it was not what I wanted. The longing for single-seater fighters, which I had remembered in Dick, was growing within me, and I felt strongly the appeal of offensive, individual operations. I had finished my time in Beauforts; perhaps if I could escape from training I could start a new lease of luck in a different game. The idea was more attractive than ever, and in my enthusiasm I almost persuaded myself that it could happen. The newspaper which I read reported fighter sweeps, three in one day over Northern France, dog-fights at dizzy heights with Me 109s, several enemy aircraft shot down. What a change it would be to fly alone and high in a clear sky, with oxygen mask on, instructions coming from the Controller over the RT, and a score or two of aircraft to keep one company. With foolish optimism rising, I read over again the short paragraph; that, I thought, is the only battle; that is where I should be.

After breakfast I went to the RAF Club in the hope of meeting a friend in Fighter Command who could help me. Spitfires flew on a circuit of my head and the rattle of eight guns sounded in my ears. I was determined to get to single-seater fighters, but, of course, I never did. I got no further than the entrance of the Club, where two friends descended on me. "Congrats, Pat" they said. "Come in and stand us a drink". And when I appeared puzzled: "What! Haven't you seen the morning papers?"; and they dragged me in to read a paragraph that had escaped me at breakfast, a paragraph which sang the sweetest of songs. "RAF Awards" was the heading, and underneath my name: "S/Ldr P. Gibbs... has been awarded the Distinguished Flying Cross for operations against enemy shipping... On one occasion he brought his extensively damaged aircraft back to base in bad weather and landed it safely..." I read the paragraph in a dream, mechanically and unbelievingly, as if it were all written about some stranger whom I had never met. Nothing could have been more unexpected than a decoration, nothing further from my mind, but nothing more acceptable and timely. The ashes miraculously arose from the floor to become a body again, one which automatically ordered drinks, dazed as if recovering from an anaesthetic. I was drunk before I had touched my drink, my feet were off the earth and I was flying. Fragments of that first flight of a year ago mingled with incidents from all my other operations to make one great marathon flight over a limitless sea, packed with incident and fraught with dangers. It was Thursday, and my own happy day. "A telegram for you, sir"; "Three telegrams for you, sir", ".... wanted on the 'phone, sir"; A visitor for you, sir". So it went on through that fantastic day, of which I can remember nothing but sublime happiness; how sweet was success, and how lucky I was to be there to taste it.

So I never got to fighters; in actual fact I would never have been allowed to make the change, and now that I was decorated I felt an allegiance to anti-shipping from which I would not try to escape. But although I could easily reject the appeal of fighters, I found it impossible to embrace the dull routine of instructing; my appointment to Training Unit was even more disappointing than I had feared it would be. I was remote from operations, never hearing how the crews fared who so quickly passed through my hands, nor did news come from the Beaufort squadrons; we were cut off, away from the war, and I hated it. Neither did instructing give the rest which I needed; there was the same sound of aircraft engines outside my office, the eternal circuits and landings at night and the everlasting battle to keep the aircraft in the air. It was steadily driving me mad, and in desperation I looked round for any loophole of escape.

Once more I was lucky; an opportunity arose to be posted abroad; I applied and was chosen.

I had long thought that the Mediterranean would be a happy hunting-ground for torpedo aircraft. Ships were continually crossing from Europe to Africa with supplies for General Rommel's army, and now Beaufort squadrons were being formed in Egypt to cut these vulnerable supply lines. These squadrons would need someone from England with experience to lead them, and I was chosen to go. While I hated the thought of leaving England, knowing that I should miss the rain and green fields and hate the desert sand and scorching sun, I knew equally well that the Mediterranean was where I should be. The ships we had attacked in European waters were relatively unimportant. But in the Mediterranean it was another story, for the fate of Egypt depended largely on the RAF being able to keep Rommel in short supply; to sink his ships was of first importance. And so I went, very reluctant to leave England, but glad to be rid of my training appointment and looking forward to the command of a Beaufort squadron which I had been promised.

The voyage out by ship was by the Cape of Good Hope, and was the pleasantest, most carefree imaginable; it was a real antidote to the worry and strain of squadron life. I embarked in January in bitter weather; soon a violent Atlantic storm was pitching and tossing the great ship, making me glad of my sea experience in aircraft carriers.

While off the Bay of Biscay the convoy was shadowed for a whole day by an enemy aircraft, one of the lethal four-engined Focke-Wulfs, yet strangely no attack was made either by aircraft or submarines. In the middle of the convoy was a warship, thought by one WAAF officer to be the *Repulsive*, by her friend to be the *Revolution*; on the flanks were destroyers, dwarfed by some great liners which had been famous in peace-time but were steaming no longer in the bright colours of former pleasure cruises but shrouded now in the drab camouflage greys of war.

I used often to look out from the boat-deck over the procession of ships that was our convoy, never tiring of the dazzling view of the changing pattern of ships, sky and sea. Sometimes it was a forest of masts, just as I had once seen an enemy convoy off Borkum; sometimes I would see individual ships merely as torpedo targets and imagine myself sighting the force from the horizon, making the critical decisions and going through all the phases of an attack. At others I would see the ships as I had known them in peace-time, the great red liners which had steamed up the Solent while I flew overhead in a floatplane from Calshot, or those which had lain at anchor in Ryde Roads during the years I had been instructing at Gosport.

As a child I had watched lesser ships steaming up the Bristol Channel and had walked fascinated under their huge hulls as they lay in dry-dock at Cardiff. It seemed ironic that the firm which bore my name was endeavouring to keep its ships afloat while I had been doing my best to sink the enemy's. I was, after all, a member of a shipping firm: "Beaufort Squadrons Ltd, Shipping Destroyers".

I wondered if the firm's fate of the last war would be repeated, and if any ships would remain sailing when it was all ended, if there would be a business left to tempt me. I wondered what would become of the service in a far-off peace-time, and if I should remain to witness a reversal of the great expansion I had known; would the tiny Air Force which I had joined, but never known, return in years to come? Would I be satisfied again with flying only, stripped of the glamour of war? I now looked on a peace-time Air Force as a shop without stocks or customers, and could not see myself dusting its shelves every day, waiting idly for another war. But I was no longer looking askance at some far-off future, as once I had done; I was contented with my lot.

The rough seas gave place to calmer waters; phosphorus gleamed in the water at night and flying-fishes played around the ship by day, their wings glistening in the sun which shone from a cloudless sky. Here was the rest to which I had looked forward through a year of fighting, a sea voyage as enjoyable as any peace-time pleasure cruise, with my heart's desire waiting at its end. So passed peaceful, uneventful days of quiet enjoyment.

One day in February I was recalled from this remote paradise by the wireless news, which told how the *Scharnhorst* and *Gneisenau* had escaped from Brest and sailed through the Channel to the North Sea. Strong forces of aircraft had gone out to attack them, great four-engined bombers, single-seater fighters, squadrons of Beauforts carrying torpedoes. Even the old and faithful Swordfish had been sent in to the attack, and a whole squadron had been lost in a very gallant effort. The enemy had made cunning use of bad weather; our fighter wings, which could so easily rule the Channel under a blue sky, found it difficult to escort our striking forces in the mist and rain which prevailed. The task set to our Air Forces was a formidable one, and while hits may have been scored, the battle-cruisers were not stopped. Yet the day could not be considered an air force failure, but a success, for bombing raids had made Brest untenable and the enemy had not dared send his ships out into the Atlantic to share the *Bismarck*'s fate. Many aircraft, both ours and the enemy's were lost in the epic Channel battle which had raged almost within sight, certainly within hearing, of England's coast.

The Beaufort squadrons had delivered their torpedo attack in the face of great opposition, but without result; it seemed sad that the opportunity which my squadron had awaited for a whole year should have been lost, and that Beauforts should have failed when they should have triumphed. Yet I knew how difficult the task must have been, could see the fast-moving targets screened by lighter craft, hear the guns firing, see the fighters overhead flying through the driving rain. I wished I had been there, leading.

The very next week, when shipping attacks had been quite forgotten in the excitement of four days ashore at Durban, the wireless again brought news which took me straight back to England, its cloudy grey skies and wind-lashed seas; Ken Campbell, who just a year ago had been missing from St. Eval was awarded a posthumous Victoria Cross. The steady voice of the announcer recounted how Ken had been ordered to attack the target in the first light of dawn, how he had arrived late in conditions of broad daylight. Ironically the objective was our old enemy, the *Scharnhorst*, which a week ago had escaped from our clutches, but at the time of the incident had been lying helpless in the harbour at Brest. To attack there in darkness was an unenviable task, but to make a torpedo attack in daylight was suicide. Nevertheless, Ken had flown into the wall of fire, from which another pilot might justifiably have turned away, and dropped his torpedo skilfully in the restricted stretch of water. As he climbed away from the attack his aircraft was hit in several places and fell out of control into the sea, killing all the crew instantly. That was Ken, who had sat in my Flight Office at North Coates the friend of Joe, who had gone the same way.

The news of this heroic effort came from secret sources, said the announcer, and the true story had only just been pieced together, hence the delay in making the award. How similar were the fates of both Dick and Ken, the one flying into Bremerhaven, the other into Brest, in the full light of day; both had been awarded decorations long after their death. They had both had their share of good luck, but it would have needed a miracle to escape from the thousand guns which Brest could bring to bear on an attacking aircraft; Ken had attempted the impossible, and almost succeeded.

But the momentary return to the past did not concern me; if I was not looking forward to my place in a peace-time of some remote future, neither was I looking back with regret on a past which it was impossible to interpret.

England is a thousand miles away, and memories have been obliterated with the change of scene. My ship, at the head of the column, rises and falls gently in tropical seas, while a steady breeze blows brine against my face. As I write, with pencil scrawling over countless sheets of paper, my right arm tires, the shoulder aches a little; it is strong, but will never be as good as new again, and games may be a thing of the past. Yet it is a reminder that I have been lucky, and brings home to me the joyful truth, that I am not dead but living.

In the Mediterranean there will be no cloud cover, the sun will shine each day from a blue sky. Hostile ships will cross the sea carrying tanks and guns and forces to the enemy; Beauforts will go out to sink them. While our hard-pressed army holds the line on land between Egypt and the foe, aircraft will attack in the rear. Malta will be a pirates' lair, the hiding-place of a horde of aircraft which will be a scourge to Rommel. Above all, the game will be worthwhile, the loss of a crew a small price to pay for saving a brigade in the field. Beauforts will fly out from Malta in strength this summer to the Italian, African and Greek coasts to seek out Rommel's ships and sink them. Bombs will be rained on their aerodrome. Enemy fighters will try to claw them from the sky, but Beauforts will fly out undaunted in fine weather. I shall be leading them.

I am fresh, you see, and young; the leaders, you know, are all peaceful in graves beneath the sea. Many brave young pilots will arise and travel that road which leads to experience, but few reach its happy end. I owe an allegiance to the dead, which I go now to repay. When engines roar, my heart will beat in sympathy; when guns flash and shells burst in the sky, I shall smile in recognition; and when my aircraft is hit, I shall bring it safely home. My hand doesn't shake any more, my voice is quite steady, my eyes are bright and smiling. There is great work to be done, and I am happy because I am going to do it. I follow the Sword, which points to the East.

MV Otranto,
   March 1942.